# Palgrave Studies in Journalism and the Global South

### Series Editors
Bruce Mutsvairo
Auburn University
Auburn, AL, USA

Saba Bebawi
University of Technology Sydney
Ultimo, NSW, Australia

Eddy Borges-Rey
Northwestern University Qatar
Ar-Rayyan, Qatar

This series focuses on cutting-edge developments in journalism in and from the Global South and illuminates how journalism cultures and practices have evolved from the era of colonization to contemporary globalization. Bringing previously underrepresented research from the Global South to the English speaking world, this series will focus on a broad range of topics within journalism including pedagogy, ethics, history of journalism, press freedom, theory, propaganda, gender, cross-border collaboration and methodological issues. Despite the geographical connotations of the term 'Global South' the series will not be defined by geographical boundaries, as Western countries are home to millions of immigrants and the contributions of immigrant journalists will be covered.

Abdullah Alhuntushi • Jairo Lugo-Ocando

# Science Journalism in the Arab World

The Quest for 'Ilm' and Truth

Abdullah Alhuntushi
Department of Media and
Communication
King Khalid Military College
Riyadh, Kingdom of Saudi Arabia

Jairo Lugo-Ocando
University of Sharjah
Sharjah, United Arab Emirates

ISSN 2662-480X  ISSN 2662-4818 (electronic)
Palgrave Studies in Journalism and the Global South
ISBN 978-3-031-14251-2  ISBN 978-3-031-14252-9 (eBook)
https://doi.org/10.1007/978-3-031-14252-9

© The Editor(s) (if applicable) and The Author(s), under exclusive licence to Springer Nature Switzerland AG 2023

This work is subject to copyright. All rights are solely and exclusively licensed by the Publisher, whether the whole or part of the material is concerned, specifically the rights of translation, reprinting, reuse of illustrations, recitation, broadcasting, reproduction on microfilms or in any other physical way, and transmission or information storage and retrieval, electronic adaptation, computer software, or by similar or dissimilar methodology now known or hereafter developed.

The use of general descriptive names, registered names, trademarks, service marks, etc. in this publication does not imply, even in the absence of a specific statement, that such names are exempt from the relevant protective laws and regulations and therefore free for general use.

The publisher, the authors, and the editors are safe to assume that the advice and information in this book are believed to be true and accurate at the date of publication. Neither the publisher nor the authors or the editors give a warranty, expressed or implied, with respect to the material contained herein or for any errors or omissions that may have been made. The publisher remains neutral with regard to jurisdictional claims in published maps and institutional affiliations.

Cover Illustration: PhotoStock-Israel / Alamy Stock Photo.

This Palgrave Macmillan imprint is published by the registered company Springer Nature Switzerland AG.
The registered company address is: Gewerbestrasse 11, 6330 Cham, Switzerland

*To both of our mothers, who brought science into our lives*

# Contents

| | | |
|---|---|---|
| 1 | Introduction | 1 |
| 2 | An Account of Science Journalism in MENA | 29 |
| 3 | Science Journalism and Media Systems in MENA | 49 |
| 4 | Science News Cultures and Journalism Practice | 77 |
| 5 | Science Journalism and Professional Autonomy | 99 |
| 6 | News Sources and Access in Science | 123 |
| 7 | Gender and Science News in the Arab World | 143 |
| 8 | Data and Statistics in Science News Reporting in the Arab World | 165 |
| 9 | Science News Audiences in the Middle East | 187 |
| 10 | Conclusion | 209 |

**Bibliography** 231

**Index** 263

# LIST OF TABLES

| | | |
|---|---|---|
| Table 4.1 | Journalistic genre of the article | 86 |
| Table 4.2 | The main topic of the article (Alhuntushi & Lugo-Ocando, 2020) | 89 |
| Table 4.3 | The main source of statistics (Alhuntushi & Lugo-Ocando, 2020) | 93 |
| Table 6.1 | Science news producers | 125 |
| Table 6.2 | Types of science news cross-tabulated with the sources | 131 |
| Table 6.3 | Provenance | 132 |
| Table 6.4 | The numbers of sources, when mentioned | 134 |
| Table 6.5 | The type of science news and number of sources mentioned | 134 |
| Table 6.6 | Correlation between the numbers of sources | 135 |
| Table 7.1 | The main source and gender | 153 |
| Table 7.2 | Gender cross-tabulated by type of science news | 156 |
| Table 7.3 | Gender of the journalist cross-tabulation | 158 |
| Table 8.1 | Mathematics performance among 15-year-olds in some Arab countries in 2015 | 176 |
| Table 8.2 | Reliability of cited sources | 178 |

CHAPTER 1

# Introduction

For journalists all over the world, one of the most dramatic events in the twenty-first century was reporting the world COVID-19 pandemic. As the virus rapidly spread across all corners of the globe and took almost everyone by surprise, it became increasingly evident how ill-prepared our societies were to deal with these types of situations. Millions across the globe were dying as the world desperately searched for a vaccine while asking people to stay at home, self-isolate and wear masks. Meanwhile, the economy was collapsing as the planet came to a halt.

Governments deployed information campaigns as part of the efforts to convince everyone to undertake precautionary measures. These efforts became, in the end, a race to win the hearts and minds of people, convincing citizens to change their lifestyles and accept what at times seemed to many as draconian measures. This included informing the public about approaches, policies and actions to be collectively undertaken to reduce the speed of the contagion so as to avoid the collapse of the public and private health systems, which were overwhelmed by the sheer numbers of people falling ill and rushing into medical emergency rooms (Ghosh & Qadeer, 2020; Muwahed, 2020).

However, these communication efforts proved to be one of the biggest challenges and, in some cases, an impossible task. Indeed, one of the biggest surprises from that event was the way the government responses to

© The Author(s), under exclusive license to Springer Nature Switzerland AG 2023
A. Alhuntushi, J. Lugo-Ocando, *Science Journalism in the Arab World*, Palgrave Studies in Journalism and the Global South, https://doi.org/10.1007/978-3-031-14252-9_1

the crisis were politicalised and faced a backlash from anti-vaccine and anti-mask movements from around the globe. Perhaps the biggest paradox was the fact that liberal democracies with an independent and free press which ought to be trusted in fact struggled to be so and failed to convince large segments of their own populations to embrace these responses and policies.

It was precisely in those political systems where information was widely available and individuals had the right to choose sources and responses where we mostly saw the spread of fake news and disinformation (Carrion-Alvarez & Tijerina-Salina, 2020; Rodrigues & Xu, 2020) as well as the embracement of conspiracy theories that led some to even question the very existence of the virus (Shahsavari et al., 2020; Stein et al., 2021). It came down to the fact that in many of these countries large segments of the public simply neither trusted the government nor the mainstream media.

These individuals fell into conspiracy theories that promoted the idea that governments and corporations were colluding for world domination and depopulation or that it was all a plot to implement a form of corporate fascism (Stecula & Pickup, 2021; Stephens, 2020). This was underpinned by irresponsible populist leaders who ignored expert advice and recommendations provided by the world's health experts, all in pursuit of their own political agendas (Matthews, 2020; Muwahed, 2020; O'Reilly, 2020). This war against scientific truth was supported in turn by important segments of the right-wing news media and a variety of voices on social media platforms, all of whom disinformation campaigns that helped to radicalise groups of the public and slow down the rates of vaccination and mask use.

At this point, one must ask why did so many ignore or distrust what governments, international organisations and the mainstream media had to say about the pandemic? As the dust settled, we came to understand that there were many variables at play. For example, one of the aspects that caused most damage during the emergency was the fact that many in society did not really understand the nature of the crisis or the science behind the virus and the responses to it (e.g., that the world already had mRNA technology which facilitated the rapid development of a vaccine). Conspiracy theories thrived from ignorance as many were unable to grasp even the most basic concepts around health while fewer understood how to assess risk in their own lives.

These shortcomings were not only a problem related to the Public Understanding of Science (PUS) but one that was also deeply ingrained in an increasingly mediatised and fragmented public sphere where journalism as a political institution had lost ground to eclectic and quasi-chimeric forms of participatory publishing—a form of citizen journalism—that present, at times, fake news and conspiracy theories as scientific truths (Carrion-Alvarez & Tijerina-Salina, 2020; Rodrigues & Xu, 2020) as these actors had little to no editorial standards to follow. Simply put, in an age of declining trust in the mainstream media, audience fragmentation and expanding social media platforms, it was very difficult for the traditional gatekeepers to retain authorial control over truth. A task that was made even harder by the irresponsible role played by some media outlets—such as Fox News in the United States—which, in search of ratings and political influence, went along with some of the craziest conspiracy theories.

Another contributing factor that had laid the ground in the long run for ample dissemination and embracement of conspiracy theories was what Chris Mooney (2007) and Shan Otto (2016) have respectively called the 'War on Science'. This refers to the systematic and at times politically orchestrated efforts to undermine public trust in science and by all accounts preceded the COVID-19 pandemic as it is a war that has been waged for decades. Over the years it has been driven mostly—but not exclusively—by political and corporative agendas, which have included deliberate attempts to question scientific consensus around issues such as man-made global warming, the risks of nuclear energy and the negative effects of smoking upon people's health (Oreskes & Conway, 2010, 2011). These wars have created doubts around scientific consensus in relation to the potential dangers of nuclear plants, the deadly impact of smoking and the effects of greenhouse emissions and man-made climate change.

More recently, disinformation around science has incorporated a variety of voices that include reptilian-world-dominated believer David Icke and right-wing newspaper columnists such as Peter Hitchens (both in the United Kingdom) as well as conspiracy-theory radio host Alex Jones in the United States, among other more credible voices such as podcast producer Joe Rogan and tennis player Novak Djokovic. This also includes a growing army of flat-earth believers and those who promote versions of the pandemic as being an elite conspiracy to dominate the world by billionaires such as Bill Gates and George Soros to implant microchips in our brains using 5G mobile technology and control world population (Oliver & Wood, 2014).

In general terms, the efforts of the mainstream news media to disseminate and explain to people the science behind the responses to COVID-19 have brought mixed results in countries such as the United States where many have lost trust in the media. Being a traditional ally of governments by helping them to 'manufacture consensus' (Herman & Chomsky, 2010 [1988]; Lippmann, 1992 [1922]) around particular policies despite normative claims of being a watchdog, the news media saw itself nevertheless in a position where it found it extremely difficult to convince many people to follow expert advice, despite overwhelming evidence and facts to support that advice.

To this we have to add, as numerous studies suggest, the fact that many journalists are not particularly good at communicating science even as they continue to be the main link between scientists and the public (Anderson et al., 2005; Peters, 2013; Trench & Junker, 2001). Indeed, one of the fundamental lessons from the COVID-19 crisis was the need not only to educate society at large but also to have better-prepared news reporters who can inform the public and deal with scientific issues more effectively (Bernadas & Ilagan, 2020; Olsen et al., 2020).

Several studies have looked at how journalists need to embrace and address these types of challenges (Bauer et al., 2013; Bauer & Bucchi, 2008; Bauer & Howard, 2009; Fjæstad, 2007). These studies suggest that in many cases, and especially in the Global South, reporters covering the science beat are poorly resourced and ill-equipped to produce science news which means basic levels of accuracy, rigour and public engagement (Martisini, 2018; Nguyen, 2017; Nguyen & Tran, 2019). Other important aspects highlighted by this body of research point towards other common challenges and issues such an increasing lack of trust by the public and also the growing presence of fake news and conspiracy theories in the past few years.

Having said that, few studies in the West have looked at the role of science journalists in the Middle East and Northern Africa Region, where around 580 million people live today (Skalli, 2006). This, despite the fact that science has historically had a central role in the development of these societies, where religion, culture and science were profoundly interconnected in public life. To be sure, one of the most under-studied paradoxes of our times is the enormous gap between a rich heritage of Islam's engagement with science against the current state of many Arab countries, which are only now starting to try to catch up with the West in terms of investment in research and development (Determann, 2015; Giles, 2006). Part of this gap is the lack of public engagement with science and the poor state of science journalism in the region.

Consequently, our book has a double task. On the one hand, we want to describe, analyse and assess the current state of science journalism as a political institution in Arab countries. This, as we want to inquire about journalism in those societies and its function in connecting people to scientific knowledge and truth. On the other, we want to critically explore the role journalism has played within the broader process of modernisation and transformation that these societies have experienced in the past decades. This last point is a task that is both welcomed and contested by the singular historical and political setting that characterises politics and the media system in this part of the world (Mellor, 2005, 2011).

In so doing, the book discusses why society's engagement with science is so crucial in the modern Arab world (Bauer & Howard, 2009; Nisbet & Scheufele, 2009). Having said that, trying to project generalised assumptions to the whole region without considering the particular and distinctive characteristics of each society would be presumptuous on our part. To say the least, science news reporters in Kuwait work under very different conditions than, let's say, Oman or Egypt. Nevertheless, by choosing what we believe to be a representative sample of countries, we have allowed ourselves to draw some general inferences that might shed light on how science news reporting happens in this part of the world.

## Preceding Debates

However, one cannot explore the topic of science journalism in the Middle East and North Africa (MENA) without first covering key and more general debates around the broader field of science communication, which has centred around two key aspects. On the one hand, there are those—particularly scientists—who have stressed the need for 'accuracy' when dealing with science news (Hansen, 2016; Murcott, 2009). For these voices, the most important issue regarding how journalists cover science and their outputs relates to the accuracy (or lack of it) among reporters of science news (Fjæstad, 2007; Seale, 2010). Many argue that the way in which science news is reported, especially when it comes to natural science, is inadequate because of its not reported or under-reporting of important scientific progress, tendency to sensationalism and negativity in wording and in presentation, and inaccurate reporting.

The other camp, on the other hand, has argued more around the need for journalists to make science news more relevant to the public while approaching stories in general in a more critical manner (Nguyen & McIlwaine, 2011). For these authors, the problem is not so much to do with accuracy—although they recognise the underlying issues around this—but the fact that many common citizens fail to engage with science news because it does not seem to be relevant enough to their individual and collective lives. In addition, and perhaps more importantly, these authors point to the lack of criticality around science news reports. For them and others, many journalists, with few exceptions, lack the necessary capabilities and tools to scrutinise science, therefore leaving it unaccountable as a news source.

In this sense, the Arab scientific news media presents deficiencies in both aspects. There is minimal scientific content and what there is seems not to live up to the standards in terms of accuracy while stories do not seem compelling enough to attract larger audiences. The overall volume of scientific information that appears in the Arab media is slight, if not negligible, when compared to the reporting of scientific information worldwide, and when considering the size of the Arab media establishment (El-Awady, 2009). Specialised scientific publications either do not exist or are just local versions of Western outlets that seldom reflect the science that is carried out in these countries. Even in Egypt, the largest media market by size, the space its daily newspapers, magazines and broadcasters allocate to science is rather minimal (Mehran, 2018, p. 101).

The credibility of scientific news is also one of the problems facing science journalism in the Arab world. Indeed, Mahmoud's (2018) study on public attitudes towards the credibility of scientific and technological news in Egyptian newspapers and electronic media suggested that science and technology news is found to be less credible on average than other types of news. This is something that we will look closer at in this book, particularly as the same study suggests that digital native news media are far more credible than the traditional printed newspapers given that the latter are strongly associated with the governments in the region. Therefore, it is important to remind ourselves that the study of science journalism cannot be performed in a vacuum but as part of a broader political and cultural context.

To be sure, many media outlets in the region continue to be owned or closely controlled by the state and as such the line between news and propaganda is at times both blurred and thin (Hamdy, 2013; Moore-Gilbert & Abdul-Nabi, 2021). Consequently, many journalists offer coverage that is often uncritical, particularly of public policy and specific issues that affect society. One example was Egypt's media coverage of the outbreak of the swine flu in 2009. As a result, there was a presidential decree that pigs in that country were to be sacrificed, even though there was no evidence of the virus in these animals. Before the epidemic hit the country, Egypt's Minister of Health at the time, Hatem El-Gabaly, asked people to perform prayers and take university exams in open spaces rather than in mosques. Uncritical coverage by Egypt's media of these policies and actions translated into fearmongering and widespread disinformation among the audiences (El-Awady, 2009).

Having said that, restrictions upon professional autonomy of journalists and gags on the news media are the least of the problems. A much bigger issue, as we will discuss in this book, is the more general lack of engagement with science by the general public and the actual lack of expertise of journalists to understand science. One of the problems we faced as researchers is that there are currently insufficient studies and surveys identifying the level of scientific awareness among the public in MENA. Moreover, some scholars agree that those working in the field of scientific media are addressing an audience about whom they know almost nothing (Abu Haseera, 2018, p. 85). The role of audiences in creating a sustainable market and deliberative space for science is indeed a very important part of the equation in understanding science news gathering, production and dissemination in the Middle East. This, as well as the existing attitudes and perceptions from the general public towards science and scientific-related issues. It is a part of the world in which scientific journalism must contend with tensions between politics, science and culture, as well as the associated spread of superstition and false science (Saber, 2013, p. 192). Let us not forget that these are a series of societies in which conspiracy theories have run wild for a very long time and continue to do so (Aistrope & Bleiker, 2018; Essam & Abdo, 2021).

Journalists in the region possess insufficient scientific backgrounds so as to allow them to truly comprehend the stories they were reporting, something that we confirmed in most of the interviews we carried out. Part of the reason is that there are very few provisions that offer science communication or science journalism courses at the university level. These practitioners often lack expertise and specialisation in science journalism and consequently their outputs do not live up to standards normally accepted in other parts of the world. As Sidqi (2009) discussed some time ago, this weakness is manifested in several ways. For instance, Arab journalists are unable to read scientific material in foreign languages, and they do not have the ability to translate it into Arabic.

Problems include a poor command of English by reporters, scarcity of scientific sources in Arabic, limitation of the information available and a weak contribution to international science by the region. All these issues come together to create the perfect storm against science dissemination in the news (Sidqi, 2009, p. 26). However, even when journalists do manage to access proper academic journals and read peer-reviewed articles, reporters still exhibit a level of functional illiteracy in science because they lack a basic comprehension of what the article actually says or do not understand the meaning of technical terminology and concepts.

In turn, scientific news written by journalists are unclear as they just reproduce the technical language of science and therefore are hardly understood by non-specialists as our own study shows in this book. Moreover, poor editing and sub-editing, as well as a deficient fact-checking system and weak post-production approach, lead to inaccuracies, oversimplifications, exaggerations or simply falsehoods.

Accuracy—or the lack of it—is not the only problem. The ability to take a science issue and turn it into a relevant and appealing story seems equally to be a problem. In many cases, as we saw in our own analysis, stories are not accessible or relevant enough and at times are even boring and longer than they need to be. To be clear, this is not only the fault of journalists as they are hardly supported by their organisations in investigating and publishing science stories.

In addition, reporters face a problem of accessing news sources. Indeed, it is difficult for reporters lacking professional skills to find good local experts and scientists willing to act as news sources given the nature of the political systems and a widespread culture of self-censorship. Journalists who regularly cover science, health, environment, and technology in Africa and the Arab world face a number of difficulties, such as the lack of elementary resources for journalistic research and the existence of newsroom environments that are not always supportive of specialised reporting (Lublinski et al., 2014).

All these issues, and others, will be discussed in this book as part of a larger debate on the role of science journalism in Arab society and the role that it plays in the construction of knowledge and truth. These are pressing issues such that each one deserves a larger discussion. Hence, our book acknowledges that it is rather a piece of a broader puzzle that will take far more research and work to solve. Hence, we have approached the following chapters as being a stepping-stone towards a better understanding of the topic rather than the definitive guide to it.

Considering the above, the first step is perhaps to agree upon a definition of both the idea of science journalism and its distinctiveness from science communication. In this sense, some authors have defined the 'science news beat' as a journalistic genre that primarily deals with scientific achievements and breakthroughs, the scientific process itself and the reporting of scientists' quests and difficulties in solving complex problems (Angler, 2017). As such, science journalism is primarily a specialisation within journalism practices that reports about the work of scientists, the research institutions in which they work, the politics around science and the processes and impacts of scientific discovery.

In so doing, journalists report science news and help the public make sense of science as a socially constructed reality in their day-to-day life. They do this not only by disseminating and sharing scientific knowledge in an accurate manner (something that science communication in its multiple forms does), but also by interpreting it in ways that make science and technology relevant, accessible, interesting, and relevant to the public. Science journalism is also, and perhaps more importantly, a practice that aims to bring about accountability to science and scientists in the ways it does in other sectors of society. That is, by questioning purposes, aims, procedures, ethics and impact.

In this book we look specifically at the science media outlets and science journalistic practices. We inquire about the role they play in exchanging science information and how they have contributed towards science debates within the community. We explore the potential to increase public access to relevant and accurate science knowledge. In our discussion, we take into consideration the disruptions within the media systems, which include, among other things, the emergence of social media and participatory publishing. However, it is important to underline that we mostly refer to the mainstream media, which in the Arab world continues to set the agenda and define public debates.

In the Arab world, the notion of science journalism as a professional and specialised field can be complex as nowadays it comprises a variety of platforms, outputs and actors that were not traditionally considered as news actors. While traditionally science was considered that which was published in the science section or produced by science journalists (Summ & Volpers, 2016), today, it is defined by a broader range of parameters and includes various types of beats such as health, technology and environment. In this sense, science journalists in MENA can be broadly defined as specialists who deliver science developments and events to their audiences, offer analysis and research background and scrutinise the sources and reliability of research.

## On Science Communication

On the other hand, science communication plays a major role in modern society by promoting scientific awareness, understanding, scientific literacy and science cultures. Accordingly, science communication is defined as 'the use of appropriate skills, media, activities and dialogue to produce one or more of the following personal responses to science: awareness, enjoyment, interest, opinion-forming and understanding' (Burns et al., 2003, p. 183).

Several scholars have argued that science communication is important to the public as it contributes to societies' renaissance and development by increasing the rationality of public debate, making it sounder and more likely to be evidence based (Bauer & Bucchi, 2008; Nelkin, 1995b). It not only informs the public about what happens in science but also provides information essential to shaping views on public policy (Nelkin, 1995; Treise & Weigold, 2002, p. 311).

Science communication has been a major factor in popularising science in the past few decades and raising societal awareness about agendas and issues relating to science. This is because the relationship between scientists and communicators is essential to making scientific knowledge accessible to the general public. Ashwell (2016) notes that the concept of science communication refers mainly to the exchange of information between two or more persons or groups using a communication medium, or channel in the pursuit of disseminating scientific truth. Hence, it mainly addresses the exchange of science information between two or more persons or groups.

The development of science communication is an important phenomenon that has helped many societies develop and create opportunities for informed-debate and rational-based public policy based on scientific inquiry. Over time, science communication efforts became accompanied by an increase in public relations professionals, which has now grown into a profession that aims to disseminate within societies the most fundamental knowledge regarding scientific facts. This has in turn laid the ground for science journalism to be able to find access to more accessible sources but that also relies more on particular agendas (Allan, 2009, 2011; Meyer, 2018).

According to Stilgoe et al. (2014), one significant problem associated with the differences in the level of science awareness in society is the public's limited knowledge of scientific facts that can help ease their lives and understand pivotal issues. This is a problem that we certainly identified also in the MENA region, where we found a lack of awareness and interest in topics relating to science as one of the key problems. In other latitudes, science communication has helped increase the public's level of engagement with science and there are some important efforts in MENA but which are so far limited in scope and impact. Nevertheless, even as limited as they are, these efforts have improved the opportunities of non-experts and even of the public to find solutions in science to common problems identifiable in their daily lives.

In addition to this, the increase in the presence of science news in the media space has promoted additional awareness. This is not only in mainstream media but also through the lenses of social media platforms. In many countries, the transformation of the media landscape has made important contributions to the dissemination of science. For example, Claussen et al. (2013) explored the digital channels, including social media, on which photographs and videos related to science news can be shared, making science knowledge accessible to wider segments of societies. These authors have underlined how the significant growth of social media sites, including Facebook, Twitter and other blogging sites, has helped to spread science news to large segments of societies. They also point out that, in addition to raising public awareness related to science knowledge, the growth of science communication helps to bridge societies' knowledge gaps regarding scientists' contributions to development.

Contributions to science communication are classified into four models, which have been described as: deficit, lay expertise, contextual and public participation (Lewenstein, 2003). These models refer mostly to the function and aim of the science communication efforts and to where they are directed. Other researchers have identified other classifications, including the dissemination model, often called the Deficit Model, the dialogue model and the participative model (Gregory & Miller, 1998; Littlejohn &

Foss, 2010; Marshall & Wickenden, 2018; Trench, 2008). Broadly speaking, we found that this theoretical explanatory framework is relevant to MENA as a region, particularly given the gaps in knowledge and limitations to participation.

In this sense, the Deficit Model is a key concept that sees scientists as experts who hold knowledge and the public as lacking in capabilities to properly understand science (Lévy-Leblond, 1992; Trench, 2008) and that we find applicable to MENA. For those who proposed this model, the public lacks sufficient knowledge to participate in, and contribute to, scientific debates (Sturgis & Allum, 2004), which is the case for Arab countries. If the public is provided with enough data about modern science and technology to overcome this 'knowledge deficit', it can view science as beneficial (Dickson, 2005). As science in Arab countries happens under the auspices of the state and there are limited options for individual decisions, then providing information to manufacture consensus is the viable path in that part of the world.

This, because the deficit model implies that science communication flows in only one direction, with scientists producing information and the public receiving it. This model of science communication sees communication as being initiated at the point where the source sends the information and as being completed when the audience receives it in an appropriate, understandable format. This implies a hierarchical structure that in many ways echoes traditional communication formats in the Arab world where there is tight control of the media.

We do have to accept, however, that this is an incomplete model given that it does not really account for the audiences' responses, interactions and receptions. Nevertheless, the deficit model is still the default choice in many areas of science in the Arab world. In these cases, the deficit model persists as the most effective way of underpinning much of the science communication efforts in the region. In fact, as some authors have argued, there is a legitimate case that can be made for retention of a dissemination model in certain circumstances (Trench, 2008) such as in MENA, we would add.

This is not to say that other models, such as the dialogue model, broadly based on the exchange of ideas, opinions, beliefs and feelings between participants—both speakers and audience—are not present in MENA. In many spaces of these societies, things are negotiated rather than imposed and dialogue is the only way forward. This model has been defined as a 'two-way, interactive and participatory' process that includes the valued aspects of mutual respect, humility and trust (Reid et al., 2018, p. 123). Accordingly, science is communicated between scientists and their representatives and other groups, sometimes to find out how science could be more effectively disseminated, sometimes for consultation on specific applications (Trench, 2008). However, in the mainstream media space in MENA, critical responses and contestation to authority are not common so the applicability of this model is limited as is the Participation Model for similar reasons.

In this sense, the Participation Model focuses on the activities that contribute to sharing and therefore to confidence in science policy. It emerged in reaction to the importance of social trust in political disputes about issues regarding science and technology. In many ways, it was a response to the lack of public involvement in the process of decision-making and public policy regarding science and technology (Joss, 1999; Lewenstein, 2003). This explains why it also has limited applicability in MENA.

Despite the fact that most people in the region are aware of the limitations imposed on the professional autonomy of journalists and on media independence, they both continue to represent the primary source of science information in the region. In the Arab world, therefore, science communication is still heavily dependent on the traditional media outlets that continue to be centralised, controlled and hierarchical. This, together with the fact that these societies have limited rights for individual choice, explains why fake news and conspiracy theories were less of an issue in that part of the world when it came to vaccination and use of masks during the pandemic. It also suggests that in that context, the deficit model is the most suitable one, in the face of political realities in the region.

## SCIENCE IN THE MUSLIM WORLD

The Arab world is situated in a large geographic area and includes countries in Asia and Africa. The word 'Arab' is a term used to describe a group of people who share the same language and certain other identifying features including religion; although certainly Islam is not the only one present. Nevertheless, the term 'Arab' is often used synonymously with 'Islam' despite the fact that Islamic countries are not necessarily the same countries as Arab ones and they include instead many others such as Indonesia, Iran, Malaysia and Pakistan, to name just a few in which in fact the great majority of Muslims live. However, the terms 'Arab' and 'Islamic' are often used to mean more or less the same thing or else they are combined into the expression 'the Arab-Islamic world'.

In reality, Arabia signifies the steppe and desert wastes bordering on the territories of the states and principalities of Egypt and the Fertile Crescent (Hoyland, 2002; Yildiz, 2018). The region is mostly identified today with Islam despite the fact that most Muslims live outside that region. Because of this, and due to the faith-based nature of the political systems that prevail in that region, many people in the West see religion as an obstacle to science. This is mostly because many are unaware of the rich scientific heritage from this religion. Historians and other scholars acknowledge the significant contribution of Islam to the contemporary world and particularly to science (Falagas et al., 2006).

In fact, today's humanity enjoys much of its modern-age development in various fields, including medicine, astronomy, mathematics and others thanks to the early scientific observations and works of several Muslim and Arab scholars and scientists. This includes al-Khwarizmi, who is known as the father of algebra, and ibn-Sina, who is considered the founder of early modern medicine (Ajwa et al., 2003; Gohlman, 1986). Dallal (2010) indicates that most historians of Islamic science agree that the beginnings of Islamic science originated with the translation movement of the earlier scientific and philosophical works of important civilisations, including ancient Greece. He also suggests that in the Middle Ages, Muslim societies were involved with pure science and knowledge in ways not seen before or again until the developments of the current era. His argument is that the number of scientists and science books produced at that time are unequalled by those of any other time or civilisation in the pre-modern era.

Moreover, Nasr and De Santillana (1968) describe the ancient sciences of the Mediterranean peoples as being the starting point of the arts and sciences in Islam. That heritage, in particular the knowledge and philosophy of the Greeks, was translated into Arabic by famous translators, including Hunain ibn-Ishaq and Thabit ibn-Qurrah (Nasr & De Santillana, 1968). Many works by Greek authors in nearly all areas and fields of knowledge were translated into Arabic.

The same view is shared by others, who argue that there was a strong translation movement after 750 CE, at the time of the Abbasid Caliphs, who sponsored this movement. Most science books were translated into Arabic. Chaney stated that 'this translation movement coincided with and served as a catalyst for the explosion of scientific output that occurred in the Islamic world over the following centuries' (2016, p. 6). This period witnessed important scientific achievements and advances in fields that included astronomy, mathematics, medicine and optics (Kennedy, 1970; Yusoff et al., 2011).

Particularly important was the 'boom in translation' during the time of the Abbasid Caliphs which was compatible with the teaching of the Prophet Muhammad (PBUH) to seek knowledge everywhere, even if you have to go to China. Baghdad, the capital of the Islamic empire at the time, was the centre stage for this movement and that translators were highly paid. This began slowly at the time of the caliphate of al-Mahdi (775–85) and Harun al-Rashid (786–809) and flourished in the time of al-Mamun. Ancient treatises and books from Greece, Persia, India and even China were brought to Baghdad to be translated into Arabic (Masood, 2017, p. 44).

The translation movement was one that led to later developments and advances in many scientific fields and other areas. Collectively, these advances are known as the 'Islamic Golden Age', a name bestowed by the 'Orientalist' movement (Said, 2003 [1978]). Renima et al. (2016) argue that there is no agreement among historians on the exact beginning and end of the Golden Age. According to them, it was a process rather than a specific period. However, that point in time was known for important events, including the establishment of the Bait el Hikma (House of Wisdom) in Baghdad in the second half of the eighth century. Scientifically, the Golden Age witnessed important breakthroughs and advances. For example, in mathematics, important developments included the decimal place value system, decimal fractions, the first systematised study of algebra (named for the work of al-Khwarizmi, a scholar of the House of Wisdom) and other developments in geometry and trigonometry (Van Sertima, 1992). By the end of the eighth century, the Abbasids applied the decimal system and invented 'Arabic' numerals. They were the first to use the zero, which facilitated operations in a highly remarkable way compared to that of Roman numerals (Renima et al., 2016). The poet Omar al-Khayyam (1048–1131 CE) is another example of the important influence of Muslim scientists at that time. He was a theologian who wrote important studies that helped to establish the principles of algebra, which formed part of the Muslim mathematics that was later passed on to Europeans (Allard, 1997).

In addition to mathematics, astronomy was an area in which Islamic Golden Age scientists made their contributions particularly useful for navigation and discovery. Muslim scholars renewed their interest in this field of knowledge and added to the heritage and contributions of other civilisations. They also noted the support for scientific efforts by the Abbasid rulers, as exemplified by Caliph al Ma'mun, who built an observatory within the framework of the House of Wisdom. The results and achievements of the House of Wisdom were so great as to influence Byzantine, European and Chinese astronomy (Rāshid & Jolivet, 1997).

In addition, alchemy, or early chemistry, is another field that grew during the Golden Age. As it did later on in Europe, where people of the time believed it was possible to transform other matter into gold using an ideal agent called an 'elixir', something that Isaac Newton himself would try centuries later (Sherwood Taylor, 1956; Westfall, 1994). There was however well-grounded research. Jabir ibn-Hayyan (721–780 CE), for example, a well-known scholar of alchemy at the time, studied the compositions of minerals and their transformations. In addition to other well-known Muslim alchemists, ibn-Hayyan developed many processes and reached important findings that served as the basis for modern chemistry.

Overall, we can firmly state that the relationship between science and religion is not a new topic of study in Islam. It is also true that most religions have had serious discussions about, and tensions with, science and we need to acknowledge that Islam is no exception. However, in many ways, Islam has had a much more positive relationship with science throughout history than Christianity, which was known for 'burning at the stake' some the most brilliant minds in history (Martínez, 2018). This is not an attempt to romanticise or simplify the complexities and tensions between two of the most important categories in society. Tensions and clashes exist but not at the antagonistic level that some authors have tried to caricature (Dawkins, 2006; Hitchens, 2008).

In fact, several Qur'anic verses indicate the importance of learning and acquiring knowledge and the Qur'an states clearly that those who know are not equal to those who know not, by adding that it is only men of understanding who will be remembered (Yusoff et al., 2011). Many Qur'anic verses highlight the importance of science, and many narrations and hadiths from the Prophet Muhammad (PBUH) offer additional encouragements to Muslims to seek scientific knowledge. The meanings of these teachings remind Muslims of the importance of searching for knowledge and that doing so is an obligation and duty of all Muslims, both men and women.

Nevertheless, there is a lack of universal agreement around science and the Qur'an. Some believe that the two are compatible while others do not.

Barbour indicates four categories of relationships between science and religion: contradiction and conflict; independence; interaction or dialogue and unity and integration (Yusoff et al., 2011, p. 54). Accordingly, such classification is useful to a scholar proving his or her point, and the same could be said about the relationship between science and the Qur'an. In addition, they refer to Qur'anic verses that have scientific references, including one that describes the mountains as stabilisers. This is accepted by, for example, El-Naggar, the author of the book The Geographical Concept of Mountains in the Qur'an, who claims that there are no contradictions between the explanations of mountain formation contained in scientific studies and those contained in the Qur'an.

In addition, Na'ik (2001) highlights the theological compatibility between science and the Qur'an. He provides many examples in which Qur'anic verses refer to phenomena that were later proved by scientific research and experiments. On the astronomical front, he discusses verses that suggested that the Earth is circular at a time when many people in Europe thought that it was flat. This is the case of the verse about the alternation of day and night which is a clear indication that the Earth is circular and not flat, or any other shape.

However, others argue that the idea of science in Islamic studies is not clear and does not have a definite meaning, as the word that is used to refer to science in Arabic, 'ilm', did not have the same significance that it has today. They add that some orthodox Muslim scholars go as far as to indicate that the definition of science should include 'religious sciences' as well as natural sciences (Guessoum, 2008, p. 416). Some argue that there is a clear difference between 'science' and 'ilm', with the latter meaning knowledge in general rather than only science. For example, Guessoum (2008) explores one disagreement among scholars about the meaning of the word 'ilm'. The object of this disagreement is whether the contemporary significance of science matches the old Islamic meaning of 'ilm'.

Regardless of the controversial nature of the definitions of the terms and the various dimensions and aspects of science in Islam, there is very little doubt that over the centuries many civilisations have interpreted from the Qur'an encouragement and motivation for Muslims to think and reflect from inside themselves about their external world and their beings. Civilisations after civilisations that have placed their faith in Islam have fallen in line with the Qur'an and Islamic teachings that promote scientific knowledge-seeking as evidence of God's creation and brilliance. In addition, Dallal argues that certain types of knowledge are considered 'collective religious obligations' (2010, p. 113). Besides fulfilling the obligations of praying, giving alms and fasting, Muslims are asked to have enough skilled people in each field of knowledge. For example, each Islamic community should have enough physicians, teachers and those skilled in the other indispensable areas of life.

Masood (2017) emphasises the important role of Islam in encouraging and supporting the pursuit of knowledge. By referring to the fact that the Prophet Muhammad (PBUH) often highlighted the importance of good health and urged people to seek medical treatment, Masood clearly shows Islam as a tradition in favour of science, learning and acquiring knowledge. Afridi (2013) notes that Islamic teachings through the Qur'an place much importance on searching for knowledge and learning. Ancient Muslim scholars were very much convinced that there is a duty and a divine instruction to be absorbed in science. Afridi makes a very important reference to the fact that the Qur'an begins with the word 'Read', followed by verses that state that God taught humans what they did not know and verses that speak about knowledge.

After all the interest in the scientific and cultural works of other important civilisations and their translation into Arabic, it is natural that many Muslim and Arab scholars and scientists achieved brilliant and significant discoveries, making contributions in a variety of fields of knowledge. In mathematics, Islamic scientific contribution is neither small nor a subject of disagreement. The numbers used the world over today in all areas of daily life are called 'Arabic numerals' because they were developed by Muslim scholars speaking and working in Arabic. In addition, algebra, a mathematics discipline developed by al-Khwarizmi, is considered one of the most useful tools in mathematics, facilitating our lives and forming the basis of most scientific disciplines. al-Khwarizmi is regarded as one of the most famous figures of Arab mathematics. His efforts in clarifying the Indian numbering system—which later became known as the Arabic system of numbers when al-Khwarizmi passed it on to Europe—are regarded as one of the most important contributions to humanity. Afridi (2013, p. 49) also discusses this mathematician's contributions, arguing that the words 'algebra' and 'algorithm' derive their names from this, and adds that some of al-Khwarizmi's books were translated into European languages and used in European universities until the sixteenth century as principal text books.

al-Khwarizmi is not the only famous mathematician in Islamic history. In eleventh-century Egypt, Hassan ibn al-Haitham was known as one of the scholars who created the basics of the integral calculus used to measure areas and volumes. His work and books on geometry, especially analytical geometry, number theory and the link between algebra and geometry, are also recognised by Europeans as having great significance (Afridi, 2013; Masood, 2017). In addition, among the Muslim scientists who left their mark on the world of mathematics, Omar al-Khayyam is highly regarded. In the early eleventh century, this scientist was able to calculate the number of days in a year. Different scholars note that his calculations were very close to the contemporary calculations achieved by modern tools, which include radio telescopes and atomic clocks. al-Khayyam is also well known for his interpretation of Euclid's geometry theories.

Furthermore, mathematics was not the only scientific area in which Muslim scientists made great developments. The discipline of physics also attracted their attention and interest. Unlike the Greeks, who relied more on theoretical and philosophical understanding and analysis of the natural sciences, Muslims relied rather on experimentation to understand physics. For instance, Muslim scientists were the first to understand the nature of sound and acoustics. They were the first to realise that bodies affect sounds and that these sounds move through the air in the form of waves. In addition, they led in dividing sounds into various categories.

With regard to physics, al-Beruni, a Muslim physicist, was able to identify the specific density of 18 types of stone (Afridi, 2013, p. 50). He also calculated the ratios between the densities of gold, silver, lead and bronze, among other metals. Afridi also notes that Mansour al-Khāzini was an unparalleled physicist, particularly in the areas of dynamics and hydrostatics. His theories, among them the Theory of Obliquity and Inclination and the Theory of Impulse, were applied by schools and universities in the field of kinetics until the modern era. Important Muslim scientists and scholars worked in nearly all areas and disciplines, and it is beyond the scope of this review to include them all, but in addition to the aforementioned, there are two important areas in which Muslim scientists did wonderful jobs: chemistry and medicine.

In chemistry, several famous scientists have been mentioned by historians, of whom Jabir ibn-Hayyan appears to be one of the most influential. He was well known for important contributions in alchemy, which he explored extensively, seeking to go beyond transmuting other metals into gold. Their work showed impressive progress in all sectors of science including chemistry and not only in the Arabian region. The rulers of Islamic Spain, in an attempt to surpass Baghdad, recruited scholars who made contributions of paramount importance to science, medicine, technology, philosophy and art (Falagas et al., 2006).

Medicine is definitely another field in which Muslim scientists left their mark, including such scholars as ibn-Sina, al-Razi and al-Baitar, who cannot be overlooked worldwide, especially by medical students or others interested in the field. For instance, ibn-Sina (980–1073) is regarded as one of the greatest Muslim doctors. Known to the West as Avicenna, ibn-Sina's famous book, *Al-Qanun fi al-Tibb*, was commonly used in Europe as a textbook for more than 70 decades (Afridi, 2013; Falagas et al., 2006). His contributions to pharmacology and public health are well recognised, including his ability to determine the communicable nature of tuberculosis and some other diseases.

Another famous Muslim physician, al-Razi, also known as Rhazes, is known for his medical achievements and for continuing the works of scientists before him and for improving their classification systems. He emphasised the need for proof by experimentation, and refined the raw processes of distillation, evaporation and filtration. al-Razi was appointed several times as the head of hospital in Baghdad. In addition, his achievements included developing a treatment for kidney and bladder stones and being among the first doctors to assess the side-effects of therapies by applying them to animals (Amr & Tbakhi, 2007; Tibi, 2006).

We could go on providing references to the history of Islam's engagement with science. However, it is enough for now to establish that there is nothing inherent to this religion's history or interpretation of tradition that precludes it from fostering the quest for scientific knowledge or embracing fully the scientific method. In this sense, Islam is not in itself an obstacle either to science communication or science in general. On the contrary, if one considers history and a variety of theological interpretations, one would need to acknowledge that there has been a supportive tradition in these societies in relation to knowledge-seeking through evidence by the many religious texts encouraging learning and teaching knowledge, that resonates today (Alexakos & Antoine, 2005; Falagas et al., 2006).

Arab societies are predominantly 'religious' in nature but as some scholars have argued this is a problematic category that has often been abused to reduce these societies to a caricature of irrationality and barbarism (Asad, 2020; Fitzgerald, 2003, 2007). Instead, a sounder analysis needs to acknowledge that these are nation-states born from the drawing of artificial borders, the clash of empires and legacy of colonialism, all of which were followed by the prerogatives of the Cold War. Consequently, they are hybrid formations that reflect a variety of forces that over the years have defined culture and politics in the region. Furthermore, the way Islam is understood today by many is defined by modernity (Gray, 2007; Sayyid, 2014). Considering all this, it would be naïve and simplistic to see these societies in their relation to science only through the prism of religious identity.

Instead, today countries in MENA thrive for modernity in multiple forms in the face of globalisation. There is ample evidence that the Arab world wants not only to eradicate illiteracy but also to engage with science in more comprehensive ways. In every single strategic document from governments in the region, there is a clear commitment to science. There is a prolific body of public policies and initiatives directed towards fostering science and technology and encouraging citizens to be more engaged with science in general.

For science journalists operating in the region this context is both a challenge as well as an opportunity. There are areas that cannot be transformed or open but there are others that are subject to intervention and change. Yes, journalism as a political institution in MENA faces important restraints in its professional autonomy and challenges exist in relation to the ability of individual reporters to cover effectively many news beats. However, the problems of science journalism in that part of the world need to be understood as a complex setting forged by history, politics and culture; a setting that nevertheless is subject to a variety of variables upon which there is potential to change.

## Arab Science Journalism

It is clear that there are distinctive settings that enhance, constrain and potentially hinder the autonomy of professional science journalists in this region. Therefore, examining how journalists operating in this part of the world—who already face very distinctive challenges associated with culture, religion, post-colonial history, politics and economics—is a promising opportunity not only to understand the subject in question, but also to contribute to the wider debates around the de-Westernisation of media studies as a whole in the context of science communication. That is the task that we have set ourselves in the following chapters.

This book is the result of two research projects that were funded by several institutions which included the Ministry of Education of the Kingdom of Saudi Arabia, the grant NPRP12S-0317-190381 from the Qatar National Research Fund, part of Qatar Foundation and Education City, the Professional Development Fund awarded by Northwestern University in Qatar and support from the University of Sharjah and the Military Academy of Saudi Arabia. We want to thank them all for their generous support, which shows the potential of the region when it comes together to facilitate research and collaboration. We also want to thank the anonymous peer reviewers for their constructive advice and feedback. This book is much better thanks to them. Our gratitude also goes to Bruce Mutsvairo, Saba Bebawi and Eddy Borges-Rey for leading this extraordinary series of books in Palgrave that highlights the contributions of the Global South to journalism studies. They have truly opened a thriving space for debate and thought. Finally, but no less important, we give thanks to our wives Alanoud and Maria Alejandra and all of our children who provided the personal and emotional support that allowed us to successfully culminate this project. It is a project that is far from perfect, but then so are most of the first steps that we take in our lives.

## Bibliography

Abu Haseera, R. (2018). *The reality of scientific journalism in the Palestinian daily newspapers: A comparative analytical and field study*. Islamic University of Gaza.

Afridi, M. (2013). Contribution of Muslim scientists to the world: An overview of some selected fields. *Revelation and Science, 3*(01).

Aistrope, T., & Bleiker, R. (2018). Conspiracy and foreign policy. *Security Dialogue, 49*(3), 165–182.

Ajwa, I. A., Liu, Z., & Wang, P. S. (2003). *Gröbner Bases Algorithm* (pp. 1–14). The Institute for Computational Mathematics.

Alexakos, K., & Antoine, W. (2005). The golden age of Islam and science teaching. *The Science Teacher, 72*(3), 36.

Allan, S. (2009). The future of science journalism. *Journalism, 10*(3), 280–282.

Allan, S. (2011). Introduction: Science journalism in a digital age. *Journalism, 12*(7), 771–777.

Allard, A. (1997). L'influence des mathématiques arabes dans l'Occident médiéval. *Histoire Des Sciences Arabes, 2*, 199–229.

Amr, S. S., & Tbakhi, A. (2007). Abu Bakr Muhammad Ibn Zakariya Al Razi (Rhazes): Philosopher, Physician and Alchemist. *Annals of Saudi Medicine, 27*(4), 305–307.

Anderson, A., Peterson, A., David, M., & Allan, S. (2005). Communication or spin? Source-media relations in science journalism. *Journalism: Critical Issues*, 188–198.
Angler, M. W. (2017). *Science Journalism. An Introduction*. Routledge.
Asad, T. (2020). *Formations of the secular*. Stanford University Press.
Ashwell, D. (2016). The challenges of science journalism: The perspectives of scientists, science communication advisors and journalists from New Zealand. *Public Understanding of Science, 25*(3), 379–393.
Bauer, M., & Bucchi, M. (2008). *Journalism, science and society: Science communication between news and public relations*. Routledge.
Bauer, M., Howard, S., Ramos, R., Jessica, Y., Massarani, L., & Amorim, L. (2013). *Global science journalism report: Working conditions & practices, professional ethos and future expectations*. Science and Development Network.
Bauer, M. W., & Howard, S. (2009). *The Sense of Crisis among Science Journalists. A survey conducted on the occasion of WCSJ_09 in London. StePS. London School of Economics and Political Science*. Institute of Social Psychology.
Bernadas, J. M. A. C., & Ilagan, K. (2020). Journalism, public health, and COVID-19: Some preliminary insights from the Philippines. *Media International Australia, 177*(1), 132–138.
Burns, T., O'Connor, D., & Stocklmayer, S. (2003). Science communication: A contemporary definition. *Public Understanding of Science, 12*(2), 183–202.
Carrion-Alvarez, D., & Tijerina-Salina, P. X. (2020). Fake news in COVID-19: A perspective. *Health Promotion Perspectives, 10*(4), 290.
Chaney, E. (2016). *Religion and the rise and fall of Islamic science*. Harvard University.
Claussen, J., Cooney, P., Defilippi, J., Fox, S., Glaser, S., Hawkes, E., Hutt, C., Jones, M., Kemp, I., & Lerner, A. (2013). Science communication in a digital age: Social media and the American Fisheries Society. *Fisheries, 38*(8), 359–362.
Dallal, A. (2010). *Islam, science, and the challenge of history*. Yale University Press.
Dawkins, R. (2006). *The God delusion*. Bantam Books.
Determann, J. M. (2015). *Researching biology and evolution in the Gulf states: Networks of science in the Middle East*. Bloomsbury Publishing.
Dickson, D. (2005). The case for a 'deficit model' of science communication. *SciDev.Net, 27*.
El-Awady, N. (2009). Science journalism: The Arab boom. *Nature, 459*, 1057.
Essam, B. A., & Abdo, M. S. (2021). How do Arab tweeters perceive the COVID-19 pandemic? *Journal of Psycholinguistic Research, 50*(3), 507–521.
Falagas, M., Zarkadoulia, E., Samonis, G., & The FASEB Journal. (2006). Arab science in the golden age (750–1258 CE) and today. *The FASEB Journal, 20*(10), 1581–1586.
Fitzgerald, T. (2003). *The ideology of religious studies*. Oxford University Press.
Fitzgerald, T. (2007). *Discourse on civility and barbarity*. Oxford University Press.

Fjæstad, B. (2007). 12 Why journalists report science as they do. In *Journalism, Science and Society* (p. 123). Routledge.

Ghosh, S. M., & Qadeer, I. (2020). Public good perspective of public health evaluating health systems response to COVID-19. *Economic and Political Weekly*, 40–48.

Giles, J. (2006). Islam and Science: Oil rich, science poor. *Nature, 444*(7115), 28–29.

Gohlman, W. (1986). *The Life of Ibn Sina*. Suny Press.

Gray, J. (2007). *Black Mass: Apocalyptic religion and the death of Utopia*. Macmillan.

Gregory, J., & Miller, S. (1998). *Science in public: Communication, culture, and credibility*. Plenum Press.

Guessoum, N. (2008). The Qur'an, science, and the (related) contemporary Muslim discourse. *Zygon, 43*(2), 411–431.

Hamdy, N. (2013). Arab investigative journalism practice. *Journal of Arab & Muslim Media Research, 6*(1), 67–93.

Hansen, A. (2016). The changing uses of accuracy in science communication. *Public Understanding of Science, 25*(7), 760–774.

Herman, E. S., & Chomsky, N. (2010). *Manufacturing consent: The political economy of the mass media*. Random House.

Hitchens, C. (2008). *God is not great: How religion poisons everything*. McClelland & Stewart.

Hoyland, R. (2002). *Arabia and the Arabs: From the Bronze Age to the coming of Islam*. Routledge.

Joss, S. (1999). Public participation in science and technology policy- and decision-making—Ephemeral phenomenon or lasting change? *Science and Public Policy, 26*(5), 290–293.

Kennedy, E. (1970). *The Arabic heritage in the exact sciences*. American University of Beirut.

Lévy-Leblond, J. (1992). About misunderstandings about misunderstandings. *Public Understanding of Science, 1*(1), 17–21.

Lewenstein, B. (2003). Models of public communication of science and technology. *Public Understanding of Science*.

Lippmann, W. (1992). *Public opinion*. Routledge.

Littlejohn, S., & Foss, K. (2010). *Theories of human communication*. Waveland Press.

Lublinski, J., Reichert, I., Denis, A., Fleury, J., Labassi, O., & Spurk, C. (2014). Advances in African and Arab science journalism: Capacity building and new newsroom structures through digital peer-to-peer support. *Ecquid Novi: African Journalism Studies, 35*(2), 4–22.

Mahmoud, N. (2018). *The credibility of scientific and technological news in electronic and paper newspapers among scientific elites and the general public.* .

Marshall, J., & Wickenden, M. (2018). Services for people with Communication Disabilities in Uganda: Supporting a new Speech and Language Therapy profession. *Disability and the Global South, 5*(1), 1215–1233.

Martínez, A. A. (2018). *Burned Alive: Bruno, Galileo and the Inquisition*. Reaktion Books.

Martisini, A. (2018). *Journalism, statistics and quality in the news*. University of Leeds.

Masood, E. (2017). *Science and Islam (Icon Science): A History*. Icon Books.

Matthews, O. (2020). *Britain Drops Its Go-It-Alone Approach to Coronavirus. Foreign Policy*.

Mehran, Z. (2018). *How to introduce science to the Arab child*. Academic Library.

Mellor, N. (2005). *The making of Arab news*. Rowman & Littlefield Publishers.

Mellor, N. (2011). *Arab media: Globalization and emerging media industries* (Vol. 1). Polity.

Meyer, G. (2018). *The Science communication challenge: Truth and disagreement in democratic knowledge societies*. Anthem Press.

Mooney, C. (2007). *The Republican war on science*. Basic Books.

Moore-Gilbert, K., & Abdul-Nabi, Z. (2021). Authoritarian downgrading,(self) censorship and new media activism after the Arab Spring. *New Media & Society*, 23(5), 875–893.

Murcott, T. (2009). Science journalism: Toppling the priesthood. *Nature*, 459(7250), 1054–1055.

Muwahed, J. (2020). Coronavirus pandemic goes viral in the age of social media, sparking anxiety. *ABC News*. https://abcnews.go.com/Politics/coronavirus-pandemic-viral-age-social-media-sparking-anxiety/story?id=69580796

Na'ik, Z. (2001). *Qur'an and modern science: Compatible or incompatible*. Dar-US-Salaam.

Nasr, S., & De Santillana, G. (1968). *Science and civilization in Islam* (Vol. 16). Harvard University Press.

Nelkin, D. (1995). *Selling science: How the press covers science and technology*. Rev. Ed. Freeman.

Nguyen, A. (2017). *News, numbers and public opinion in a data-driven world*. Bloomsbury Publishing.

Nguyen, A., & McIlwaine, S. (2011). Who wants a voice in Science issues—And why? A survey of European citizens and its implications for science journalism. *Journalism Practice*, 5(2), 210–226.

Nguyen, A., & Tran, M. (2019). Science journalism for development in the Global South: A systematic literature review of issues and challenges. *Public Understanding of Science*, 28(8), 973–990.

Nisbet, M., & Scheufele, D. (2009). What's next for science communication? Promising directions and lingering distractions. *American Journal of Botany*, 96(10), 1767–1778.

O'Reilly, A. (2020). *Trump calls for restarting economy by Easter: 'We have to get back to work.'*

Oliver, J. E., & Wood, T. J. (2014). Conspiracy theories and the paranoid style (s) of mass opinion. *American Journal of Political Science, 58*(4), 952–966.

Olsen, R. K., Pickard, V., & Westlund, O. (2020). Communal news work: COVID-19 calls for collective funding of journalism. *Digital Journalism, 8*(5), 673–680.

Oreskes, N., & Conway, E. M. (2010). Defeating the merchants of doubt. *Nature, 465*(7299), 686–687.

Oreskes, N., & Conway, E. M. (2011). *Merchants of doubt: How a handful of scientists obscured the truth on issues from tobacco smoke to global warming.* Bloomsbury Publishing.

Otto, S. L. (2016). *The war on Science: Who's waging it, why it matters, what we can do about it.* .

Peters, H. P. (2013). Gap between science and media revisited: Scientists as public communicators. *Proceedings of the National Academy of Sciences, 110*(Supplement 3), 14102–14109.

Rāshid, R., & Jolivet, J. (1997). *Oeuvres philosophiques et scientifiques d'Al-Kindi: L'optique et la catoptrique* (Vol. 29). Brill.

Reid, M., Walsh, C., Raubenheimer, J., Bradshaw, T., Pienaar, M., Hassan, C., Nyoni, C., & Le Roux, M. (2018). Development of a health dialogue model for patients with diabetes: A complex intervention in a low-/middle income country. *International Journal of Africa Nursing Sciences, 8*, 122–131.

Renima, A., Tiliouine, H., & Estes, R. (2016). The Islamic golden age: A story of the triumph of the Islamic civilization. In H. Tiliouine & R. Estes (Eds.), *The State of Social Progress of Islamic Societies* (pp. 25–52). Springer.

Rodrigues, U. M., & Xu, J. (2020). Regulation of COVID-19 fake news infodemic in China and India. *Media International Australia, 177*(1), 125–131.

Saber, N. (2013). The scientific media crisis: A study of the scientific press discourse in Al-Ahram newspaper from October–December 2012. *Arab Journal for Media and Communication Research, 2*, 192–215.

Said, E. (2003). *Orientalism: Western conceptions of the Orient*. Penguin Books Limited.

Sayyid, S. (2014). *Recalling the Caliphate: Decolonisation and world order*. Oxford University Press.

Seale, C. (2010). How the mass media report social statistics: A case study concerning research on end-of-life decisions. *Social Science & Medicine, 71*(5), 861–868.

Shahsavari, S., Holur, P., Wang, T., Tangherlini, T. R., & Roychowdhury, V. (2020). Conspiracy in the time of corona: Automatic detection of emerging COVID-19 conspiracy theories in social media and the news. *Journal of Computational Social Science, 3*(2), 279–317.

Sherwood Taylor, F. (1956). An alchemical work of Sir Isaac Newton. *Ambix, 5*(3–4), 59–84.

Sidqi, H. (2009). *Scientific journalism between theory and practice*. Academic Library.

Skalli, L. (2006). Communicating gender in the public sphere: Women and information technologies in the MENA. *Journal of Middle East Women's Studies*, 2(2), 35–59.

Stecula, D. A., & Pickup, M. (2021). How populism and conservative media fuel conspiracy beliefs about COVID-19 and what it means for COVID-19 behaviors. *Research & Politics*, 8(1), 2053168021993979.

Stein, R. A., Ometa, O., Shetty, S. P., Katz, A., Popitiu, M. I., & Brotherton, R. (2021). Conspiracy theories in the era of COVID-19: A tale of two pandemics. *International Journal of Clinical Practice*, 75(2) https://www.ncbi.nlm.nih.gov/pmc/articles/PMC7995222/

Stephens, M. (2020). A geospatial infodemic: Mapping Twitter conspiracy theories of COVID-19. *Dialogues in Human Geography*, 10(2), 276–281.

Stilgoe, J., Lock, S., & Wilsdon, J. (2014). Why should we promote public engagement with science? *Public Understanding of Science*, 23(1), 4–15.

Sturgis, P., & Allum, N. (2004). Science in society: Re-evaluating the deficit model of public attitudes. *Public Understanding of Science*, 13(1), 55–74.

Summ, A., & Volpers, A. (2016). What's science? Where's science? Science journalism in German print media. *Public Understanding of Science*, 25(7), 775–790.

Tibi, S. (2006). Al-Razi and Islamic medicine in the 9th century. *Journal of the Royal Society of Medicine*, 99(4), 206–207.

Treise, D., & Weigold, M. F. (2002). Advancing science communication: A survey of science communicators. *Science Communication*, 23(3), 310–322.

Trench, B. (2008). Towards an analytical framework of science communication models. In *Communicating science in social contexts* (pp. 119–135). Springer.

Trench, B., & Junker, K. (2001). *How scientists view their public communication*, 1–3.

Van Sertima, I. (1992). *The golden age of the Moor* (Vol. 11). Transaction Publishers.

Westfall, R. S. (1994). *The Life of Isaac Newton*. Cambridge University Press.

Yildiz, M. (2018). *Historiography development in Arabic-Islamic history writing*.

Yusoff, M., Yakub, M., & Danehsgar, M. (2011). Islam and the relation of science and the Qur'an. International Conference on Humanities, Society and Culture, Singapore.

CHAPTER 2

# An Account of Science Journalism in MENA

From all the avenues and forms used to communicate science to the general public, science journalism continues to be one the most influential and central in underpinning the efforts to provide access to, and engage, common people with scientific knowledge (Al-Qafari, 2009; Bauer, 2013). So much so, that while other forms of media entertainment content—for example, films, television shows and others—might reach mass audiences or be very comprehensive and accurate, such as museums and exhibitions, they struggle to deliver both (accurate information as in the first case or reach the mass public as in the second case) at the same time.

Indeed, only science journalism seems capable of combining both. This, as it encompasses comprehensive and accurate aspects of science while, at the same time, is able to disseminate accurate and accessible information across large segments of the public (Nguyen & McIlwaine, 2011; Nguyen & Tran, 2019) in ways that can be used and trusted on a daily basis.

This very important function of news reporting of science has been widely acknowledged both by experts, scholars and the overall scientific community, despite important reservations about the capacity of journalists to report accurately and comprehensively both the findings and process of producing scientific knowledge (Allan, 2011; Hermida, 2010). In democratic societies, there has been more or less a move towards the consolidation of science and technology as permanent news beats in

© The Author(s), under exclusive license to Springer Nature Switzerland AG 2023
A. Alhuntushi, J. Lugo-Ocando, *Science Journalism in the Arab World*, Palgrave Studies in Journalism and the Global South, https://doi.org/10.1007/978-3-031-14252-9_2

mainstream media outlets. That is, today many newspapers, broadcasters and online digital native media dedicate resources and have space and people dedicated to cover a variety of topics relating to natural sciences and health. To be sure, areas such as health, astronomy, the environment and even mathematics receive regular news coverage by journalists who are fully dedicated to write and produce stories about these topics.

Although the field of science communication is a broad one and encompasses multiple dimensions and areas, it is the role of the news media in reporting science that has received most attention by scholars (Bauer, 2013; Bucchi, 1998; Fischhoff & Scheufele, 2013; Fjæstad, 2007; Nelkin, 1995; Treise & Weigold, 2002). This is because the news media have an important role in communicating science to the public, and in doing so, it not only raises awareness about science and its methods but also makes science relevant to people and, subsequently, it can have an impact on both policy and allocation of resources. It is in this context that science journalism becomes relevant as it helps shape public opinion and engagement with science.

Moreover, science communication in general has been a major part of journalism throughout the past few decades. In this sense, science journalism is the third most prolific news beat after social science and life science, with 15% of all news stories (Al-Qafari, 2009). This is mostly because it includes sub-areas such as health and technology in its news beat. Moreover, science journalism has a significant role in developing countries (Bauer, 2013; Mbarga et al., 2012). This, as it is considered a platform for the introduction of ideas, innovations and exchanges of expertise and experiences while fostering creative ability (Al-Qafari, 2009 p. 89). In addition, in developed countries, science news is considered one of the most trusted types of news. A YouGov survey revealed that print and online news stories about science and sports are considered the most trustworthy by the British public, with sport having 17%, while science accounts for 14% of the total of trust (Matter, 2017). This was, however, a survey carried out before the COVID 19 pandemic, which we now know altered fundamentally public perceptions of science news and trust in the media among large segments of the audiences.

In addition, scholars argue that science communication is important to the public not only because it fosters civic engagement with science as a topical issue, but also because it introduces a degree of further rationality into all public debates, making these discussions sounder and more prone to evidence-based discussion (Bubela et al., 2009; Nisbet & Scheufele,

2009). For sure, science communication not only informs people about what happens in science, but it can also provide the public with essential information to shape their views about public policy (Treise & Weigold, 2002, p. 311). Nelkin, for example, pointed out that science communication supports 'the individual's ability to make rational choices'. Thus, science communication can aid people in making better decisions about their society and their own lives (1995, p. 2). In this sense,

> We all need science for making effective decisions in our lives. Are the expected benefits of a medical procedure worth its risks? Does it make sense to rebuild homes along the seashore after a hurricane? How good are the predictions for storm surges? Should we sign a lease for hydrofracking on our property? What are the risks to our drinking water? Science is, potentially, the best source for the evidence needed to answer these questions. Realizing that potential will require effective two-way communication with those whom science hopes to serve—so that it produces relevant information and conveys it in a credible, comprehensible form. (Fischhoff & Scheufele, 2013, p. 1413)

The ability of journalists to report science news in an accessible and accurate manner, while making these topics relevant to the general public, allowing people to engage and actively participate in science discovery, is, therefore, of vital importance given the reasons enunciated above in relation to the need for society's engagement with science.

In relation to this, the debate within the science communication field has mostly centred around two key aspects. On the one hand, there are those—particularly scientists—who have stressed the need for 'accuracy' when dealing with science news (Hansen, 2016; Murcott, 2009). For these voices, the most important issue relates to the accuracy of media reporting of science (Seale, 2010). Fjæstad (2007 p. 123) suggested some time ago that the way in which science news is reported, especially when it comes to natural science, is inadequate because of its non- or under-reporting of important scientific progress, tendency to sensationalism and negativity in wording, presentation and inaccurate reporting.

The other camp, on the other hand, has argued around the need for journalists to make science news more relevant to the general public while approaching science news in general in a critical manner (Nguyen & McIlwaine, 2011). For these authors, the problem is not so much to do with accuracy—although they recognise the underlying issues around this—but the fact that many ordinary citizens fail to engage with science news because it does not seem to be relevant enough to their individual and collective lives. In addition, and perhaps more importantly, these authors point to the lack of criticality around science news reports. For them, many journalists, with few exceptions, lack the necessary capabilities and tools to scrutinise science, therefore leaving it unaccountable as a news source. It is because of these two camps in particular, and the wider debates around science communication in general, that we have decided to explore in my study the importance of statistics in the articulation of science news.

In these settings, science news has become central in the questioning of power and policy such as the use of genetically modified organisms in the food production chain, the emissions of CO2 gases and the link between smoking and cancer, to mention a few. Indeed, in many liberal societies, science has become an ally of journalists seeking truth and performing a role of watchdog to power in society. In places such as Australia, Europe, Japan and the United States, science journalists use science to challenge power relations and help improve the wellbeing of society.

However, the role of science journalists is by no means limited to science dissemination and providing access to scientific knowledge but also, and perhaps more importantly, it extends to bringing accountability to science itself and putting it under the public microscope in the same manner as it does with the actors of other news beats. Hence, journalists' function is also to question science itself. Particularly, when its ethics are compromised by greed, power or disdain for others. This was the case, to use a notorious historical example, of the Tuskegee Study where members of the Afro-American community were allowed to die in order to carry out scientific observations of the effects of syphilis (Jones, 1993; Reverby, 2005). Science journalists therefore are not just there to help popularise science and make complicated notions accessible, but also to ask important questions in relation to the impact of scientific work upon the rest of society.

However, the question remains, how much of this function is applicable to societies where news reporting operates in a completely different framework? What happens in places in which journalists are restricted politically, face important cultural limitations or where the political economy of the news media is insufficiently developed so as to sustain science as a permanent and specialised news beat? What other limitations and challenges do journalists face under these circumstances?

To explore these questions, this chapter looks at the case of science journalism in MENA, where many of these limitations are present on a daily basis. The idea is to assess through a combination of research strategies the current state of science journalism in that region, while inquiring about its function in society. In so doing, the chapter aims to examine the role and performance of science reporting in the context of societies that have limited freedom of expression and that are politically and culturally defined in many instances by colonialism and religion.

An important caveat in this analysis of the Middle East and North Africa is the need to provide a comparative approach that is both intra-regional as well as transnational. This, because of the need to explore commonalities between science journalism roles and performances within the Arab world and the way it is practised in the so-called West. Our own comparative content analysis between news pieces published in Arab and US newspapers discussed in this book shows a remarkable convergence around the final outputs that reporters covering this news beat produce when their work become juxtaposed with that of their counterparts in other countries in Europe and the United States. Equally, interview after interview with news people in the MENA region highlights the great degree of affinity that Arab journalists express with Western normative professional aspirations relating to quest for truth in science news, something that is also supported by other research in the field (Bebawi, 2016; Douai & Moussa, 2016; Pintak, 2014).

In addition to this general view of journalism, one tends to find that many science news stories published and broadcast in the Middle East are very similar or literally the same as the ones that appear in the Western media. This is either because they come from international news agencies and sources or because the reporter in one of these countries adopted the same approach and angle when producing the story. This should not come as a surprise given the overall remarkable convergence of journalistic practices and news cultures across the globe (Hanitzsch, 2007; Hanitzsch et al., 2019; Mellado, 2015). Journalists all over the world share seemly universal and deontological universal normative values about what makes something newsworthy and how to present this to the public.

Having said that, we also noticed exceptional characteristics and, overall, a very distinctive nature on the ground in relation to both outputs and roles. For example, reviewing mainstream legacy news media outlets in the Arab world, one does not find certain news stories that are present and even prevalent in the West. They either remain invisible and completely missing from the public debates or one reads them with a very different tone or angle to the point that it is almost unrecognisable from the same story published in another country. In some cases, for obvious reasons, certain stories have been suppressed or ignored while in others they are presented fundamentally changed. Our own comparative data, discussed in this book, shows that science journalism in Arab countries has both common and distinctive agendas when reporting science to those of their western counterparts.

Overall, and despite many similarities, Arab science journalism seems to be a very different political institution altogether. Not only because it operates within a very discrete cultural context and political framework but also because the nature itself of journalism as a social practice in these countries is widely different (Al-Najjar, 2011; Mellor, 2007). To understand this better, we have looked at the historical formation of journalism as a political institution and examined the development and current state of science journalism in the Arab world. In so doing, we aim to provide a grounded assessment of how it became to be and how it reflects and, also, diverges from other political institutions in those societies.

The chapter accounts for those aspects that define and shape science journalistic practices. Aspects that include elements such as religion, culture and politics. However, as we also argue here, we inquire too into how other historical aspects have also been equally influential such as colonialism, economics, technology and globalisation. We do not pretend to offer an overall history of science journalism in the Arab world, which would merit a book in its own right, but we do try to provide elements that allow us all to better understand how and why it is distinctive from related professional areas such as science communication in the region. In so doing, we explore how news audiences around science developed in the region while providing a theoretical framework as to how science journalism reached its current state.

## History, Post-colonialism and Science

However, before we can do that, we need to explain further the development of journalism as a political institution in the modern age in the Arab world. This is a history that is intrinsically linked to the development of the institutional and political framework that today defines the region. And, one that has been equally shaped by local traditions and norms, colonialism, resistance and globalisation. Consequently, we cannot situate the development of science journalism in the region without accounting for the historical and political contexts in which it emerged.

As with many societies in the Global South, the modern institutions in Arab countries were shaped by the forces of colonialism and resistance. This, as the colonial powers created a legacy that shaped the trajectory of state development within the Arab region. To be sure, during the decline, and later, collapse of the Ottoman Empire, the colonial powers imposed the system of nation-states that exists today in the region. These were, with the exception of Egypt that had a long history of territorial unity, artificial political entities that imposed new political realities and identities for many of its citizens (Pratt, 2007). This process of imposition, which started under colonial rule, also meant the incorporation of the region into the global capitalist system while cementing its subordinate position within that system of producers of commodities and consumers of industrial goods (Ateş et al., 2005; Tignor, 1980). This was even the case in those areas on the periphery of MENA that escaped direct colonial control, such as Turkey and Iran. This, as they were, nevertheless, dependent on commodities that needed to be sold on the international market and as any attempts to redeem national rights were met with military interventions and/or externally orchestrated coups.

In many of these countries, local elites were commissioned by the colonial powers to oversee their interests there and in such circumstances these elites were allocated variable degrees of power and autonomy as well as the ability to concentrate resources in their own hands.

During the colonial era, European powers imposed strict rules and norms against freedom of speech and kept the media tightly controlled as part of their efforts to keep a grip on these societies. To be sure, these powers exercised directly—or through their local representatives—widespread media control. Censorship was in fact a central feature of colonial rule (Tibi, 1997; Watenpaugh, 2014), which explains why many nowadays accuse the West of having double moral standards as a great deal of the current legislation that today limit freedom of speech and professional autonomy of journalists in MENA was actually developed or inspired by the then colonial former masters (De Baets, 2016). In many of these countries, the British and French either implemented censorship or left in place the one that the Ottoman Empire had imposed in the first place (Tillier & Nicholson-Smith, 2012; Yosmaoğlu, 2003) and through the independence struggles freedom of speech became a central cry by locals.

Having said that, the end of colonial rule did not mean the termination of censorship and many of the calls for greater freedom during the struggles for independence remained unanswered following liberation. Moreover, many of the newly independent states saw an expansion in the legal mechanisms to control and restrict freedom of the press despite what many of their leaders had promised during the independence struggles. This was partly due to the tensions, conflicts and confrontations that arose after independence, which forced or enabled the leaders to impose emergency legislation that limited individual freedoms while setting the basis of future authoritarianism (Ghalioun, 2004; Hanssen & Weiss, 2018). The postcolonial Arab societies saw many wars and struggles, including the occupation of Palestine by a neo-colonial state that still today imports settlers with the excuse of Judaism and that since then has provoked havoc across the region. The role of these conflicts in preventing democratic and institutional development needs to be considered too as central factor in the implementation of the restriction of individual and collective freedoms (Pratt, 2007; Wolfsfeld, 1997).

Another very important force shaping the institutional framework that served as a context for the emergence of modern science journalism in the region was undoubtedly the imperatives imposed by the Cold War. This, because the superpowers of the time, the United States and the Soviet Union, projected their struggles in proxy conflicts and propaganda efforts (Slater, 1990; Vaughan, 2005). As nationalist movements and monarchies took sides in the Cold War and gained support and assistance from the superpowers, they were also subjected to the tensions and issues derived from the proxy confrontations (Katsakioris, 2010; Scott & Carter, 2015).

Meanwhile, the region witnessed the emergence, expansion and consolidation of nationalist and religious political movements such as the Ba'ath Party, with a strong secular intake as well as others such as the Muslim Brotherhood, which embraced Islam as part of its political ideology. These movements had several common characteristics despite their obvious ideological differences. Firstly, they were both transnational with a presence in many of the countries in the region where they operated in the form of political parties or affiliated organisations. Secondly, they embraced a different form of modernisation even when in some cases they claimed to be anti-Western or had a longer tradition present in their views (Citino, 2008; Iqbal et al., 2021). Thirdly, in those cases where they achieved power, they became increasingly authoritarian.

Once in power, many post-independence regimes responded to the challenge of modernisation by initiating heavy state involvement in the economy. Consequently, not only political but also economic power became concentrated in the hands of the elites that controlled the new independent states. This, together with the fact that the military became central in the allocation of power in the context of the Cold War paving the way for the type of authoritarianism that would come to dominate the region for most of the twentieth century (Ghalioun, 2004; Pratt, 2007, p. 27) and which became the norm for both secular regimes and monarchies.

This in turn had a profound effect on the development of journalism as a political institution in the Arab world, which adopted distinctive, and at times polarised, forms across the region. On the one hand, mainstream journalism became attached to the powerful elites and subordinated to the central state. This expressed itself as a body of news media outlets that had little discretionarily to say what they wanted while individual reporters enjoyed limited professional autonomy in their work. Yes, we can find a variety of examples of independent journalism that even managed to contest power, but more often than not they were short-lived experiments in the vast desert of co-opted media.

It is in this context that we can place the formation of science journalism in the Arab world as we know it today. It is a constructed practice that reflects both the forces of imposition and contestation that shaped all the institutions in the region. It is also one that carries with it a tradition of scientific knowledge creation and dissemination that goes back to the foundation of Islam. Indeed, let us not forget that the land that Western colonisers found in the nineteenth century was never an empty space but instead one rich in science engagement that had a very long tradition of universities and centres of research that provided spaces for knowledge exchange (Iqbal, 2007; Nasr & De Santillana, 1968).

In fact, the Ottoman Empire had left in the region a strong legacy of scientific engagement (Citino, 2008; Inalcik, 2019; Ortaylı, 2019 [2004]). Even if it was a legacy that reflected the Ottoman decline itself. During the last decades of the empire, the region saw a mass exodus of scientists and researchers who left the scholarly world to undertake other jobs and tasks in order to look for better salaries. More broadly speaking, what one could call a scientific community of scholars slowly disintegrated as the empire became politically weaker, economically poorer and intellectually disperse. The subsequent European colonial power did little to nothing to revive culture and science in their new domains. By the time the Arab states became completely independent, any form of public science communication was a shadow of its former past and new existing manifestations of journalism practice started to be recreated in the image of the new Western institutions. This context provides a good idea of the historical roots for the challenges that science journalism faces today in that region.

## Science News Cultures

Science journalism faces several issues in this region. To start with, there is a lack of specialisation among reporters trying to cover this news beat (Al-Qafari, 2009; El-Awady, 2009; Mahmood, 2008). The existing gap is exacerbated by poor working conditions and precarious salaries in several news media outlets across the region, declining revenues in the news media, lack of interest to train reporters in the field of science journalism, constraints when trying to access sources and systematic undermining of the professional autonomy required to produce independent news. To be fair, many of these are conditions that we tend to find in many countries in the Global South, as has been recorded by some scholars (Bauer et al., 2013; Calvo Hernando, 2002; Massarani & Boys, 2007; Nguyen & Tran, 2019).

To this we have to add the lack of scientific communication culture in the Arab region, which is far from showing similar levels of engagement as in other countries. Consequently, that part of the world lacks the necessary driving elements that tend to foster a market for science news that in turn fosters more news content in that beat. Without sufficient demand, professional and organisational dynamics to produce science news, which is present in other societies, simply do not happen. To be sure, to foster a news culture around science, there needs to be a particular level of demand from the public to the point of creating a political economy that can push for journalists [and their editors] to engage with science information on a regular basis (Long, 1995).

Equally pervasively present, are some institutional structures and dynamics left behind by history. Science journalists in MENA operate in the context of tensions provoked by the imposition of modernisation, post-coloniality and illiberal regimes. These dynamics have created a unique dimension in the Arab world for the way journalists act as an interpretative community that produces and shares knowledge and information (Mellor, 2008). In some cases, these dynamics are a historical by-product of tensions, imposition and contestation, which consequently have shaped particular forms of journalism in the Global South (Lugo-Ocando, 2020). Hence, journalism as a political institution in Arab societies reflects the sociological constructs that are derived from culture, politics and history.

We should also acknowledge how the imposition of modernity as a legacy of colonialism and the Cold War also helped generate the types of tensions and limitations that science journalism faces today in the Arab world; even more so, given the actual historical legacy of the role of science in these countries. This need to historicise our discussion must be a dialectical exercise in the face of the present, given the preconceptions and quasi-axiomatic assumptions around science communication in the Arab world. To contextualise Arab science journalism in history can allow us to understand it not only as a post-colonial construction that intends to mirror the West, but also as a political institution that has a long and rich history of science communication that dates back centuries and that over the years has linked these societies and knowledge in ways that would take many centuries for Europe to reach.

It is not our intention to romanticise either religion or culture of the past but to show how the imposition of modernity by means of colonial rule, particularly in the aftermath of the dissolution of the Ottoman Empire (Levy-Aksu et al., 2017; Lewis, 1980; Vorderstrasse, 2014), and the subsequent prerogatives of the Cold War had an equal stake in creating the problems that science journalism in the Arab world confronts today.

Considering the above discussion, we need not only to provide some history of science journalism in Arab countries—incorporating the link between Islam and science—but, additionally, we need to explain the context in which present political institutions in the Arab world, including journalism, reflect history, politics, cultures and disruptions created by modernity itself while acknowledging why these matter to the present and future of science journalism in the region. This, because we cannot analyse these issues simply through Western lenses, that are often distorted by Orientalism (Said, 2003 [1978]; Thompson, 2016), but instead through a more integrated, transactional and comprehensive analysis.

## Some Historical Background

Even though it developed alongside other newsbeats in the Arab nations, science journalism grew more modestly and slowly in the region than in other parts of the world. It started with science publishing in a time in which 'science in general was dominated by books and not journals' (Khun, 2012). One of its first recorded manifestations was the Bulaq printing press (Ekmeleddin İhsanoğlu, 2020; Verdery, 1971). Established in 1821 in Cairo, it made a significant contribution to the popularisation of science. It ran until the middle of the nineteenth century, publishing nearly 100 books, which helped disseminate important works among the public. It was followed by *Al-Waqa'i' al-Misriyya*, which in 1828 effectively became the first magazine devoted to spreading science in the Arab world (Sidqi, 2009, p. 177).

One of the first registered attempts at scientific news in the press in modern times began with the Egyptian newspaper *Al-Ahram* in the 1950s, which published some scientific subjects and translated scientific news (El-Awady, 2009). These news items were published by some Egyptian journalists, most notably Fawzi Sheiti and Mahmoud Abdul Aziz, who had the scientific stories translated from English and French into Arabic. In 1954, Salah Jalal, one of the pioneers of modern scientific journalism in the region, introduced a new genre in the *Al-Akhbar* newspaper where writing science news was all about simplifying science to educate the community. He then moved to another newspaper, *Al-Ahram*, in the early 1960s and formed a team of scientific editors in collaboration with Mohamed Hassanein Heikal who was the then editor-in-chief of *Al-Ahram* (Badran, 2014).

The first Egyptian Association of Scientific Writers and Editors was established in 1980, which was formed by a group that included all scientific editors, media outlets and writers concerned with the issue of simplifying science. The society, headed by Salah Jalal, conducted studies on the role of scientific media in Egypt and investigated ways the media could improve the development of scientific culture in Egyptian society. Then, in 1993, the first association of environmental writers and editors, chaired by the journalist Salama Ahmed Salameh, was established (Badran, 2014). The association included the editors responsible for coverage of the environment at *Al-Ahram* and other Egyptian newspapers and magazines, and it aimed to shed light on pressing environmental issues at the local and international levels.

Over the years, there have been several initiatives in science journalism in the Arab region. These included some publications and the fact that mainstream newspapers in these countries have always carried stories on health, technology and other areas of science. For example, 1969 saw the publication of *Tabibak El Khas* or 'Your Private Doctor', which is the oldest medical magazine in Arabic. The magazine is directed at the general public and aims to disseminate general medical knowledge.

The following year, Egypt saw its first non-specialist science magazine or mini-encyclopaedia, the popular *El Ma'rifa* (Knowledge), which was translated from a Swiss version in 1971. Other technical magazines also saw the light of day thanks to the professional association that issued them but that were mostly directed towards specialists in fields such as engineering, pharmacy and health (Gamal, 2020), and in 1986, the Kuwait Foundation for Scientific Advancement launched the Arabic version of *Scientific American*. However, most of the scientific publications in the Arab region were 'translated' versions of existing content produced in other parts of the world.

In more recent times there have been additional coordinated attempts to establish initiatives to support science journalism and incentivise local production of knowledge and content on a greater scale. One of them is the Arab Science News Agency that had an electronic portal on the World Wide Web. This agency is managed by the Arab Science and Technology Foundation (ASTF), in association with the *Technical Magazine*. The project was launched in the form of an electronic portal on the Internet on October 28, 2008, in the context of a conference on the prospects of scientific research in the Arab world, which was held in the city of Fez in Morocco. Among its most prominent objectives was to bring all scientific news from various fields in the Arab world to Arab citizens, in clear and easy Arabic (Bibbo, 2008; Hamwi, 2009).

The news agency was an attempt to fill a gap in the reporting and development of research in the region. Indeed, although there are many universities in the Middle East, reports about research in that region of the world seem to be quite sparse. Fedaa' El-Gendy, the website's manager, pointed out that 'the Arabic website, called the Arab Agency for Science News, will collect stories from around the Arab region through an extensive network of reporters'. Adding that its main aim was to 'communicate research news to the public' (Rowe, 2008; Yahia, 2008).

However, from the start, the agency faced difficulties and important limitations. These included the scarcity of locally produced content, not enough Arab scientific media outlets possessing both the media talent and the scientific background to contribute and, the problem derived from the difficulties of incorporating particular terminology and jargon into Arabic (Hamwi, 2009). Today the agency no longer operates, although the online domain is still there.

It is also important to say that the development of science journalism has also come with attempts to organise associations of news reporters. Perhaps the most important of all is the Arab Science Journalists Association (ASJA), which is a regional Arabic, non-profit network that aims to develop the field of science and technology in the Arab world through developing the scientific Arabic mass media and its role in the fields of technology and science. The ASJA operates under the umbrella of the Arab Science and Technology Foundation (ASTF), which is non-profit non-governmental organisation that works regionally and internationally to encourage investment in science and technology created in 2000 with the support of Sheikh Dr Sultan Bin Mohammed Al-Qassimi, Member of the Supreme Council of the UAE and Ruler of Sharjah. The ASJA created the 'Tawasol' training centre for journalists. However, to this day, both the association and centre are no longer active.

Over time, there have also been other organisations worth mentioning, such as those local initiatives supported by the World Federation of Science Journalists and the local correspondents of the news agency SciDev.Net, which has reporters and editors based in the region. Having said that, it is clear that there is an important gap in terms of who does science journalism in that part of the world. This, as neither the legacy mainstream media nor individual independent digital-natives seem to dedicate sufficient resources to have a wider presence of science in the news.

This initial account suggests that science journalism in the Arab world has developed within institutional and political frameworks that have come to define how it operates but that also reflects the realities on the ground, which are equally defining. As we have seen above, there are several organisations that support and educate science journalistic practices across the region. However, these are few and far between while important gaps remain in relation to the ability to foster news culture around science that not only promotes informing about science but also that debates and brings accountability to it. This institutional framework will not happen overnight and, if it did, it might be very different among each one of these societies as they present very distinctive characteristics.

Overall, the historical and political contexts that gave birth to science journalism in MENA as we know it today account for a diversity of forces that include the same elements that have also shaped the rest of society. What we have discussed in this chapter is how much we can attribute to each of these forces.

## Conclusion

A key question that remains unanswered here is which of these forces have been more prevalent and which have enhanced and hindered science journalism the most in the region. To answer this, we have to explore, albeit briefly, the different manifestations of science journalism practices within the diversity of media systems that we find in MENA. Then we can pinpoint the overlaps and also distinctive features within the region so as to understand more broadly the opportunities and challenges for the newsbeat.

This because, as we have seen here, the problems and issues that science journalism faces in the Arab region have mostly historical roots. In the past, there was no interest in science journalism in the manner required by governments and newspapers in addition to the lack of interest of some members of the public in science journalism to the present day. Despite more recent efforts, science journalism in Arab societies remains weak in terms of its ability to set an agenda and produce content that reflects local interests and promotes discussions and debates about Science, Technology, Engineering and Mathematics (STEM) subjects happening locally despite a good amount of stories originating at the national level.

The reasons for the current state of science journalism in the Arab world are multiple, as we will discuss in subsequent chapters. For now, it is sufficient to say that they include a scarcity of specialised journalists, particular political constraints often justified by religion and a general lack of interest from the public in science issues (Al-Qafari, 2009; El-Awady, 2009). However, and despite multiple overlaps, it is crucial to understand that each country in the region has its own settings and that the challenges they face might be common but also, in many cases, distinctive on the ground. A brief analysis of the state of science journalism in each one of these countries is therefore an important step in the direction of better understanding science journalism in MENA.

# Bibliography

Allan, S. (2011). Introduction: Science journalism in a digital age. *Journalism, 12*(7), 771–777.

Al-Najjar, A. (2011). Contesting patriotism and global journalism ethics in Arab journalism. *Journalism Studies, 12*(6), 747–756.

Al-Qafari, A. (2009). *Science media in Saudi journalism*. King Abdul-Aziz City for Science and Technology (KACST).

Ateş, H., Es, M., & Bayraktar, Y. (2005). Dependency Theory: Still an appropriate tool for understanding the political economy of the middle-east? *Atatürk Üniversitesi İktisadi ve İdari Bilimler Dergisi, 19*(2), 247–262.

Badran, A. (2014). *The reality of scientific journalism in Kuwait from the perspective of journalists working in Kuwait*. Middle East University.

Bauer, M., Howard, S., Ramos, R., Jessica, Y., Massarani, L., & Amorim, L. (2013). *Global science journalism report: Working conditions & practices, professional ethos and future expectations*. Science and Development Network.

Bauer, M. W. (2013). The knowledge society favours science communication, but puts science journalism into a clinch. *Science Communication Today, Paris, CNRS*, 145–166.

Bebawi, S. (2016). *Investigative Journalism in the Arab World: Issues and Challenges*. Springer.

Bibbo, B. (2008). *Call for creation of journalists' association in Qatar*. World Gulf. https://gulfnews.com/world/gulf/qatar/call-for-creation-of-journalists-association-in-qatar-1.84882

Bubela, T., Nisbet, M. C., Borchelt, R., Brunger, F., Critchley, C., Einsiedel, E., Geller, G., Gupta, A., Hampel, J., & Hyde-Lay, R. (2009). Science communication reconsidered. *Nature Biotechnology, 27*(6), 514–518.

Bucchi, M. (1998). *Science and the media: Alternative routes in scientific communication*. Routledge.

Calvo Hernando, M. (2002). El periodismo del tercer milenio. Problemas de la divulgación científica en Iberoamérica. *Interciencia, 27*(2), 57–61.

Citino, N. J. (2008). The Ottoman Legacy in cold war modernization. *International Journal of Middle East Studies, 40*(4), 579–597.

De Baets, A. (2016). Censorship by European states of views on their past as colonizers. In *La censure des États européens sur leur passé colonial* (pp. 229–245). Presses Universitaires de Rennes.

Douai, A., & Moussa, M. B. (2016). *Mediated identities and new journalism in the Arab world*. Palgrave Macmillan.

Ekmeleddin İhsanoğlu, H. A. (2020). The birth of the tradition of printed books in the Ottoman Empire Transition from manuscript to print (1729–1848). In *Studies on Ottoman Science and Culture*. Routledge.

El-Awady, N. (2009). Science journalism: The Arab boom. *Nature, 459*, 1057.

Fischhoff, B., & Scheufele, D. (2013). The science of science communication. *Proceedings of the National Academy of Sciences, 110,* 14031–14032.

Fjæstad, B. (2007). 12 Why journalists report science as they do. In *Journalism, Science and Society* (p. 123). Routledge.

Gamal, M. Y. (2020). *The Earth turns and the world has changed: Egyptian and Arab Science journalism in the digital age.* Arab Media & Society. https://www.arabmediasociety.com/the-earth-turns-and-the-world-has-changed-egyptian-and-arab-science-journalism-in-the-digital-age/

Ghalioun, B. (2004). Debate: The persistence of Arab authoritarianism. *Journal of Democracy, 15*(4), 126–132.

Hamwi, A. (2009). Translation and the problem of the scientific term in media. Science Media. *Journal of Scientific Progress,* 67–72.

Hanitzsch, T. (2007). Deconstructing journalism culture. Toward a Universal Theory. *Communication Theory, 17,* 367–385.

Hanitzsch, T., Hanusch, F., Ramaprasad, J., & de Beer, A. (2019). *Worlds of journalism: Journalistic cultures around the globe.* Columbia University Press.

Hansen, A. (2016). The changing uses of accuracy in science communication. *Public Understanding of Science, 25*(7), 760–774.

Hanssen, J., & Weiss, M. (2018). *Arabic Thought Against the Authoritarian Age: Towards an Intellectual History of the Present.* Cambridge University Press.

Hermida, A. (2010). Revitalizing science journalism for a digital age. In D. Kennedy & G. Overholser (Eds.), *Science and the Media* (pp. 80–87). American Academy for Arts and Sciences.

Inalcik, H. (2019). *The Ottoman Empire and Europe.* Kronik.

Iqbal, F., Khaliq, A., & Al-Ain, M. N. (2021). An evaluation of political modernization of Asian Islamic states in postmodern era. *Journal of Religious Studies, 3*(2), 163–172.

Iqbal, M. (2007). *Science and Islam.* Greenwood Publishing Group.

Jones, J. H. (1993). *Bad blood.* Simon and Schuster.

Katsakioris, C. (2010). Soviet lessons for Arab modernization: Soviet educational aid towards Arab countries after 1956. *Journal of Modern European History, 8*(1), 85–106.

Khun, T. (2012). *The structure of scientific revolutions.* University of Chicago Press.

Levy-Aksu, N., Lévy-Aksu, N., & Georgeon, F. (2017). *The Young Turk Revolution and the Ottoman Empire: The Aftermath of 1908.* Bloomsbury Publishing.

Lewis, B. (1980). The Ottoman Empire and its aftermath. *Journal of Contemporary History, 15*(1), 27–36.

Long, M. (1995). Scientific explanation in US newspaper science stories. *Public Understanding of Science, 4*(2), 119–130.

Lugo-Ocando, J. (2020). *Foreign aid and journalism in the global south: A mouthpiece for truth.* Lexington Books.

Mahmood, S. (2008). *Scientific media.* Alfagar Publishing.

Massarani, L., & Boys, B. (2007). La ciencia en la prensa de América Latina: Un estudio en 9 países. *Reunión de La Red de Popularización de La Ciencia y La Tecnología En América Latina y El Caribe, 10*, 1–12. Retrieved March 11, 2022, from https://www.cientec.or.cr/pop/2007/BR-LuisaMassarani.pdf

Matter. (2017). *Science news most trusted by British public.*

Mbarga, G., Lublinski, J., & Fleury, J.-M. (2012). New perspectives on strengthening science journalism in developing countries: Approach and first results of the 'SjCOOP' mentoring project. *Journal of African Media Studies, 4*(2), 157–172.

Mellado, C. (2015). Professional roles in news content: Six dimensions of journalistic role performance. *Journalism Studies, 16*(4), 596–614.

Mellor, N. (2007). *Modern Arab journalism: Problems and prospects: Problems and prospects.* Edinburgh University Press.

Mellor, N. (2008). Arab journalists as cultural intermediaries. *The International Journal of Press/Politics, 13*(4), 465–483.

Murcott, T. (2009). Science journalism: Toppling the priesthood. *Nature, 459*(7250), 1054–1055.

Nasr, S., & De Santillana, G. (1968). *Science and civilization in Islam* (Vol. 16). Harvard University Press.

Nelkin, D. (1995). *Selling science: How the press covers science and technology.* Rev. Ed. Freeman.

Nguyen, A., & McIlwaine, S. (2011). Who wants a voice in Science issues—And why? A survey of European citizens and its implications for science journalism. *Journalism Practice, 5*(2), 210–226.

Nguyen, A., & Tran, M. (2019). Science journalism for development in the Global South: A systematic literature review of issues and challenges. *Public Understanding of Science, 28*(8), 973–990.

Nisbet, M., & Scheufele, D. (2009). What's next for science communication? Promising directions and lingering distractions. *American Journal of Botany, 96*(10), 1767–1778.

Ortaylı, İ. (2019). *Ottoman studies, 10*, Kronik.

Pintak, L. (2014). Islam, identity and professional values: A study of journalists in three Muslim-majority regions. *Journalism, 15*(4), 482–503.

Pratt, N. C. (2007). *Democracy and authoritarianism in the Arab world.* Lynne Rienner Publishers.

Reverby, S. M. (2005). 'Misrepresentations of the Tuskegee Study'—Distortion of analysis and facts? *Journal of the National Medical Association, 97*(8), 1180.

Rowe, A. (2008). Meet the Arab Agency for Science News [Magazine]. *Wired.* https://www.wired.com/2008/11/meet-the-arab-a/

Said, E. (2003). *Orientalism: Western conceptions of the Orient.* Penguin Books Limited.

Scott, J. M., & Carter, R. G. (2015). From cold war to Arab Spring: Mapping the effects of paradigm shifts on the nature and dynamics of US democracy assistance to the Middle East and North Africa. *Democratization, 22*(4), 738–763.

Seale, C. (2010). How the mass media report social statistics: A case study concerning research on end-of-life decisions. *Social Science & Medicine, 71*(5), 861–868.

Sidqi, H. (2009). *Scientific journalism between theory and practice.* Academic Library.

Slater, J. (1990). The Superpowers and an Arab-Israeli political settlement: The cold war years. *Political Science Quarterly, 105*(4), 557–577.

Thompson, T. (2016). Conducting the Conversation: Insights from the Historical and Theological Contextualization of Edward Said's Orientalism. *The Muslim World, 106*(2), 255–270.

Tibi, B. (1997). *Arab nationalism: Between Islam and the nation-state.* Palgrave Macmillan.

Tignor, R. L. (1980). Dependency Theory and Egyptian Capitalism, 1920 to 1950. *African Economic History, 9,* 101–118.

Tillier, B., & Nicholson-Smith, D. (2012). The impact of censorship on painting and sculpture, 1851–1914. *Yale French Studies, 122,* 79–103.

Treise, D., & Weigold, M. F. (2002). Advancing science communication: A survey of science communicators. *Science Communication, 23*(3), 310–322.

Vaughan, J. R. (2005). *The Failure of American and British Propaganda in the Arab Middle East, 1945–57.* Palgrave Macmillan.

Verdery, R. N. (1971). The Publications of the Būlāq Press under Muḥammad 'Alī of Egypt. *Journal of the American Oriental Society,* 129–132.

Vorderstrasse, T. (2014). The archaeology of the Ottoman Empire and its aftermath in the Middle East. *Near Eastern Archaeology, 77*(4), 292–298.

Watenpaugh, K. D. (2014). *Being Modern in the Middle East.* Princeton University Press.

Wolfsfeld, G. (1997). *Media and political conflict: News from the Middle East.* Cambridge University Press.

Yahia, M. (2008). Arab world debuts its first science news website. SciDev.Net. https://www.scidev.net/global/news/arab-world-debuts-its-first-science-news-website/

Yosmaoğlu, İ. K. (2003). Chasing the printed word: Press censorship in the Ottoman Empire, 1876–1913. *The Turkish Studies Association Journal, 27*(1/2), 15–49.

CHAPTER 3

# Science Journalism and Media Systems in MENA

In the past few decades, several states in the region have set their 2030 Vision. This is a strategic attempt to modernise and diversify their economies, in an attempt to move away from their fossil-fuel dependency. MENA countries have adopted an explicit commitment to transition towards a more diversified economy, making them less dependent on fossil fuels and geared instead towards a 'knowledge' society. Part of these efforts has meant that governments in MENA have started to invest more heavily in science and technology and push towards more general engagement with Science, Technology, Engineering and Mathematics (STEM) subjects.

To be sure, these policies have incorporated the notion of transition into a knowledge society in almost all the national strategic plans. This translates in most cases in explicit calls to improve general knowledge and understanding of science and technology among the public and increasing general literacy rates as well as the number of young individuals, particularly women, studying STEM areas as to improve Public Engagement with Science (PES).

This explicit strategic commitment carries with it a commitment with wider dissemination of science, particularly among members of the Cooperation Council for the Arab States of the Gulf or better known as Gulf Cooperation Council (GCC). Established in 1981, this is as a regional intergovernmental union. Its members are the Kingdom of Bahrain, the

© The Author(s), under exclusive license to Springer Nature Switzerland AG 2023
A. Alhuntushi, J. Lugo-Ocando, *Science Journalism in the Arab World*, Palgrave Studies in Journalism and the Global South, https://doi.org/10.1007/978-3-031-14252-9_3

Kingdom of Saudi Arabia, the Sultanate of Oman, the United Arab Emirates (UAE), the State of Kuwait and the Emirate of Qatar. The GCC not only groups some of the biggest investors in science and technology in the region but also hosts some of the most powerful and reputable universities and research centres in the whole of MENA, which also include many western universities that have branches and campuses in those countries. The other powerhouse in the region is of course Egypt, given the sheer size of its population and economy.

These facts alone could allow us to aspire for a more developed form of science journalism practice in that country. Moreover, one would expect a concentrated effort to promote science communication within these countries to underpin these goals of raising awareness and understanding of science among their publics. However, efforts to communicate science are, overall, scarce and not sufficiently present. Particular efforts tend to derive more from particular individuals and organisations than from state policy. In this context, as we explore the case of each country in this chapter, science reporting in the region does not rank highly among the news agenda, editorial priorities and newsroom hierarchies nor does there seem to be a substantial audience for that type of news (Reinisch, 2010).

Each country in the region has a particular set of characteristics that came to define the nature of its media system and that of journalistic practices, as we will see here. To explore these and other related aspects, we try to offer an overview of the history and current state of science journalism, country by country, attempting to pinpoint the key characteristics that make a news beat unique in a particular nation as well as how approaches and practices overlap with other nations in MENA.

## Science Journalism in Algeria

Algeria has had scientific press since the second half of the nineteenth century, when the *Algerian Medical Journal* was published in 1856 in Algiers by one of the doctors working in the French-occupation colonial army. We know that there was oversight and censorship on this publication as the records show that the editor-in-chief of the magazine was supervised by medical officials of the then known 'the Army of Africa' at the Dey Hospital (Bouhaila, 2017). During French colonial occupation, we found a series of publications that focused on science and technology, some of which survived independence but were then discontinued or ceased publication over the years.

It would not be until the 1990s that the country would again see the emergence of timid media pluralism and with that some attempts to establish scientific journals for the public. However, as records show, most failed because of economic reasons, lack of interested audiences and poor readability. In fact, one of the key problems they faced, put simply, was the inability of their publishers to make the content accessible and understandable for the general public. Having said that, the general Algerian press has had a continuous and almost uninterrupted engagement, both in Arabic and French, with scientific information, providing space directed to readers in general that addresses issues on health, astronomy and more general issues regarding natural sciences and technology (Abdel Rahman Qanchouba, 2021).

Our brief assessment of capabilities and outcomes of the Algerian media by analysing content and semi-structured interviews with journalists and editors suggests the absence of specialised scientific journalists and the non-appointment of a scientific editor in any of the key publications. The journalists interviewed confessed that they felt unable to prepare or at times even distinguish certain scientific files, neither did they feel that their readers were sufficiently engaged with these topics or that there was a more general desire to know more about the nature of science and technology. As one of the journalists said,

> *At times what I write about science it seems to be wasted. My editor shows little interest and I have almost no feedback ever from readers. It would have to be something extraordinary, such as at the start of COVID. Everyone wanted then to know more. But if I write something about astronomy or even other issues in biology, there is literally almost no interest.*[1]

In reference to technology, most of the media does dedicate space and time but in a way that mostly focuses on new products rather than the issue itself. These stories, as we observed in a sample of 156 selected stories in 2020 for the *Echourouk* and *Ennahar* newspapers, were not written by science correspondents, but by reporters who normally cover other news beats. Our analysis of a subgroup of 20 of these groups of news stories about health showed the absence of simplified language that could be understood by non-specialist audiences.

---

[1] Interview with Algerian journalist on May 12, 2020, identity withheld.

Instead, at times most of these stories showed a high degree of convoluted language, confusing terminology and a level of complexity that makes it difficult to understand. The key problems we identified in this country are limited resources, absence of general knowledge and capabilities in science, not h having enough experience or degree of specialisation, being restricted to a timetable, and almost no editorial prerogatives to dedicate time and space to science.

The country does not have a sufficient number of scientific media professionals with the skills, capabilities and tools that enable news organisations to prepare and distinguish scientific reports, understand the scientific activities and fields of research centres and scientific bodies, and approach with confidence scientists and researchers in those institutions and at scientific conferences so as to be able to create meaningful, relevant and accessible content (Azzouz, 2016).

Overall, there are some general obstacles that pose a challenge to scientific news reporting in Algeria. According to some authors, these can be condensed in to some broad areas (Abdel Rahman Qanchouba, 2021; Azzouz, 2016; Bouhaila, 2017).

They include the absence in most of the Algerian news media of a well-defined scientific section, at least in the way that other newsbeats such as economics and sport have. This suggests a low interest in providing science with a home from where to publish and broadcast stories in this beat. It also includes weak training and poor specialisation among potential scientific journalists. There are no specialisations on offer and hardly any provision in the existing media departments in the universities of that country that pay sufficient attention to scientific journalism or sufficient continuing education provision for those in fulltime jobs. In addition, it is important to pinpoint poor qualification regarding translation and Arabisation, given that the sources concerning scientific knowledge are often in foreign languages. This requires the qualification of cadres specialised in translation and in scientific disciplines. However, the problem of translation is not limited to crossing different languages but also the inability to translate in accessible ways scientific terms into Arabic; this, as much scientific writing is full of technical terms in foreign languages that are hard to Arabise.

Other issues that we observed include the dominance of information from abroad over locally produce science news stories despite the fact that most stories are produced locally. It was also very rare to see longer feature articles and during that period we could not find in either of the two newspapers a local science story that was the product of investigative reporting. In the few pieces we found on science, we mostly saw the reporting of events and, on occasion, scientists and researchers as the key news sources in those stories. In this sense, most of the journalists we interviewed—six out of eight—complained about 'time pressures' and 'strict deadlines' as the underlining reasons for the lack of engagement with proper investigative reporting and the production of feature articles relating to science.

All of the journalists admitted to possess limited abilities to keep pace with science issues. They argued that their work demands—particularly tight deadlines and overwork—stopped them from attending scientific forums and conferences or being able to keep up with the latest developments. One of the reporters pointed out the 'lack of pathways to professional development in their own news organizations' and the fact that they 'were constantly and routinely asked to cover different newsbeats', which hindered their ability to specialise in a particular area in the long run.

Another important problem we saw in the case of Algeria's media ability to increase the number and quality of local science stories is the challenge posed by the lack of available news sources. That is, scientists and experts who are readily available to speak to the press about their own work or matters surrounding science and technology. This refers to the scarcity of specialists in scientific expert voices in media that could offer careful examination and documentation for wider discussion, which is a key problem. The elephant in the room is that in illiberal regimes common members of the public—which includes scientists and experts—are reluctant to speak freely to the media. This results in the absence of recognisable expert voices in the public sphere that can shape the narratives about science with substantiated and grounded knowledge.

Algeria presents in many ways several of the features of the other MENA countries in terms of lack of capabilities, low public interest in science by the audiences and similar dynamics and issues around the gathering of science news and access to expert voices. In the subsequent analysis of the other countries, we will not be repeating these issues unless it is to underline differences. Be it sufficient to say that these problems are widely present all over the region with very few exceptions, regardless of the state of science itself as a whole.

## Science Journalism in Egypt

Egypt is by far the most important media space in the Middle East, both in terms of the potential size of the audience and in relation to the nature of its own media system (De Angelis, 2015; Halabi, 2015; Jebril & Loveless, 2017). In terms of professional autonomy, despite years of colonial and military rule, the Egyptian press was considered until relatively recently as more open than others in the region, particularly in its ability to engage with important issues and develop newsbeats. Part of the reason for this was that it successfully merged the tradition of 'street discussion' (Saber, 2013) and an adaptation of the colonial press to its own context, which in many places brought its own practices and organisational cultures (Spurr, 1993; Worth, 2014).

With regard to the scientific press, Egypt has passed through four historical stages (Saber, 2013). The first stage, also known as the functional stage, was the period from the First World War until the late 1920s and represented the childhood of Egyptian scientific journalism. The reporting of science in general newspapers, such as *Al-Ahram* was functional and did not enter criticism or analysis, nor was it considered a tool for education or enlightenment.

The second stage was one of prosperity and the emergence of the critical trend. It developed from the 1930s until the end of the Second World War and represented a period of prosperity for the scientific press in Egypt. During this time, several cultural and scientific newspapers were published that, in responding to the interest of the Egyptian public, used science to address culturally relevant questions. In this sense, we should highlight some of the initiatives and publications led by reformers such as Salama Moussa (1887–1958) and Ismail Mazhar (1891–1962) who advocated for a wider dissemination of science among the public, particularly in relation to ideas from Europe and promoted the creation of science publications (Yari, 2016; Ziadat & Jallow, 1986).

However, over the next years, most efforts to report science according to western standards based on objectivity and neutrality towards social, political, and cultural problems of Egyptian society, were abandoned. For Saber (2013), this represented in part a return to the Islamic legacy that promoted a more critical engagement with science in the broader context of challenges in society. This abandonment of neutrality and the adoption of advocacy responded in many ways to the quest to promote decolonisation and independence that started to emerge and that rejected the imposition of Western values and costumes (Rugh, 2004; Sharkey, 1999; Spurr, 1993).

Despite this, the period saw a scientific press that continuously expressed progressive ideas. This would bring it into conflict with the reactionary and conservative forces in Egyptian society at that time. This conflict led to the disappearance of these newspapers by the end of this period and other newspapers which survived the backlash preferred not to enter in to such battles. Moreover, the intellectuals who carried the banner of spreading scientific thinking among the public withdrew from the press, a legacy that even today helps partially explain the reluctance of many scientists in the Arab world to engage with the media (Saber, 2013).

The third stage was one of intellectual regression and repression. During the post-Second World War period, from the mid-1940s until the early 1950s, scientific journals were battered by the changes that affected most Egyptian intellectuals. It was during this period that the scientific publications of Mazhar and Moussa came to an end, and the situation returned to one similar to the first stage of infancy. The hindering of the Egyptian scientific press during the 1940s was the direct result of stricter laws, censorship, and the circumstances of war. However, some Egyptian intellectuals also blamed the public, which seemed to have abandoned them in their battles for enlightenment (Saber, 2013).

The fourth stage or 'survival stage' came last and reflected the post-Second World War and Cold War political landscapes. During this period, science publications in Egypt continued to engage with societal issues and problems but by then had toned down criticality or cultural and social engagement between science and society. In exchange for preservation and continuity, they abandoned the intellectual and philosophical aspect of their scientific presentation, and once again went back to performing a straightforward science dissemination function. At the same time, newspapers dedicated to highlight 'the cultural significance' of science ceased to be published and critical engagement with knowledge and its relevance to society disappeared. The general press became 'responsible' for the introduction of science to the public but in such a way that lacked the depth and the philosophical and theoretical aspects that the cultural magazines had once offered.

In this stage, scientific topics became increasingly practical and decontextualised. For instance, science news favoured topics such as astronomical phenomena related to weather conditions and scientific discoveries. In doing so, science journalism in the Arab world followed suit with its western counterparts and became all about 'practical links to daily life' as a way to gain relevance (Nguyen & McIlwaine, 2011). Science news became, therefore, 'objective' and deprived of meaning and relevance to societies for which knowledge has historically been a way of challenging power structures.

We argue that this conundrum was not only a product of the new political landscape but also a direct result of the westernisation of the press. By this we mean that by embracing the notion of objectivity in order to survive, science journalism became stripped of its intellectual and critical philosophical context that once allowed it to be a part of change and reform in the region. In addition, the professionalisation of science journalism translated into side-lining scientists as intellectuals in the public and media spheres, something that in the past Islamic societies had allowed but that the new rulers did not. Hence, the emergence of editors of scientific journalism with little or no academic backgrounds in the fields of natural and applied sciences or who are unable and unwilling to take science to society as a space for wider discussion, cannot be seen just as an isolated issue but needs to be assessed as a greater historical problem in these societies.

## SCIENCE JOURNALISM IN IRAQ

What today we call Iraqi has had a rich history in terms of both science and science dissemination. The first outlet of the Iraqi scientific press, as it is known today, was established in Iraq in 1869 as a scientific supplement to *Al-Zawraa* newspaper in the fields of space, technology and inventions. This was one of the earliest examples of a science-dedicated news outlet, not only in the region but also in the world.

By 1910, the country saw the publication of *The Science Journal*, which despite the diversity of interests between science, religion, philosophy, culture and sociology, became nevertheless to be dominated by natural science. Perhaps this coincides with the fact that the founder and owner of the magazine was a well-known science communicator who had an avid scientific interest. The name chosen for the magazine, *Al-Ilm* (The Knowledge), was, by all accounts, a reflection of that focus in science.

This predominance of scientific interest can be considered a step towards journalistic specialisation, which, however, did not find a clear place in the news spectrum in subsequent years (Al Rawi, 2010). This magazine managed to last two years, as it was dependent upon the personal financial capabilities of its owner and the devotion of the clerics and journalists (AL-Salem & Abu-Saab, 2007). This publication fought a war against ignorance and for the sake of knowledge until it met the obstacles and problems that prompted its owner was forced to leave the country (Metab, 2019).

The city of Mosul, on the other hand, saw the publication of the magazine *Al-Nadi Al-Ilm*, as its first issue appeared on January 15, 1919. The magazine described itself as a scientific journal and only eight issues were issued, the last of which was on April 10, 1919 (Al Rawi, 2010). Some years later on June 10, 1921, Iraq would witness the creation of the *Al-Falah* newspaper as a scientific publication. Established by Abdul Latif Al-Falahi, a virtuous scholar of that era, it strived for editorial independence by establishing its own board. A year later, the newspaper *Tawila* was established, which also managed to last two years and after that the *Iraqi Scout* magazine, published in June 1924, brought in a disciplinary scientific journal (AL-Salem & Abu-Saab, 2007; Shaaban, 2009).

Overall, this period of a scientific press was characterised by short-lived scientific publications that nevertheless created an important space for science dissemination and debates (KoKaz, 2008). However, from what we know, these publications had limited audiences and the number of copies was low. The archival revision also showed a lack of interest from advertisers, which in turn led to a decrease in the financial income of the newspaper.

The 1958 revolution and the republican era meant a profound change in the institutional framework of the country. Part of that change translated into a more secular and centralised form of government that started by issuing its own official newspapers with a certain specialisation and editorial direction. Although scientific newspapers continued to be published until the end of the year 2000, they would never achieve the degree of professional autonomy that their predecessors had.

The Gulf War of 1991, and subsequent invasion of Iraq in 2003, meant that the country as a whole became increasingly fragmented and that the institutional framework in which journalists operate became fragile at best. However, even today we can recognise some of the same problems and challenges that this country has faced in relation to science communication in general and science journalism in particular. For example, a survey conducted by KoKaz (2008) highlights that the scientific press in Iraq receives the attention of only 2% of the public while sport gets 70% of readers' interest. As the audience for the specialised press in science is limited, so are the chances of having a properly developed science news beat.

## Science Journalism in Kuwait

As was the case of other Arab countries, the beginning of the press in Kuwait was modest (Alyan, 2012). Several factors contributed to the delay in the development of the media system in Kuwait, which include an underdeveloped educational system, scarce economic resources (before the advent of oil discovery), as well as the legacy of colonialism that hinder the creation of an independent institutional setting (Badran, 2014). However, all that changed in the last decades of the twentieth century, when the media in Kuwait started to follow the global trend towards the allocation of media to suit the interests of different segments of society, especially in the fields of sport, economics and culture.

This was the case particularly after the Gulf War of 1991 in which the liberation of Kuwait by the US–UN-led coalition led to important changes in the political and media systems in the aftermath of the conflict. The post-invasion setting translated into a more general push for liberal institutions and for fewer restrictions on all political institutions in society, including newspapers and other media outlets (Alqudsi-Ghabra, 1995; Meyer et al., 2007; Yetiv, 2002). Today, its media systems are perhaps one of the most sophisticated and open in the region (Odine, 2011; Onyebadi & Alajmi, 2016).

The Kuwaiti media started to regularly offer a scientific section, including the daily *Al-Rai*, which began to run a weekly page dedicated to the environment in 1995—although the page was suspended a year later. The daily *Al-Qabas* ran a two-page environmental supplement entitled 'Our Environment, Our Lives'. The scientific pages of the Kuwaiti papers dealt primarily with technology and agriculture (Alyan, 2012). Over the years, there have been sporadic attempts to offer space to STEM subjects and with the COVID-19 pandemic there was a great surge in the space dedicated to biological and health sciences.

According to Badran (2014), nevertheless science journalism in the state of Kuwait continues to be a rare phenomenon and of low quality in general. This, he explains, has several reasons. Despite its relative openness and being one of the better resourced media systems in the region, the media in Kuwait still exhibits low standards and limited levels of professionalism. In the case of the science news beat, this includes the lack of specialised journalists in this field and low appetite for science news among audiences, which are major factors contributing to the current state of science journalism in that country.

Another important factor is the late establishment in the country of scientific institutions and research centres concerned with theoretical and applied sciences. Moreover, it was only after the Iraqi invasion of 1990 that officials in Kuwait allowed a greater degree of independence in terms of professional autonomy for science and technology institutions and scientists themselves. Most of the officials linked to universities and research institutions we contacted were unequivocal and unanimous in saying that it will still take years to have a better established space to discuss science in that country and for them to feel completely free to speak to the media without supervision or controls.

## Science Journalism in Lebanon

Over the years, the scientific press in Lebanon has relied on two fundamental pillars. The first is the technical development and the emergence of the art and printing industry, and the second is the development of the scientific research movement, with a high rate of education and an increase in sub-disciplines in various sciences. In this sense, the scientific press appeared in Lebanon in the form of scientific articles in public newspapers and then developed into scientific supplements inserted in these newspapers (Qabbanji, 2011).

Meanwhile, the country saw an increase in the number of institutions that produced science or that facilitated common people to engage with science. Science, over the years, became a central teaching topic in schools and universities, which in turn had a significant impact on the emergence of a segment of writers who produced articles and scientific research, especially translated ones in the field of science or prepared locally in the humanities. This placed Lebanon way ahead of other countries at the time even thought it might be difficult for some to see that in hindsight, given the current crisis that engulfs that country today.

With the increase in missionary missions to Lebanon at the beginning of the nineteenth century, these missions came with modern means such as printing presses and the establishment of modern schools that contributed to the emergence of the Lebanese press. In 1858, it was the first Lebanese newspaper under the name (*The News Garden*) by Khalil Al-Khoury. In the same year, Count Rasheed issued the second Lebanese newspaper called *Berges Paris*, which meant 'Paris Star', as it was the most elegant of Arab newspapers. It was also requested by the French Emperor Napoleon III (Hassan, 2013). *Al-Jawa'ib* newspaper, which was established by Ahmed Al-Shidyaq, is considered one of the most powerful newspapers in terms of influence and spread in the Arab world because of its transmission of European thought, Western civilisation and modern urbanisation to the Arab world (Hassan, 2013).

The first scientific journal was published in 1902 in Beirut by the Syrian Evangelical College of the American University. This was followed decades later by the Jesuits, who in 1951 established the *Oriental Society*—dedicated to the study of science—and with it they issued a magazine bearing the same name, which can be accredited as the first Lebanese science news publication. The magazine was concerned with publishing various scientific articles that were characterised by human content more than pure and applied sciences, but that nevertheless centred on science (Hassan, 2013). Only a few years later, in 1955, Minbar Baalbaki and Bahij Othman, two strong advocates of science in that country, went on to publish *Al-Ulum* magazine in Beirut, but ceased publication very shortly thereafter.

The late 1960s and early 1970s saw an exposition of science news publications that included the *Journal of Science*, published in Beirut in 1968 by the Syrian Scientific Society but which also ceased publication after a short period. After that, scientific journals spread in Lebanon. This included the university magazine, which was published by Farah Antoun, one of the pioneers in this area. At the time, the country saw the publication also of the magazine *The World of Chemistry*, which was published in Beirut by the Syndicate of Chemists.

Lebanese scientific journals continued to be issued and enjoyed a relatively brief period of success among publishers. In 1870, the magazine *Al-Jinan* appeared in Beirut, issued by Boutros Al-Bustani, and it took the initiative to publish a scientific article by the scientist 'Van Dyck' titled, 'Animals and Girls'. In later years, the *Dunia Al-Alam* magazine appeared in Beirut under the ownership of Farid Ayman, which was followed that same year by the Arab Scientific Journal, also in Beirut (Abu Saiba, 2016). This was followed by the magazine *Arab Water World*, which was published also in the capital, which cantered upon water issues in the Middle East and Africa (Bou Tebakalt, 2013).

Some important milestone publications include several works from intellectuals and journalists. Besides *Al-Muktataf* (1876–1952), a number of Arabic periodicals have been very influential in science popularisation. They are, among others, *Al-Hilal* (The Crescent, est. 1892), *Al-Machriq* (The Orient, 1898–1971), *al-Manār* (The Lighthouse, 1898–1935), *Arrissalah* (The Message, 1933–53), *Al-Arabi* (est. 1958), *Aldoha* (Doha, est. 1969) and *Alfaisal* (est. 1977), among others. More recently, scholars should pay attention to websites Al-Fanar Media and Nature Middle East, both making today significant contributions by enhancing PUS.

The 1980s saw a shift towards more niche-focused scientific journals and less focus on science dissemination to the general public. This decade saw the first issue of the Science and Technology Journal in 1982. This was a monthly scientific magazine issued by the Arab Union in Beirut that had the aim of spreading scientific and technological culture among the educated public in the Arab world. This was done by keeping pace with scientific and technological developments worldwide, focusing on applicable scientific and technological achievements and drawing attention to the reality of development and its obstacles in the field and providing the Arab region with scientific contribution that could help it reach solutions and options when addressing issues faced by these societies (Qabbanji, 2011).

It is perhaps important to underline that the journal's publishing policy was directed to cater for three segments of the audience, which included individuals who work in the field of science and technology in the public and private sectors, as well as those who deal with the fields of development and education; university students and graduates in the educational and scientific fields to create a mechanism for scientific thinking, view global technological achievements, and learn about scientific developments in the specialisations of these students and graduates; and, the more general audiences such as educated readers interested in learning about the latest inventions and general scientific developments (Hassan, 2013; Qabbanji, 2011).

## Science Journalism in Palestine

Since the end of the British mandate in 1948 and the Nakba against the people who until then inhabited those lands, Palestine has been under the colonial occupation of an apartheid state created with the support and funding of Western powers and referred to as Israel (Davis, 2003; Kasrils et al., 2015). Palestinians have been constantly attacked and their homes destroyed over successive decades as well as having to live under a perpetual and brutal state of military intervention (Allen, 2008; Quigley, 1991). Under these conditions, it has been literally impossible for the Palestinian people to build any type of stable framework that allowed journalism to operate as a viable political institution in today's world.

Therefore, it is easy to forget that before the Zionist occupation, the Palestinians had a well-established scientific press in the 1930s and 1940s of the twentieth century. One that was rich and robustly independent, which created multiple spaces for scientific exchanges and dialogue. Archives show newspapers, magazines and other publications in the cities such as Jaffa and Jerusalem. In these archives, we find a variety of scientific articles that reflected discussions and ideas and, which appeared regularly. Palestine also had other science news content that appeared in the form of scientific articles in magazines in Jaffa, such as the *Palestinian Medical Journal* and the *Arab Journal* that were published during the British mandate (Abu Haseera, 2018).

Over the years of resistance and pushbacks, Palestine has managed to open new spaces for journalism although they remain contested both by the Israeli occupation and internal tensions among its political forces. A new wave of print press began in the 1990s that included daily newspapers and other types of publications. The country also saw the airing of the radio broadcaster Palestine Air as well some local news agencies that dedicated space and airtime to science. Particular attention was paid to health sciences and alternative medicine as well as information technology and natural sciences (Abu Haseera, 2018).

Among the outlets that emerged in the occupied territories it is important to mention some scientific journals in Palestine such as the *Balsam* Magazine, a monthly scientific and cultural publication. Other, during this era, included the magazine of the Palestinian Red Crescent Society, which was published in Beirut, and *Balsam Al-Youm* magazine, which was published in 1994 to deal with medical health affairs and medical issues (Abu Haseera, 2018).

Another important publication was the *Science and Knowledge Journal*, a scientific magazine published in the Gaza Strip since 1994. It was a monthly magazine for the Scientific Studies and Research Committee in Al-Azhar. It covers a diversity of topics including physics, chemistry, mathematics and health. The pieces are written by specialised researchers, and its journalistic forms are varied, including interviews, press interviews and scientific reports, articles, competitions and cartoons. However, the magazine was discontinued in 1995 and then reappeared in 2000, but in a non-paper electronic format. Since then, it was transformed into the Industrial Physics Journal as an electronic magazine.

*Amwaj* Magazine, another example, was a periodical scientific journal also published in the Gaza Strip since 1998. Its topics included medicine, health, and psychological, social and health safety. It has appeared in both print and electronic forms via the Gaza Mental Health website, albeit not constantly, since its creation.

Having said all this, it is in the daily newspapers themselves where science in Palestine found a space for dissemination of its scientific sections. For example, although the *Al-Quds* newspaper didn't have a specialised scientific journalist, nevertheless it dedicated pages to these issues though mostly publishing/reproducing articles from international scientific agencies and journals. It is also important to mention the *Al-Ayyam* newspaper which included subjects around science and health on a regular basis.

Overall, as we can see, Palestine is often credited with having a much richer history in science journalism but science journalism in general has the core problem of not operating under a framework that guarantees the professional work that reporters do. To be sure, the country faces important obstacles such as the lack of scientific cadres specialised in scientific media, language barriers that can allow the transfer of knowledge between Arabic and English as well as insufficient numbers of editors and producers who have the capabilities and skills to access scientific knowledge. There is insufficient educational and vocational provision to train newer generations of science reporters and, crucially, the audience for science news is simply not there in terms of the size needed to make it viable, which in turn affects funding for science news outlets and science news spaces.

## SCIENCE JOURNALISM IN QATAR

Over the years, the State of Qatar has developed two institutions that can potentially foster a great deal of science journalism. On the one hand the Qatar Foundation for Education, Science and Community Development (or simply known as QF). This is a state-led but semi-autonomous organisation, which was established to promote education, science, and cultural development on both a regional and global scale. The foundation created Education City where international higher education (HE) institutions, research centres and think-tanks have operated independently from state interference since 1995. In addition to that, QF organises the World Innovation Summit for Health (WISH) and World Innovation Summit for Education (WISE) as well as sponsoring a series of other events and activities.

Alongside QF, Qatar has also created what is perhaps the most powerful and influential news media outlet to have emerged from the Global South,

*Al-Jazeera*. Indeed, the network is one of the most widely watched news channels in the world (Figenschou, 2013; Maziad, 2021; Miles, 2010) and despite controversy it has made important inroads around the world due to the reach and trust it enjoys among most of its audiences. The network has achieved pre-eminence among the Arab public sphere in areas such as politics, foreign policy and other domestic issues pertinent to the region.

In their own way these two institutions have provided important conditions for science journalism to flourish. On the one hand, QF has created a truly exceptional critical mass of expert sources, events and HE institutions that offer content and voices for any journalist reporting on science discovery, issues, and controversies. On the other, *Al-Jazeera* not only has developed its own specialised section for science and technology but has also hired over the years some of the most talented professionals in that field. In addition to this, QF has offered resources and support such as research grants through its different arms to promote science dissemination and science communication. Meanwhile, by pushing the boundaries of what is 'tolerated' or not, the network also allows other local media to operate passing those boundaries and enjoying greater independence.

The question remains however as to why then is science journalism so underdeveloped in that country? To answer that, researchers at Northwestern University in Qatar have looked at the Qatari news media's capacities for fostering public understanding of, and engagement with, science issues, challenges and opportunities in that country (Lugo-Ocando et al., 2019). Although at the time of writing this book the project is still in progress—given the restrictions imposed by COVID—it is already possible to suggest that at least at the level of the local media, science reporting is still underdeveloped and facing very similar issues as its counterparts in other MENA countries.

## SCIENCE JOURNALISM IN THE KINGDOM OF SAUDI ARABIA

The publication of scientific news in Saudi Arabia also had a modest start (Al-Qafari, 2009). The history of the modern Saudi press dates back to 1924, when *Umm al-Qura*, the first Saudi newspaper, was published. In its early stages, the Saudi press faced many physical and social struggles and media outlets came and went with the market. Until the beginning of the 1950s, most of the press was owned by individuals but by the end of the decade, mergers with state-owned outlets were imposed and many got integrated into larger publicly owned conglomerates or simply disappeared. Over the years, the laws were relaxed and today most newspapers are again privately owned but are subsidised and regulated by the government.

There was a paucity of scientific news that coincided with the Saudi press at the beginning, specifically regarding spreading awareness and education about some of the diseases that were prevalent at the time (Al-Qafari, 2009). After a period, interest in scientific news increased in the Saudi newspapers through their publication of stories concerning health, the environment, and information technology, in addition to following up on scientific conferences. Currently, one can find scientific pages in some Saudi newspapers produced on a regular basis as well as reports about science, but none have a dedicated space or section as such.

Al-Qafari's (2009) study about science media in Saudi Arabia found that some Saudi newspapers allocated daily or weekly pages to publishing scientific news and many other Saudi newspapers published it either regularly or irregularly. The study indicates that around 20% of all news articles fall into the broadest category of scientific news. Health news, as expected, accounts for more than 60%, therefore dominating that newsbeat. Having said that, there are no sections specifically dedicated to science news in Saudi newspapers, but the scientific editor is responsible for other sections of the newspaper and they decide whether or not to publish such pages.

In interviews with journalists themselves, they argued that the media organisations do not seem to be too concerned with specialisation or the qualifications and training of scientific journalists. Most of the interviewees confessed to having little or no experience of science. As one of them said,

*"There are simply no specialists in scientific writing. Saudi newspapers rely instead on freelance editors from outside the newspaper who edit scientific news. Journalists writing scientific news are not expected to abide by quality standards. Nevertheless, the presentation of scientific news tends to be simple and easy for readers to understand, which is characteristic of the Saudi press"*, said one of the editors interviewed. *(interviewed on October 14, 2020)*

## SCIENCE JOURNALISM IN SUDAN

Sudan sits at the other end of the spectrum in relation to general income and welfare in the countries analysed in this chapter (Ballon & Duclos, 2016; Yagoob & Zuo, 2016). Indeed, despite rising income in Sudan, almost half of the population lives below the poverty line. In Khartoum,

26% of people live in poverty, while in North Darfur and South Darfur the figure is 70% and 61%, respectively. More significantly for this study, almost four out of every ten adult Sudanese cannot read and write, a percentage that is much higher among women and the elderly.

So, the question remains, is there any sense in talking about science journalism in a country in which a very significant segment of its population cannot access or afford science news or even science knowledge itself? Although we have discussed this in other chapters of the book, it is important to remind ourselves why science journalism is important—and perhaps even more important—in a country such as Sudan. The answer is two-fold. First, we have the fact that journalists continue to be, in most societies, the gatekeepers between scientific knowledge and the general public. They decode and recode science content and provide meaning through appealing, interesting and relevant narratives that allow the audiences to engage, read and interpret science in the context of their daily lives (Baker & Scott, 2018; Jjuuko, 2020).

This last point is made, despite an increasing rich media environment that now provides multiple platforms and which are often said to be crucial in enhancing the way we communicate science to the public (Abd Al-Elah & Al-Saraj, 2021). Secondly, it is precisely because of the lack of capabilities among the Sudanese to connect directly with scientific knowledge through the emerging platforms in useful and meaningful ways that science journalists are needed more than ever. They are crucial not only in terms of their news-gathering capacity but also, and mostly, for their ability to select news that is accurate and trustworthy for the audiences.

Having said that, Abdul Hafeez (2016) has concluded that there is no daily or periodical scientific newspaper that meets the needs of readers with regard to the existence of scientific material with an explanatory and simplified press treatment of the scientific content in that country. The only exceptions are what is published in science magazines affiliated with institutions working in a scientific field but that have limited scope and reach.

As in the case of other MENA countries, we find the paradox of a Sudan that actually has a rich tradition in science news. In fact, the Sudanese press arose when the first Sudanese modern newspaper appeared in 1903. It did not originate in the same way as the news press of Egypt and Europe, but rather the Sudanese press mixed the news with what we would call today op-eds. The Sudanese press, since its inception, was interested in various journalistic newsbeats and gave particular attention to science.

Moreover, in the decades that followed colonial rule, the Sudanese press witnessed a relative liberalisation and loosening up of political controls that brought increasing diversity of content in social, cultural, sports, economic and scientific topics, as well as a more independent newspaper editorial policy in many of the existing media outlets at the time (Malik, 2012; Sharkey, 1999). Over the years, the Sudanese press has been devoid of scientific journalism experiences and has not had any mainstream or far-reaching daily newspaper or periodical dealing with science topics or magazine specialised in this subject. The only exceptions are very niche journals such as *Your Medical Health Journal*, which is issued by the Kuwaiti Patients Benefit Fund in Sudan, *The Scientific Life* magazine, which is issued by the Authority for the Care of Scientific Creativity, and the *Sadd Muroori* newspaper, which is issued by the Dams Implementation Unit (Abdul Hafeez, 2016).

Statistics from the National Council for Press and Publications in that country on the report verifying the spread of Sudanese newspapers for the year 2014 indicate that the number of Sudanese newspapers issued until December 2015 reached 57 newspapers, including 39 that cover general topics, 11 focused on sports and 7 focusing on more general social issues. However, none of these newspapers had a scientific focus. The only exception was the *Meroe Dam* magazine (monthly) affiliated to the Dams Implementation Unit, which is distributed among various institutions but without general public reach and, a magazine specialised in water, dams and energy called the *One Scientific Journal*, which is a specialised quarterly magazine issued by the Ministry of Minerals.

General daily newspapers and mainstream broadcasters in that country have shown a degree of interest in scientific topics by providing space offering separate pages or airtime to the environment, medical issues and technology as well as for university maters (although not necessarily dealing with science produced there but rather general issues affecting higher education in that country). This attention in the mainstream media however has been irregular, sporadic and at times eclectic. When interviewed about this, Sudanese editors and journalists came with the same two answers as other Arab countries: lack of specialised reporters and lack of sufficient interest on the part of their audiences.

Our own content analysis of a sample of two of the leading newspapers in Sudan in the first four months of 2019 suggests that the presence of scientific opinion articles in the Sudanese press is limited to events and occasions that require discussion from a scientific point of view. The sample also indicates that even dialogue with a scientific personality is hardly found in the Sudanese press except in the case of an event that calls for dialogue with a scientific interest (or connection) such as weather events, earthquakes, floods, the emergence of an environmental problem and other similar disaster-driven events. Only in those circumstances its seems will the press actually sit down to interview scientists.

Several reasons contributed to the deterioration of the scientific press in Sudan and have hindered successful scientific journalistic experiments in that nation. This, with the exception of a handful of initiatives affiliated with government, mining corporations or specific research agencies. According to Abdul Hafeez (2016), there is a lack of enthusiasm among media business people to invest in science media—and who perhaps do not see a market opportunity—given the low interest of audiences in this topic. This might partially explain a great deal for the gaps in the media provisions around science. In addition, scientific newspapers have noted there is a lack of qualified and specialised journalists in scientific affairs who can be relied upon. As one of the interviewees expressed in Hafeez's own sets of interviews,

> *There are structural issues that we face that makes it difficult to establish a proper science journalism practice in this country. This includes the lack of scientific media specializations in science and scientific journalism in Sudanese universities. This as well as the absence of cadres that could establish the experience of specialized scientific journalism.* (Abdul Hafeez, 2016)

Our own interviewees highlighted the absence of scientific journalism federations and unions that could benefit from qualifying and training media professionals to work in the field of scientific journalism as well as the lack of support and encouragement by the state and scientific institutions for the scientific press in Sudan, confirming Hafeez's earlier findings.

## Science Journalism in Syria

The scientific press accompanied the public press in Syria in terms of its establishment and development, albeit slowly and modestly. In 1855, the Syrian Society for the Dissemination of Science and Revitalization of the Arts began establishing a specialised magazine under its banner. The publication included a number of scientific, artistic, astronomical and historical articles as well as covering scientific discoveries and modern inventions (Sedki, 2018).

During its modern history, the scientific press in Syria suffered from multiple problems and setbacks that hindered its development. One of the most important of these problems was its inability to use accessible and translatable language. This, as it struggled to translate scientific terms into the Arabic language as it lacked the technical and professional cadre for press production. One that could combine journalistic craftsmanship and scientific expertise in ways that could do these translations and make the content more widely accessible (Hassan, 2013).

Other publications have made important inroads, such as the scientific journals in Syria (Bou Tebakalt, 2013; Hassan, 2013). One example is the *Atomic World Magazine*, which before the start of the civil war, has been published three times a year since 1986 by the Atomic Energy Authority in Syria. It is a publication concerned with the dissemination of scientific knowledge in the field of atomic science in Arabic. Other scientific journals include the *Geological Journal*, which is issued by the General Organization for Geology and Mineral Resources in Syria and, the *Energy and Development Journal*, which has been published since 1980 as a monthly scientific journal.

As in most countries, science news in Syria is mostly produced today not by journalists themselves but by communication professionals and press officers who pitch content to the newsrooms in several forms (Sedki, 2018). Press releases are perhaps the most common form of delivering potential news stories to journalists and editors/producers. Our own analysis of over 50 press releases in that country suggests that they mainly centred on the discovery and invention of the institution or government dependency that produces that science. In most cases, we can see press releases about health and, to certain degree, news about technology. On the other hand, most science press reports in that country come from news agencies and refer to science abroad. On occasion, although sporadic, one finds op-eds and columns as well as commentary around science news.

However, since the start of the civil war science news reports in the press and other broadcast media have greatly diminished. The country is now torn apart and most of the media operate under government control as before but with even tighter forms of censorship. We did not have equal access to Syria in terms of our ability to interview journalists or editors and the content analysis was limited to the newspapers *Tishreen* and *Al-Thawra*, both based in Damascus. This included a one-month sample: June 2020. The sample suggests that stories on COVID were mostly about government policy and actions and some international dispatches from the region but we did not find any locally produced articles about science in our non-representative sample.

## SCIENCE JOURNALISM IN THE UAE

The United Arab Emirates, together with Egypt, exhibits one of the most sophisticated media systems in the region. Many media corporations have offices in Dubai Media City, including the Financial Times, CNN and Reuters. These media companies have received guarantees that they would be exempt from national legal restrictions and for years in that country have had the biggest concentration of dedicated news bureaus in the region (Komorowski, 2017; Picard & Barkho, 2011; Reinisch, 2010).

The UAE was also among the first of the GCC countries to strategically move towards economic diversification and to push for greater engagement with science and technology. In addition to this, it has one of the highest levels of literacy and higher education attendance per capita. The nation has attracted many leading international universities, think-tanks and research centres as well as establishing their own HE institutions that today rank among the best in the region, placing it in a particular position to have a well-developed practice of both science communication and science journalism.

Moreover, the country has a strong tradition of science journalism. Indeed, the UAE became known to the scientific press with the publication of the *Petroleum and Industry News* magazine in 1964 by the then Ministry of Petroleum in the United Arab Emirates. Years later this publication became the *Energy and Industry Journal*, a periodical magazine that aimed at raising awareness about energy matters and that then focused on natural and clean energy for the Arabian Gulf.

The UAE, again with Egypt, are perhaps the countries that have done visibly more to promote science journalism in the region. For example, Sultan bin Muhammad Al Qasimi—Sheikh Sultan III, member of the Supreme Council of the United Arab Emirates and the Ruler of Sharjah—has been a very active advocate of science journalism by promoting and supporting the association of Arab science journalists, although at the moment the organisation's website remains inactive. With perhaps the biggest concentration of universities per capita in the region and one of the highest ratios of graduates, the UAE provides solid ground for science communication in general and science journalism in particular.

In 2017, the Dubai Press Club announced the launch of the 'Science Journalist Program' in cooperation with the Emirates Scientists Council. This had the aim of training specialised journalists concerned with the science and technology sector in local and Arab media outlets, providing them with basic concepts that would help them absorb scientific content (Al-Suaid, 2016). The duration of the training programme extends for four months and consists of holding practical lessons, workshops, discussion sessions and interactive lectures, through which trainees can learn about new professional visions and ideas about scientific journalism (Al-Hassan, 2010).

The programme includes introductory tours for journalists in scientific institutions in the country to get closely acquainted with the scientific branches of specialised fields and how to formulate news and related press reports and to simplify some terms and information that may seem complicated to non-specialists and develop language that readers from different cultural backgrounds can understand (Nafadi, 1996).

Having said all this, science news in the UAE remains largely underdeveloped. Our own content analysis shows that local newspapers, broadcasters and digital-native media continue to pay scarce attention to science and technology and that most of the stories published and broadcast come from abroad even in the face of the Expo Dubai mega-event. Despite having access to a number of university and research centres, locally produced science news stories remain dependent on press releases and that many potentially interesting and relevant news stories remain broadly ignored.

## Conclusion

One of the most striking paradoxes that we find in this chapter is the inability of the MENA region to see the emergence of a robust practice of science journalism despite seemly having all the conditions in place for that to happen. After all, the region has a rich tradition and legacy in terms of its engagement with science that not only relates to Islam's so-called Golden Age, but that also links to more recent times in which many media outlets and individuals have engaged profusely with science and science dissemination.

Moreover, the region has witnessed literacy rates that have grown exponentially in the past decades, and the vast incorporation of women into scientific and technological professional spheres. To be sure, a much higher percentage of women in countries such as Qatar and the United

Arab Emirates today study STEM subjects than in most western countries—for example, Qatar's percentage of female engineering students is double that of the United States (Abdallah, 2021; Rizvi, 2018). There is also an increasingly robust scientific community made up of local and international universities and research centres that can provide expert sources and that is constantly generating innovations and discoveries. In addition, journalism in the region has become overall more professionalised, while journalists operate in a richer media ecology that provides a greater number of options for the public. All this despite persistent political limitations to the practice of news reporting and to academic freedom that journalism education in MENA equates to 'walking on eggshells' (Saleh, 2010, p. 78). However, even those limitations should not hinder the development of science journalism. After all, it is an area that enjoys broad political consensus and that avoids problems of censorship or self-censorship usually found in that region.

So, the question remains as to why then science journalism in the region has failed to achieve its full potential? As we will discuss in the following chapters, there are structural and contextual issues that undermine the potential of science journalism in the region. These conditions include, as we have seen in most cases, a lack of specialised journalists, editors and producers, limited economic viability of media outlets specialised in science and technology, a weak institutional framework for the practice of news reporting, not enough expert sources, limited scientific activity in some countries and, perhaps most importantly, a general apathy among the greater regional public to science itself. Overall, as we have discussed here, science news reporting in MENA lacks what the ancient Greek philosopher Aristotle called the 'entelechy'—that which realises or makes actual what is otherwise merely potential—to turn normative aspirations into a reality.

## Bibliography

Abd Al-Elah, H. R. H., & Al-Saraj, S. K. (2021). Science Journalism within the framework of Media Richness Theory. *PalArch's Journal of Archaeology of Egypt/Egyptology, 18*(7), 2835–2844.

Abdallah, H. (2021). Qatari women 'outnumber men' at local universities [News]. *Doha News*. Retrieved May 12, 2022, from https://www.dohanews.co/qatari-women-outnumber-men-at-local-universities/

Abdel Rahman Qanchouba, K. R. (2021). COVID-19 crisis: The need for science media. *Journal of Human Sciences, 21*(1), 824–840.

Abdul Hafeez, H. (2016). Journalistic treatment of scientific topics in the Sudanese Press. *Journal of the Humanities, 1*(1), 109–118.

Abu Haseera, R. (2018). *The reality of scientific journalism in the Palestinian daily newspapers: A comparative analytical and field study.* Islamic University of Gaza.

Abu Saiba, S. N. (2016). The Lebanese press in the stage of leadership and establishment: A study in the archives of the Lebanese National Archives. *Journal of the College of Education for Girls for Human Sciences, 10*(18), 401–448.

Al Rawi, K. H. (2010). *History of the press and media in Iraq from the Ottoman era until the second Gulf War.* Pages House for Studies and Publishing.

Al-Hassan, I. M. (2010). *Specialized press.* Zahran Publishing and Distribution House.

Allen, L. (2008). Getting by the occupation: How violence became normal during the Second Palestinian Intifada. *Cultural Anthropology, 23*(3), 453–487.

Al-Qafari, A. (2009). *Science media in Saudi journalism.* King Abdul-Aziz City for Science and Technology (KACST).

Alqudsi-Ghabra, T. (1995). Information control in Kuwait: Dialectic to democracy. *Journal of South Asian and Middle Eastern Studies, 18*(4).

AL-Salem, K., & Abu-Saab, A. (2007). Science Magazine. *AAL—Bahith AL—A'alami, 1*(3), 31–48.

Al-Suaid, I. M. (2016). Emirati media: Its origin and development. *The Scientific Journal of Public Relations and Advertising Research, 2016*(8), 437–467.

Alyan, H. (2012). History of science journalism in Kuwait. *Al Taqaddum Al-Ilmi Journal, 76.*

Azzouz, H. (2016). The Algerian press specialized in the era of the French occupation. *Al-Turath Magazine, 22*(1), 190–181.

Badran, A. (2014). *The reality of scientific journalism in Kuwait from the perspective of journalists working in Kuwait.* Middle East University.

Baker, N., & Scott, H. (2018). Media capacity building in Sudan: A measure of success? *African Journalism Studies, 39*(2), 130–137.

Ballon, P., & Duclos, J. (2016). A comparative analysis of multidimensional poverty in Sudan and South Sudan. *African Development Review, 28*(S2), 132–161.

Bou Tebakalt, T. (2013). The role of the press in the modern Arab renaissance or when cultures cross. *Turjuman Magazine, 22*(2), 11–48.

Bouhaila, R. (2017). History of the specialized written press in general and sports in particular in Europe and the Arab world: Egypt and Algeria as a model., Issue 15. *Al-Maaref Journal for Research and Historical Studies, 15*(1), 289–309.

Davis, U. (2003). *Apartheid Israel: Possibilities for the struggle within.* Zed Books.

De Angelis, E. (2015). Introduction: The hybrid system of Egypt and 'cultural chaos'. *Égypte/Monde Arabe, 12,* 21–33.

Figenschou, T. U. (2013). *Al Jazeera and the global media landscape: The South is talking back.* Routledge.

Halabi, N. (2015). Media privatization and the fate of social democracy in Egypt. *Arab Media & Society, 21,* 1–10.

Hassan, I. M. (2013). *Specialized Press.* Zahran House for Publishing and Distribution.

Jebril, N., & Loveless, M. (2017). Media audiences and media consumption during political transitions: The case of Egypt. *Interactions: Studies in Communication & Culture, 8*(2–3), 151–167.

Jjuuko, M. (2020). Environmental journalism in East Africa: Opportunities and challenges in the 21st century. In *Routledge Handbook of Environmental Journalism* (pp. 354–365).

Kasrils, R., Ben-Dor, D. O., Cook, J., Farsakh, L., Löwstedt, A., Badran, A., Friedman, S., Tilley, V. Q., & Greenstein, R. (2015). *Israel and South Africa: The many faces of Apartheid.* Bloomsbury Publishing.

KoKaz, S. (2008). The specialized press in Iraq after the events of April 9. *AL—Bahith AL—A'alami, 1*(4), 126–145.

Komorowski, M. (2017). A novel typology of media clusters. *European Planning Studies, 25*(8), 1334–1356.

Lugo-Ocando, J., Mohsin, A., Nguyen, A., & Hamadeh, S. (2019). *Assessing the Qatari news media's capacities for fostering public understanding of and engagement with science: Issues, challenges, opportunities and their socio-political implications.* QNRF, Doha. NPRP12S-0317-190381.

Malik, S. I. (2012). Writing from inside out: Accounts of Sudanese women working in the media. *Journal of Arts and Humanities, 1*(2), 68–83.

Maziad, M. (2021). Qatar in Egypt: The politics of Al Jazeera. *Journalism, 22*(4), 1067–1087.

Metab, H. S. (2019). *Haider Shallalientific press in Iraq.* Karbala Channel. https://www.youtube.com/watch?v=kxSsK7itcPk

Meyer, K., Rizzo, H., & Ali, Y. (2007). Changed political attitudes in the Middle East: The case of Kuwait. *International Sociology, 22*(3), 289–324.

Miles, H. (2010). *Al Jazeera: How Arab TV news challenged the world.* Hachette UK.

Nafadi, A. (1996). *Press Emirates upbringing and artistic and historical evolution.* Publications of the Cultural Foundation.

Nguyen, A., & McIlwaine, S. (2011). Who wants a voice in Science issues—And why? A survey of European citizens and its implications for science journalism. *Journalism Practice, 5*(2), 210–226.

Odine, M. (2011). Middle East media: Press freedom in Kuwait. *Journal of Advanced Social Research, 1*(2), 177–190.

Onyebadi, U., & Alajmi, F. (2016). Gift solicitation and acceptance in journalism practice: An assessment of Kuwaiti journalists' perspective. *Journalism, 17*(3), 348–365.

Picard, R. G., & Barkho, L. (2011). Dubai media city: Creating benefits from foreign media developments. In *Media Clusters*. Edward Elgar Publishing.

Qabbanji, J. A. (2011). Research in Lebanon: Scientific groups, researchers and creativity: The current situation in the social sciences. *The Arab Journal of Sociology—Additions, 15*(1), 173–176.

Quigley, J. (1991). Apartheid outside Africa: The case of Israel. *Indiana International & Comparative Law Review, 2*, 221.

Reinisch, L. (2010). Environmental journalism in UAE. *Arab Media & Society, 11*, 1–19.

Rizvi, A. (2018). UAE bucks global trend as women lead the way in science studies [News]. *The Nation*. https://www.thenationalnews.com/uae/uae-bucks-global-trend-as-women-lead-the-way-in-science-studies-1.745043

Rugh, W. (2004). *Arab mass media: Newspapers, radio, and television in Arab politics*. Greenwood Publishing Group.

Saber, N. (2013). The scientific media crisis: A study of the scientific press discourse in Al-Ahram newspaper from October–December 2012. *Arab Journal for Media and Communication Research, 2*, 192–215.

Saleh, I. (2010). Journalism education in MENA: Walking on eggshells. *Brazilian Journalism Research, 6*(1), 78–88.

Sedki, H. (2018). *Scientific journalism between theory and practice*. Academic Library.

Shaaban, A. M. (2009). The trends of the Iraqi press in the first decade of the royal era: A descriptive study of the newspapers of Baghdad. *Al-Adab Journal, University of Baghdad, 88*(1), 492–511.

Sharkey, H. J. (1999). A century in print: Arabic journalism and nationalism in Sudan, 1899–1999. *International Journal of Middle East Studies, 31*(4), 531–549.

Spurr, D. (1993). *The rhetoric of empire: Colonial discourse in journalism, travel writing, and imperial administration*. Duke University Press.

Worth, A. (2014). *Imperial media: Colonial networks and information technologies in the British literary imagination, 1857–1918*. The Ohio State University Press.

Yagoob, A., & Zuo, T. (2016). Patterns of economic growth and poverty in Sudan. *Journal of Economics and Sustainable Development, 7*(2).

Yari, Y. (2016). A study on the thought and political action of Salama Moussa in the realm of Socialism. *A Quarterly Journal of Historical Studies of Islam, 8*(29), 151–169.

Yetiv, S. (2002). Kuwait's democratic experiment in its broader international context. *The Middle East Journal*, 257–271.

Ziadat, A., & Jallow, B. (1986). *Western science in the Arab world: The impact of Darwinism 1860–1930*. Palgrave Macmillan.

CHAPTER 4

# Science News Cultures and Journalism Practice

Despite the disruptive technological and societal changes in recent years, the mainstream media continues to play a central role in communicating science to the public and setting the news agenda around science and technology (Angler, 2017; Bucchi, 1998; Mahmood, 2008). Moreover, despite the public's growing engagement with social media platforms, journalists who work in the mainstream media continue to be pivotal in bridging between the scientific community and the general public (Barel-Ben David et al., 2020; Dunwoody, 2020). They remain an 'interpretative community' (Zelizer, 1993) that is core to the construction of social reality in the minds of the public and continue to act as key gatekeepers who not only select the events and facts that are to be disseminated but also interpret the world outside in order to provide meaning while sharing information with the public.

The functions of sharing knowledge and articulating meaning are particularly relevant as science reporters work nowadays within an evolving media ecosystem that is pluralistic, participatory and highly networked (Splendore & Brambilla, 2021). Driven by economic imperatives and technological changes, science journalists perform a wider variety of roles, including those of curator, convener, public intellectual and civic educator, in addition to more traditional journalistic roles of reporter, conduit, watchdog and agenda-setter (Fahy & Nisbet, 2011). Therefore, it is inconceivable to provide any insight into the role of science journalists in

© The Author(s), under exclusive license to Springer Nature Switzerland AG 2023
A. Alhuntushi, J. Lugo-Ocando, *Science Journalism in the Arab World*, Palgrave Studies in Journalism and the Global South, https://doi.org/10.1007/978-3-031-14252-9_4

MENA without first understanding the role itself of both journalists and the media in the gathering, production, dissemination and consumption of news.

A series of studies have addressed the role of the Arab media in science communication and, in some cases, also looked at science journalism in the region. Most of these scholarly works suggest that science communication in general remains underdeveloped and deficient, and presents important limitations in terms of existing capabilities and a lack of specialised reporters (Alhuntushi & Lugo-Ocando, 2020; Al-Qafari, 2009; El-Awady, 2009). In addition, the work of science journalists in MENA countries has been singled out as being inaccurate and showing a lack of specialised sources (Mahmood, 2008, p. 50). This criticism extends to inaccurate reporting and the inability to substantiate important claims with hard evidence and data. It also pinpoints the use of inaccessible terminology and language when writing news stories, which makes it very difficult for the public to understand what is being said.

However, one of the biggest challenges in the region, according to these authors, is the absence of a comprehensive and robust scientific communication news culture in the Arab region. In other words, neither the general public speaks sufficiently and comprehensively about science nor journalists report this beat with sufficient expertise, credibility and accessibility. Without a cultural space for scientific exchange and dialogue, science journalism is a practice that sees itself limited in its ability to disseminate science and technology discovery, debates and issues (Al-Qafari, 2009; El-Awady, 2009; Mahmood, 2008; Mawlawi, 1988).

Therefore, it is important to start by recognising that news cultures that foster the professional and organisational dynamics to produce science news and promote public interest in science are quintessential for that practice. These news cultures, which take different forms in each society, are also an essential source of science information for many people and are critical in underpinning public awareness and engagement with science in general (Khairy, 2020; Long, 1995). This because, in many ways a news culture is a sort of ecosystem that not only depends on the providers of news but also relies upon those at the receiving end who consume science news.

Take for example Atwater's classical study, which found that newspapers and the mainstream media in general were a significant source of environmental information for Michigan residents (Atwater, 1988, p. 34). Other studies over the years have confirmed these findings, while providing further cross-cultural and cross-national evidence of people's reliance on the media for scientific information (Brossard & Scheufele, 2013; Pierce et al., 1988; Scheufele & Krause, 2019). More recently, newer studies have started to suggest that there is a displacement from traditional media to social media as the main source of news about science in the region (Dennis et al., 2020). However, even this being the case, the content that is disseminated and which is mostly influential in setting the agenda is still produced by a handful of mainstream media outlets that continues to be present and dominating across all types of platforms.

The notion of news cultures and their relation to journalism practice cannot therefore only be seen in terms of the media ecology that defines exchanges and process, but also through the lenses of its relation to the audiences. Hence, it additionally requires to be understood in the context of political power and societal context. That is because the media systems in which science reporters work do not operate in a vacuum. They are instead shaped and respond to a multiplicity of factors present in each society, which in turn are the making of the prevalent news cultures in each society discussed in this book.

This chapter provides a general assessment of how science reporting is defined as a professional practice by the imperatives established by the prevalent news cultures. In so doing, the chapter offers an exhaustive and comprehensive analysis of how journalists producing science news in MENA interact and engage with science topics in the face of contextual factors that play a role in shaping journalism itself and the relationship that reports have with both news events and their audiences. These contextual factors—or background issues—in our view influence the capabilities of journalists when producing and presenting science news stories to the public.

The concept of 'News Culture' places the media within a historical framework of a particular society. In this sense, there is an ample body of literature around the structural issues and background that define the way and ability of journalists to gather, disseminate and produce news as well as about the expectations of news audiences (Allan, 2004; McNair, 1998; Schudson, 2003). This literature refers to a 'sociology of journalism' that contextualises news reporting practices in societies, which in turn upholds values and procedures that are used to inquiry into society's issues (McNair, 1998; Schlesinger, 1999 [1978]). This creates a news culture in which those who report are expected to produce news in a certain way and those who consume news expect this to be presented and provided within news that meets certain standards. In countries such as the United States and the United Kingdom, to name two, these normative expectations are summarised by the notions of objectivity and impartiality (Allan, 2004, 2011; Galison, 2015).

However, in other contexts—such as in MENA—one can broadly point to very distinctive practices and normative expectations and assumptions in relation to their news culture. These features have been defined by a series of aspects present in the political and societal context in which each media system has emerged. Something that has forged the news cultures in each one of these countries. These elements include the political system, religion and culture, economics, media ownership, and the background, education and training of journalists in that region (Mellor, 2005, 2010; Rugh, 2004).

Among these elements, it is perhaps religion, culture and politics that are mostly cited by external observers as sources of differentiation with news cultures in the west. Indeed, they are considered the most relevant categories influencing news cultures and journalistic practices in the MENA region. Overall, of these elements, politics is considered the most important factor affecting the media in this region. Three aspects of politics come out as most influential; the illiberal nature of the regimes in the region, the way media ownership is structured and, the role of religion in society. Until recently, most scholarly analysis about science news reporting has been performed from the perspective of secular liberal democracies; hence, part of the contributions of this chapter is to examine the formation and nature of a type of news culture that is different from that Weberian ideal type (Hamdy, 2013, p. 71).

Indeed, when looking at the Arab media, the analysis from scholars and experts has often been closely associated with the context in which reporters operate, which, to a great extent is defined by illiberal regimes and the role of Islamic culture (Lynch, 2015; Rugh, 2004). In addition, and despite the proliferation of media outlets operating in the region, Arab governments continue to largely be the main owners and funders of the mainstream media outlets. This is not new but a historical occurrence that can be observed in the first Egyptian papers, the journals *al-Khadyu* and *al-Waqa al Masriya*—published in 1827 and 1828, respectively—which were published by the government at a time when private proprietors already owned the commercial press in places such as England and the United States with robust legislation to secure independence.

Today, Arab media outlets tend to operate under official government guidance and follow authorised editorial policies, even when they are in the hands of private proprietors (Rugh, 2004, p. 6) and in so doing, their main role has been to promote government policies (Hamdy, 2013, p. 71). Hence, rather than to scrutinise policy or challenge power, they remain subservient to state narratives. The media in MENA functions within political systems that, as a result of post-colonial settings and the legacy of the Cold War, continue to be mostly illiberal.

In these societies the distinctions between the private and public spheres and between religion and secularism have never truly occurred, at least not in the same ways they happened in Europe (Asad, 2003; Fitzgerald, 2003). This is not to say that one must fall into the intellectual trap of assigning rationality to the secular while ascribing irrationality to the religious. As these scholars have debated in Critical Religion Studies, these dichotomies are profoundly problematic and unrepresentative as categories of analysis.

Therefore, as we argue in this section, there is a need for a particular analytical category that recognises that the news culture in the Arab world is fundamentally different. This is not to say, however, that science reporting is not practised in the MENA region but to clarify instead that it is carried out within a different cultural and professional context. Consequently, the relationship of professional journalism with science in the context of the tensions provoked by modernisation and post-colonialism means that news about science is gathered, produced and disseminated in a way that might seem alien to those reporters working in the West. It also means that the audiences expect, and are accustomed to, a different deontology and aesthetics in science news.

This, because in journalism, the MENA region reflects the sociological dynamics that are present in many of the nations in that region. These dynamics are historical by-products of larger and broader political events and therefore cannot be analysed simply through western lenses, which overall tend to 'orientalise' any scrutiny and assessment of those societies (Said, 2003 [1978]; Thompson, 2016). Our work tries instead to assess science reporting in its own context and approach 'what journalists do' and 'how the public reads science news' in their own terms. At the end, the way people engage with news is defined by news cultures that are at times ambivalent towards science and contextualise 'truth' within broader systems of belief. It is a science news culture that over time has been converging with the west in an increasingly globalised world but that remains anchored to particular political and cultural values and professional dynamics.

## Science News in the Arab World

These issues raise a key research question: How can we best define the news cultures in the MENA region in relation to how they shape and define science-reporting deontology and practices? In asking and unpacking this question, we should notice the historical and sociological context for the formation of news cultures in that region. We should also account for the relationship between Islam and society by acknowledging that it is one of the many features that characterises that context. Perhaps one way to start is by detailing and describing the current state of science journalism in the region from the point of view of the elements that structure reporting practices.

To start with, perhaps one of the most important challenges in these countries is the scarcity of science journalists themselves (Al-Qafari, 2009; Plackett, 2020), which is aggravated by the lack of specialised editors and producers in the newsrooms. Indeed, like in many countries in the Global South, the lack of professionalisation of journalists in general, let alone the specialisation of science reporters, has been a concern in the Arab region (Bebawi, 2016; Hamdy, 2013; Lublinski et al., 2014). Some authors single out the political context in which journalists operate, the historical relation to the prevalent political system and cultural/idiosyncratic framework (namely, religion) as some of the main reasons (Mellor, 2005; Rugh, 2004).

We concur with this view as it is impossible to disassociate the way science journalism is practised in these countries from the way politics, culture, the economy and history have defined their specific media systems. In addition, it is important to note that the scarcity of professional science reporters is exacerbated by both a lack of general knowledge about science in the newsroom and a wider public disinterest in science news compared to other beats such as politics and sports (El-Awady, 2009; Mbarga et al., 2012). This vicious circle in which journalists do not engage with science because, allegedly, their audiences are not interested in science has the inevitable consequence that, as a whole, science communication tends to be neglected and remains un-professionalised and underdeveloped.

Another aspect to highlight is that the news media coverage of science news in the MENA region is not homogenous even within the same country. Our own research shows, to cite an example, that even among Saudi newspapers there are significant differences. While *Al Riyadh* published

308 articles that can be considered as science stories, its counterpart, *Oqaz*, only published less than a third of that, with just 101 in the same time period, despite being similar media outlets. These intra-national disparities within a single country suggest also that there are different understandings in the region as to what constitutes newsworthy issues and events in relation to science and technology. It also indicates that far from the broad assumptions among many in the west that the media in MENA is a monolithic and homogenous entity, there is instead—at least in relation to science—a diversity of news values and criteria that define what is selected and shared with the public.

Interviews with journalists and editors/producers in the region show that the criteria considered as to whether or not to incorporate science news in their agenda is viewed differently among media outlets and that the way these outlets pay attention to science has more to do with organisational dynamics and local news cultures than with national trends or media systems. Our study in the region shows a distinct gap in relation to the number of science news stories which appear in the press. The numbers not only vary between each country but also within each country itself.

So, one of the first questions we should ask is what it is exactly understood in MENA as 'science news'? Despite the seeming simplicity of a possible answer, it is not just about defining it as the reporting of scientific issues. This, because any answer to that question also demands the exploration of general news values and the implicit understanding that to be in the news, science must be 'newsworthy'. Hence, one also has to ask what makes—or possibly enables—science and technology to be considered by the gatekeepers as newsworthy enough to be incorporated into their agenda of inquiry? One also must ask about the criterion that is taken into consideration when assessing what makes the headlines.

Scholars have for years examined what constitutes news, while inquiring about the values that are prevalent in determining the selection of what stories to bring to the public (Bro & Wallberg, 2014; Galtung & Ruge, 1965; Harcup & O'neill, 2001). These studies suggest a professional criterion that includes several aspects such as: timeliness, is the event/issue immediate or 'new'; proximity, if it is geographically or culturally 'close to home'; does it reflect enough conflict or controversy; how much human interest can be conveyed; and 'relevance' to the audiences' interests.

In this sense, what is considered to be 'news' for journalists is not necessarily relevant to scientists and vice versa. The traditional reference of Charles Anderson, Dana editor and proprietor, New York Sun, who in 1882 allegedly said 'when a dog bites a man that is not news, when a man bites a dog, that is news' is often used to illustrate the phenomenology of what becomes headlines or not. Overall, the question of what makes something newsworthy has been debated in media and journalism studies by experts (Harcup & O'neill, 2001; Schudson, 2003). These and other scholars have highlighted a set of criteria that suggest there are aspects in an event or issue that make the story appealing and relevant to both the media and the general public. These criteria can help to explain why a particular science story can become news while others do not. In science, this refers to events, discoveries and research in science, which might be of interest to the scientific community but not intrinsically newsworthy for the general public.

Despite persisting political controls over the news agenda in the case of MENA, there has been, nevertheless, a convergent trend towards embracing a more universal ideal of what is newsworthy. Most newsrooms in the region today tend to embrace the global notion of news, as shown by studies regarding journalists' normative expectations (Hamdy, 2013; Hanitzsch et al., 2019; Mellor, 2005), although at times this would not be apparent for the average reader who will still find many pages dull and unappealing. That convergence is applicable in most news beats such as sport, science and entertainment but not in others such as politics or sensitive areas where they are restricted by the nature of the political systems in which they operate. Consequently, journalists report in ways that can be similar to those in the west but that at the same time stay away from controversial issues or which are perceived to be adversarial.

Consequently, the tone and aesthetics of news in the region, characterised by deference to power. This central feature of the news culture in the Middle East is particularly significant as it is closely linked to issues around the professionalism and professional autonomy of news reporters and also highlights the need to pay careful attention to not only the existing 'media systems' (Hallin & Mancini, 2011) and the news organisations as units of analysis, but also the individual and collective news practices as both components and manifestations of the news cultures in those countries.

## Journalistic Genres

Among these units of analysis, we can start by exploring one central defining feature of a news culture; that is, the aesthetics of news. The aesthetics of news is the way journalists are expected to present the news and audiences read it (Glasser, 1980). Over the past 150 years, news aesthetics have been defined by a global trend set originally in the United States and Europe, which under colonialism and then the Cold War expanded across the Global South (Lugo-Ocando, 2020; Wasserman & de Beer, 2010). This trend reflects in many parts of the world the Associate Press stylebook and, furthermore, the notions of 5WH and inverted pyramid. This aesthetics have translated, among other aspects, into narrativising news stories in genres such as hard news, feature articles and op-eds, among others.

The mostly widely used genre is the so-called hard news, which refers to a style mostly present in English-language journalism that is characterised by the authorial 'neutrality' and use of the 'inverted pyramid' structure that allow journalists to assert their 'objectivity' and 'impartiality' when they write their stories (Dowling, 2020; Hovden & Kristensen, 2021). Hard news refers not only to the way the story is structured and written but also its focus in terms of news that directly affects society and that is of interest or relevant to the community.

Over the years, hard-news practices diffused across borders and led to the formation of distinct news cultures that had, nevertheless, important global overlaps (Esser & Umbricht, 2014; Thomson et al., 2008; Umbricht, 2014). News media in Arab countries have in that same period converged towards hard news and made it into the predominant genre for the reporting of news in both their Arabic and English-speaking newspapers in MENA. The prevalence of this genre conveys an approach that aspires to neutrality by presenting facts instead of opinions.

Our findings highlight that science news reporting in Arabic newspapers is mostly present through the genre of 'hard news'. Not surprising given that hard news is the most widespread genre in news stories overall (Rudin & Ibbotson, 2002, p. 52). The study indicates that almost 98% of science news in MENA is presented in the form of hard news, while just 2.3% of such articles came in the form of beat feature articles, reportage or op-eds (Table 4.1).

One explanation for the prevalent character of this genre is that most science news stories in the region are based on actual events happening, press conferences or press releases, rather than investigation or inquiry

**Table 4.1** Journalistic genre of the article

|  |  | Frequency | Per cent | Valid per cent | Cumulative per cent |
|---|---|---|---|---|---|
| Valid | Hard news | 911 | 97.7 | 97.7 | 97.7 |
|  | Beat reportage | 21 | 2.3 | 2.3 | 100.0 |
|  | Total | 932 | 100.0 | 100.0 |  |

Source: Authors' data

from the journalists themselves. In other words, the predominance of 'hard news' indicates that science news depends on external agendas and an 'external' push or interest (e.g., from those producing press releases or organising a press conference) to get those stories out. This, instead of reporters' own quest for stories. As a central aesthetical feature, it also denotes a marked difference with western science journalism, which also depends on external inputs but in ways in which journalists can be more proactive in searching for the stories and be less event driven. For example, one of the main sources for science news in the west are academic peer-reviewed journal articles (Kiernan, 2003, p. 903).

In these cases, many western journalists are really translators of very specialised information and are able to assess the work of scientists and turn specialised work—that is either too technical or complex so as to be understood by the general public—into accessible material to which common people can relate and decipher. However, in our own sample of the Arab media, we could not find a significant number of stories produced locally and that were based in science in which there was any indication that journalists accessed scientific journals to produce the stories.

The prevalent use of hard news also suggests a more day-to-day coverage that follows events—as indicated above—rather than setting the news media's own agenda. In other words, it indicates that in relation to science news, journalists in MENA tend to follow and not to lead when setting the agenda. It also denotes a far more descriptive rather than analytical and critical approach towards the news. Its prevalent use may also suggest that it is a news beat dominated by immediacy and pressures of time, as most stories are published the very same day or the next day after the event happened. This means that journalists have less time to process and understand well the science in the stories and, therefore, are more prone to mistakes.

The fact that journalists tend to over-rely on event-driven issues to produce science news, together with the fact that they are ill-prepared to critically assess the external inputs—such as press releases or information packages given to them by their sources—can help explain why many mistakes and inaccuracies in science news reporting in MENA do not come from the journalists themselves, but rather from the press releases of organisations featured in the reporting. We are not blaming the use of hard news genre for these mistakes but arguing that the use of it reflects a specific work dynamic that fosters uncritical dependency towards what the sources supply to the reporters and that gives little room to properly scrutinise those inputs.

We looked at 20 news stories across different newspapers in Kuwait and Saudi Arabia in which we found mistakes or factual errors. Then we managed to find the original press releases coming from the science organisations, official sources or universities that produced the news story. In all but 4 of the 20 stories, we found that the mistakes or factual errors could be traced back to the original press release. This is a finding that corresponds with similar studies from around the world (Autzen & Weitkamp, 2018). In saying this, we are not making any excuses for the reporters in the newspapers of our sample who should, nevertheless, have properly fact-checked the stories. However, given their lack of training and expertise, plus the time pressures and, the decreasing number of resources in the newsrooms, the likelihood that these mistakes will just be passed on to the public is all but certain.

The fact remains that hard news stories in our sample are largely from external professional communication efforts. By 'professional communication efforts' it is meant items such as press releases produced by public relations professionals or strategic communication officials. In the sample, we can see that both *Al-Riyadh* and *Al-Ahram* produced science news in the form of hard news only, while other Arabic newspapers produced different percentages of both hard news and beat reportage. Over 81% of beat reportage news came from the Kuwaiti newspapers *Al-Qabas* and *Al-Rai*; *Al-Masry Al-Yuom* came next with 14.2%; and finally, in last place, was *Oqaz*, with nearly 5% of science news in the form of beat reportage (Fig. 4.1).

What this data suggests is that within the prevalent news culture in MENA journalists reproduce rather than create science news in the sense that they depend upon what external third-party content providers input into the newsroom. Contrary to what happens in the west, the

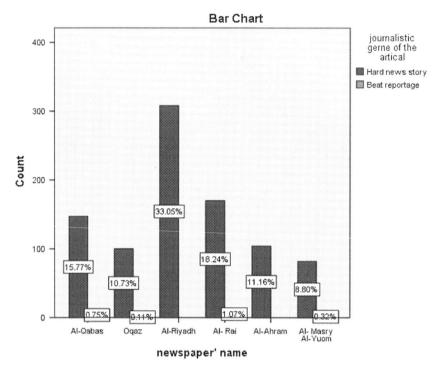

Fig. 4.1 Source: Authors' data

dependency on press releases is a result of not only the news deficit due to market failure—scarce allocation of resources to properly cover serious news given a weak demand market (Davies, 2011; Doyle, 2013; Lewis et al., 2008a)—but also a series of factors present in the settings in which journalists in MENA operate, such as restrictions and self-censorship. Hence, to avoid political hazards, reporters in the region tend to reproduce the materials that they are provided by officials and this practice has become in time a widespread culture that applies to all news beats, not just politics or sensitive matters.

In this sense, reporter and editors in MENA follow official agendas and this means reflecting inputs from officials that are mostly related to policy announcements. Newsrooms in the region are closely aligned with governments and consequently peg themselves to official agendas that are focused on disseminating public policy. Therefore, they are prone to publish related material supporting these efforts and policies. A trend that is reinforced by the fact that governments there spend large amounts of money and are, in some cases, the biggest advertisers.

Science news in MENA is vastly dominated by health as a central theme and as such it provides insightful understanding of the features that characterise science news cultures in MENA. For example, the fact that health news is so present in the science news beat indicates that there are important overlaps between Arab and Western science news agendas. Moreover, as these are findings from a pre-COVID sample.

Within health news, our study found that the media outlets in the sample were mostly focused on publishing news specifically related to disease. By this we mean that stories appearing in the press tend to be about threats and risks to individuals and society or they tended to be about treatments and discoveries to address those diseases (Table 4.2).

This suggests that, as is the case of other countries (Allan, 2002; McCluskey & Swinnen, 2011), risk is also a central feature of the science news culture in MENA. Both reporters and news audiences seem to be attracted to those news items that highlight potential hazard or that create 'moral panic'. Now, there is a slight difference as in many Arab countries there are strict regulations or accepted norms regarding the media's role in inciting havoc or contributing to public fear that could lead to disorder. In countries such as Qatar, for example, there is a broad agreement between the government and journalists to approach particular types of news in ways that are institutionally sound, and which do not create unnecessary alarm. In that country, from the start of the COVID pandemic of 2019, there were regular meetings between government officials and media owners to coordinate communication efforts. Indeed, given

Table 4.2 The main topic of the article (Alhuntushi & Lugo-Ocando, 2020)

| Frequency | Per cent | Valid per cent | Cumulative per cent |
|---|---|---|---|
| Public health | 358 | 38.4 | 38.4 | 38.4 |
| Health policy | 23 | 2.5 | 2.5 | 40.9 |
| Diseases | 496 | 53.2 | 53.2 | 94.1 |
| Other tech devices | 44 | 4.7 | 4.7 | 98.8 |
| Computer software | 11 | 1.2 | 1.2 | 100.0 |
| Total | 932 | 100.0 | 100.0 | |

the political context and the nature of the media systems in which reporters in MENA operate, risk within science news receives a very different treatment.

Very closely intertwined to the reporting of diseases in terms of risk, we find 'public health' as a key theme accounting for 38.4% of all the published health stories appearing in our sample. By 'public health' we mean, journalists describing and explaining long-term issues that affect the public, such as an increasing propensity to develop diabetes, lifestyle or any other matter that can affect the health of the community. In many ways, 'public health' is also about risk but rather than focusing on the outcomes—the disease itself—the theme is all about societal context. Hence, stories deal with issues such as lifestyle and diet, which surveys show are very popular among segments of the public (Dennis et al., 2020).

However, the science news culture in MENA does not seem one that tends to highlight approaches and policies to tackle these issues and address health risks. News related to 'health policy' barely made it to the headlines and did not receive the same level of interest despite being central to debates and discussions that bring scrutiny and assessment of collective efforts to address health issues. News on 'health policy'—including stories that were uncritical to policy and that just reflected government views—constituted just 2.5% of the total.

In other words, it is not just that journalists and editors in MENA follow official agendas and do not adopt an adversarial model, but the fact that health policies do not seem to be up for public debate, not even in places such as Kuwait where there is an elected parliament. Yes, journalists' work reflects—as expected—the inputs and views from officials, which are mostly about policy announcements, and yes, they reproduce both narratives and perspectives from those in power. However, the key is that there is very little debate or mention of policy. Further studies need to be undertaken to re-assess if this has changed post-COVID-19 pandemic as health policy might by now have become a more central theme in the news.

In addition, as we suggested before, it is no secret that the illiberal nature of the political systems in which the news media operates makes criticism of public policy unwelcome in public and media debates. Therefore, news media outlets are prone to publish materials supporting government proposals and rarely questioning them or scrutinising public policy. In interviews with journalists, there was no indication that these patterns are not seen other than 'normal' as there is a normative expectation that, at least in health, the function of reporters is 'to support efforts to preserve public health', as articulated by one of the interviewees. Thus, this raises the issue of professional autonomy (or the lack of it) in relation to the reporting of science in this part of the world.

Besides health, another area that we used to assess news cultures in science was that of technology, although it had far fewer occurrences than health-related topics. Key technology categories such as 'computers' and 'machines' which are widely reported in the western media make up less than 6% of the science stories in MENA. Indeed, the Arab media does not seem to keep pace with the more global media coverage of technology and is far from keeping up with technological developments, especially in the digital industry.

For countries that are aspiring to transition to sustainable and non-fossil-based economies, this situation must be a concern. In our sample, the news on technology is scarce and mostly reduced to sporadic announcements about the odd invention and particularly emphasising on gadgets in the market. In interviews with journalists, it became clear that there are not enough links established between the research and development centres in MENA and the newsrooms. Few reporters knew about their own technological parks or were able to name any person working in nanotechnology—two cases we used to explore this issue—which tends to highlight another problem in relation to the science news culture in the region, that of engaging with science news sources.

## News Sources in Science

For years, scholars have highlighted the importance of news sources for journalists in their daily routine (Berkowitz & Beach, 1993; Lewis et al., 2008; Tuchman, 1972). Reporters base their stories on information they extract from their sources through interviews. That is, by speaking directly to officials, experts or witnesses who can provide both the facts and the context for the subject being explored in a particular news story. In so doing, reporters access primary sources, such as the central actors of the story and, secondary sources, such as other pieces of news already published or archival materials that can offer additional information and context (Berkowitz & Beach, 1993; Manning, 2000).

However, studies around science journalism practices and professional dynamics suggest that the relationship between scientists and journalists is not direct but instead nowadays tends to be mediated by professional communication. That is, reporters rarely speak to scientists directly and when they do so, it is a conversation that tends to be arranged by public relations professionals working for the research institution, corporate organisations or universities in which that scientist works (Anderson et al., 2005; Autzen & Weitkamp, 2018).

In addition, the relationship between reporters and scientists is characterised by mutual suspicion with each side being critical of the other. On the one hand, scientists constantly complain about the inability of journalists to grasp basic science and highlight how reporters get it wrong most of the time by exaggerating particular issues or just being inaccurate in their reporting. On the other, reporters tend to resent the inaccessible and convoluted language used by scientists and their inability to understand the time pressures and limitations of space reporters face to do their job (Ashwell, 2016).

News coverage of science presents a particular challenge for the prevalent deontology of journalism in relation to how reporters relate to their sources. This is because journalists operate within a news culture in which reporters are expected to counterbalance oppositional views remain neutral, question the fundamentals of any position and try to avoid uncertainty in their stories. All this is precisely contrary to what news coverage of science is about, which, instead, is about consensus, accepting uncertainty, dealing with objective truth beyond opinions and ideology and through which dissent is resolved through experimentation. In news beats such as politics or economics, on the other hand, there are opposing views despite dealing with the same facts and ideological interpretation of some accepted criteria to assess the facts, and news stories are there to solve the unknown rather than to create more questions.

In the case of MENA countries, these tensions are also present, but they happen in the context of a different news culture, which we have described above. So, examining aspects such as how journalists interview scientists, how many sources o they use on average for each story and what is the nature of the sources, is key to understanding these tensions and the actual layout of science journalism professional cultures and practices in the region.

In this sense, our study is about the engagement, nature and use of news sources in the science beat and how journalists use them to gather and present accurate information, something that is a normative requirement in journalistic practice (Manning, 2001; Soloski, 1989). The content analysis highlights that in more than half of science articles in Arab newspapers (521 of the 932), reporters use mainly official sources. In this category, we have included both government institutions and organisations closely associated with the central government. Needless to say, most of these stories related to health. There is in fact a high dependency on official news sources in these countries despite science and technology being somehow a newsbeat that one expects to be outside the realm of politics or other sensitive issues. Overall, these findings support the views from authors that journalists tend to rely on official sources to produce their news stories (Goldacre, 2009; Lewis et al., 2008; Manning, 2001).

One possible explanation for this is the fact that governments in the region often pass their own agenda in sensitive areas such as politics and economics (Khazen, 1999; Mellor, 2011) which creates a news culture that extends to all newsbeats and in which the self-perception of reporters, regardless of the topic or area, is that their own professional autonomy is limited (Table 4.3).

Another interesting observation from the data is the number of articles in which the sources are 'unknown' or not explicitly presented in that piece, accounting for 25% of all science articles. The fact that there is a high percentage of news items lacking a source can be attributed to the fact that journalists in the region tend to reproduce press releases from government or other official institutions with almost no changes. We extracted a small non-representative sample of 25 news articles with unknown sources in order to undertake a reconciliation between the same news story in different newspapers. What we found is that not only did the same story appear in several newspapers in 19 of the cases, but that in all of these cases the source was unknown. This suggests that the story came from the same press release. We then did a close reading of these articles in both their Arabic and English versions, which indicated that in all cases they all came from the same press release. It is important to highlight that

**Table 4.3** The main source of statistics (Alhuntushi & Lugo-Ocando, 2020)

|  | Frequency | Per cent | Valid per cent | Cumulative per cent |
| --- | --- | --- | --- | --- |
|  |  | Valid |  |  |
| Official statistics | 521 | 55.9 | 55.9 | 55.9 |
| Non-official statistics | 178 | 19.1 | 19.1 | 75.0 |
| Unknown | 233 | 25.0 | 25.0 | 100.0 |
| Total | 932 | 100.0 | 100.0 |  |

Arab press releases do not always follow the traditional AP style and in many cases press officers write in an essay or op-ed style, which leaves sources out.

Finally, it is important to remark that non-official sources, such as those from universities, research centres and non-governmental organisations, came last on the list. In the case of science news, non-official sources stand for independent and scientifically driven sources. Indeed, while official sources such as the Ministry of Health would be communicating policy, approaches or challenges that their society is facing, the non-official sources tend to talk about science discovery and scientific issues.

This prevalent use of official sources can relate to both limited professional autonomy but also to the lack of training and understanding of how to develop an independent news agenda that takes into account unique editorial considerations. That is, science news is perhaps one of the few areas in which journalists in the region face little or no external pressures. Nevertheless, we see in the region that most media outlets tend to mostly access official sources and do not make enough use of independent scientific sources. That is the case of *Al-Riyadh* in the Kingdom of Saudi Arabia, which was the outlet that mostly used official sources, with 160 articles. This was followed by the Kuwaiti newspapers *Al-Rai and Al-Qabas* with 113 and 85, respectively, and then the Egyptian newspapers *Al-Ahram* and *Al-Masry Al-Yuom* that had 64 and 53, respectively. It is interesting to note in this sample that while the main Saudi newspaper *Al-Riyadh* led in the use of official sources, it was another Saudi newspaper, *Oqaz*, that had the fewest of these with only 46 articles. This suggests that the culture of deferring to official sources in science reporting is not a national phenomenon but one that is circumscribed to the media outlet itself.

The findings confirmed initial assumptions that Arab governments exercise the most important degree of influence in defining what science journalists do in the region and shaping the way the news beat is covered. It also shows that despite the fact that science and technology is not a sensitive or highly regulated area, reporters nevertheless continue to behave in the way their peer do in areas such as politics and economics. In interviews with reporters of these media outlets, we asked them about exploring more thoroughly non-official sources such as universities and research centres. Most of the interviewees highlighted that universities did not send enough information to them, and it was difficult to know exactly what was taking place in those institutions. However, it was the lack of time and pressures from deadlines that were mostly underlined as culprits for the lack of engagement with independent sources from the scientific world.

Overall, these findings suggest that the news culture in relation to science reporting in the region is one that underpins dependency towards official narratives, rarely questions the issues being covered and reproduces non-adversarial approaches from areas such as politics and economics. If, well, the organisation of mega-science events such as World Innovation Summit for Education (WISE) and the World Innovation Summit for Health (WISH), both in Qatar, as well as the presence of international universities in the Education Cities in Doha and Sharjah, among others, create an important expectation for the development of a news culture around science and technology, the reality on the ground seems to indicate that there is still a long way to go before we can see a comprehensive and critical science journalism practice in the region.

Having said that, most of our research predates COVID-19, a very significant event that might have changed the dynamics between journalists and scientific sources in the region. It is for future research projects to determine to what extent the pandemic has changed the way reporters and audiences perceive what science journalism ought to be and to what degree science reporting has been able to change and adapt to the new scenario.

## Bibliography

Alhuntushi, A., & Lugo-Ocando, J. (2020). Articulating statistics in science news in Arab newspapers: Cases of Egypt, Kuwait and Saudi Arabia. *Journalism Practice*. https://doi.org/10.1080/17512786.2020.1808857

Allan, S. (2002). *Media, risk and science*. Open University Press/McGraw-Hill Education.

Allan, S. (2004). *News culture*. Cambridge University of Press.

Allan, S. (2011). Introduction: Science journalism in a digital age. *Journalism*, 12(7), 771–777.

Al-Qafari, A. (2009). *Science media in Saudi journalism*. King Abdul-Aziz City for Science and Technology (KACST).

Anderson, A., Peterson, A., David, M., & Allan, S. (2005). Communication or spin? Source-media relations in science journalism. *Journalism: Critical Issues*, 188–198.

Angler, M. W. (2017). *Science Journalism. An Introduction*. Routledge.

Asad, T. (2003). *Formations of the secular: Christianity, Islam, modernity*. Stanford University Press.
Ashwell, D. (2016). The challenges of science journalism: The perspectives of scientists, science communication advisors and journalists from New Zealand. *Public Understanding of Science, 25*(3), 379–393.
Atwater, T. (1988). Reader interest in environmental news. *Newspaper Research Journal, 10*(1), 31–38.
Autzen, C., & Weitkamp, M. (2018, June 7). *Science communication, public relations, journalism: Exploring blurry boundaries*. Current Challenges to Mediatised Science Communication Conference, Rostock.
Barel-Ben David, Y., Garty, E. S., & Baram-Tsabari, A. (2020). Can scientists fill the science journalism void? Online public engagement with science stories authored by scientists. *PloS One, 15*(1), e0222250.
Bebawi, S. (2016). *Investigative Journalism in the Arab World: Issues and Challenges*. Springer.
Berkowitz, D., & Beach, D. W. (1993). News sources and news context: The effect of routine news, conflict and proximity. *Journalism & Mass Communication Quarterly, 70*(1), 4–12.
Bro, P., & Wallberg, F. (2014). Digital gatekeeping: News media versus social media. *Digital Journalism, 2*(3), 446–454.
Brossard, D., & Scheufele, D. A. (2013). Science, new media, and the public. *Science, 339*(6115), 40–41.
Bucchi, M. (1998). *Science and the media: Alternative routes in scientific communication*. Routledge.
Davies, N. (2011). *Flat earth news: An award-winning reporter exposes falsehood, distortion and propaganda in the global media*. Random House.
Dennis, E., Martin, J., & Allagui, I. (2020). *Media Use in the Middle East*.
Dowling, D. O. (2020). When news became literature: The tumultuous ascent of narrative journalism in the twentieth century. *American Periodicals: A Journal of History & Criticism, 30*(2), 168–172.
Doyle, G. (2013). *Understanding media economics*. Sage.
Dunwoody, S. (2020). Science journalism and pandemic uncertainty. *Media and Communication, 8*(2), 471–474.
El-Awady, N. (2009). Science journalism: The Arab boom. *Nature, 459*, 1057.
Esser, F., & Umbricht, A. (2014). The evolution of objective and interpretative journalism in the Western press: Comparing six news systems since the 1960s. *Journalism & Mass Communication Quarterly, 91*(2), 229–249.
Fahy, D., & Nisbet, M. C. (2011). The science journalist online: Shifting roles and emerging practices. *Journalism, 12*(7), 778–793.
Fitzgerald, T. (2003). *The ideology of religious studies*. Oxford University Press.
Galison, P. (2015). The journalist, the scientist, and objectivity. In F. Padovani, A. Richardson, & J. Tsou (Eds.), *Objectivity in Science. New perspectives from Science and Technology Studies* (pp. 57–75). Springer.

Galtung, J., & Ruge, M. H. (1965). The structure of foreign news: The presentation of the Congo, Cuba and Cyprus crises in four Norwegian newspapers. *Journal of Peace Research, 2*(1), 64–90.

Glasser, T. L. (1980). The aesthetics of news. *ETC: A Review of General Semantics, 37*, 238–247.

Goldacre, B. (2009). *Bad Science*. Harper Perennial.

Hallin, Daniel C., & Paolo Mancini, eds. (2011). *Comparing media systems beyond the Western world*. Cambridge: Cambridge University Press.

Hamdy, N. (2013). Arab investigative journalism practice. *Journal of Arab & Muslim Media Research, 6*(1), 67–93.

Hanitzsch, T., Hanusch, F., Ramaprasad, J., & de Beer, A. (2019). *Worlds of journalism: Journalistic cultures around the globe*. Columbia University Press.

Harcup, T., & O'neill, D. (2001). What is news? Galtung and Ruge revisited. *Journalism Studies, 2*(2), 261–280.

Hovden, J. F., & Kristensen, N. N. (2021). The cultural journalist around the globe: A comparative study of characteristics, role perceptions, and perceived influences. *Journalism, 22*(3), 689–708.

Khairy, L. (2020). Applying the four models of science journalism to the publics' interaction with coronavirus news. *Arab Media & Society, 28*(6), 71–88.

Khazen, J. (1999). Censorship and state control of the press in the Arab world. *Harvard International Journal of Press/Politics, 4*(3), 87–92.

Kiernan, V. (2003). Embargoes and science news. *Journalism & Mass Communication Quarterly, 80*(4), 903–920.

Long, M. (1995). Scientific explanation in US newspaper science stories. *Public Understanding of Science, 4*(2), 119–130.

Lublinski, J., Reichert, I., Denis, A., Fleury, J., Labassi, O., & Spurk, C. (2014). Advances in African and Arab science journalism: Capacity building and new newsroom structures through digital peer-to-peer support. *Ecquid Novi: African Journalism Studies, 35*(2), 4–22.

Lugo-Ocando, J. (2020). *Foreign aid and journalism in the global south: A mouthpiece for truth*. Lexington Books.

Lynch, M. (2015). How the media trashed the transitions. *Journal of Democracy, 26*(4), 90–99.

Mahmood, S. (2008). *Scientific media*. Alfagar Publishing.

Manning, P. (2000). *News and news sources: A critical introduction*. Sage.

Manning, P. (2001). *News and news sources: A critical introduction*. Sage.

Mawlawi, R. (1988). Arab scientific journalism: Achievements and aspirations. *Impact of Science on Society, 38*(4), 397–409.

Mbarga, G., Lublinski, J., & Fleury, J.-M. (2012). New perspectives on strengthening science journalism in developing countries: Approach and first results of the 'SjCOOP' mentoring project. *Journal of African Media Studies, 4*(2), 157–172.

McCluskey, J., & Swinnen, J. (2011). The media and food-risk perceptions: Science & society series on food and Science. *EMBO Reports, 12*(7), 624–629.

McNair, B. (1998). *The sociology of journalism*. Oxford University Press.

Mellor, N. (2005). *The making of Arab news*. Rowman & Littlefield Publishers.

Mellor, N. (2010). More than a parrot The case of Saudi women journalists. *Journal of Arab & Muslim Media Research, 3*(3), 207–222.

Mellor, N. (2011). *Arab media: Globalization and emerging media industries* (Vol. 1). Polity.

Pierce, J., Lee-Sammons, L., & Lovrich, N., Jr. (1988). US and Japanese source reliance for environmental information. *Journalism Quarterly, 65*(4), 902–908.

Plackett, B. (2020). [News]. Al-Fanar Media. https://www.al-fanarmedia.org/2020/03/talk-to-me-urges-a-science-journalist-working-in-the-arab-world/

Rudin, R., & Ibbotson, T. (2002). *An introduction to journalism: Essential techniques and background knowledge*. Focal Press.

Rugh, W. (2004). *Arab mass media: Newspapers, radio, and television in Arab politics*. Greenwood Publishing Group.

Said, E. (2003). *Orientalism: Western conceptions of the Orient*. Penguin Books Limited.

Scheufele, D. A., & Krause, N. M. (2019). Science audiences, misinformation, and fake news. *Proceedings of the National Academy of Sciences, 116*(16), 7662–7669.

Schlesinger, P. (1999). Putting 'reality' together: BBC News. In H. Tumber (Ed.), *News. A Reader* (pp. 121–133). Sage.

Schudson, M. (2003). *The sociology of news*. Norton.

Soloski, J. (1989). Sources and channels of local news. *Journalism Quarterly, 66*(4), 864–870.

Splendore, S., & Brambilla, M. (2021). The hybrid journalism that we do not recognize (anymore). *Journalism and Media, 2*(1), 51–61.

Thompson, T. (2016). Conducting the Conversation: Insights from the Historical and Theological Contextualization of Edward Said's Orientalism. *The Muslim World, 106*(2), 255–270.

Thomson, E. A., White, P. R., & Kitley, P. (2008). 'Objectivity' and 'hard news' reporting across cultures: Comparing the news report in English, French, Japanese and Indonesian journalism. *Journalism Studies, 9*(2), 212–228.

Tuchman, G. (1972). Objectivity as strategic ritual: An examination of newsmen's notions of objectivity. *American Journal of Sociology, 77*(4), 660–679.

Umbricht, A. (2014). *Patterns of news making in Western journalism*.

Wasserman, H., & de Beer, A. S. (2010). Journalism in the global South: South Africa and Brazil., *36*(2), 143–147.

Zelizer, B. (1993). Journalists as interpretive communities. *Critical Studies in Mass Communication, 10*(3), 219–237. https://doi.org/10.1080/15295039309366865

CHAPTER 5

# Science Journalism and Professional Autonomy

In the previous chapters, we have highlighted that the limitations to journalistic and editorial independence do not apply equally to all areas and newsbeats. Some topics, such as politics and economics or foreign policy, are far more sensitive and subject to control and editorial restrictions than others, such as fashion and sport. Science, however, sits somewhere in between. In most cases, journalists are given ample space to debate around a series of issues with almost no interference or editorial restrictions.

Nevertheless, there are some particular topics in science news which might generate sufficient controversy as to attract attention—and intervention—from the authorities or media owners. In the MENA region, these interventions might be related to areas of science that clash with religious views, government policy or corporate interests, among others. This is all made even more complex by the very blur distinction between what is private ownership and state control of the media in these countries, which furthers the complexity around the professional independence of reporters.

Generally speaking, professional autonomy is perhaps one of the most important dimensions of professionalism in relation to the production of independent news (McNair, 1998; Waisbord, 2013). It has been defined as 'the degree of judgment or ability to make personal decisions without being affected by external or internal influences' (Mellado & Humanes, 2012, p. 985). Several elements may affect the autonomy of a journalist in

© The Author(s), under exclusive license to Springer Nature Switzerland AG 2023
A. Alhuntushi, J. Lugo-Ocando, *Science Journalism in the Arab World*, Palgrave Studies in Journalism and the Global South, https://doi.org/10.1007/978-3-031-14252-9_5

their journalistic work, such as the media organisation in which they work or their professional experience and capability to understand and engage with particular issues without having to over depend upon some expert voices and official (Nygren, 2012, 2015; Nygren et al., 2015). This is in addition to the context in which both the media and individual journalists operate.

Sjøvaag has observed that professional autonomy 'is restricted at the political, economic and organizational levels of news production, negotiated at the editorial level and exercised at the level of practice' (2013, p. 78). Thus, autonomy is a fluid concept that is continually adjusted to manage the daily task of reporting the news. Nygren, (2012, p. 78) divided journalists' professional autonomy into two levels.

Professional autonomy can be studied at different levels such as external autonomy, internal autonomy, autonomy of the ideal, perceived autonomy and factual autonomy. Internal autonomy, to mention one of these levels, refers to the way the individual reporter can operate independently from the media organisation in which they work. Internal autonomy, therefore, is the ability to perform and operate with a substantial degree of freedom and independence in a particular news media outlet without too much oversight from the owners and top managers. It concerns also possible financial pressure from owners, other sections within the firm and advertisers.

Another level is that of external autonomy, which is linked to the situation of journalists as a group in terms of power in society (2012, p. 78). This refers to the relationships between the professions as a collective group that share a set of values and practices and those who hold power in society (Nygren, 2012). This level has to do with the political influences and the capacity that the media in general and reporters in particular have for being truly independent from government and corporations. It is important to mention here that in journalism studies' literature, autonomy is also referred to as the degree of independence that is required to consider journalism a separate field (Benson & Neveu, 2005). Consequently, the notion of perceived autonomy targets decisions that must be carried out in the daily work of media companies and raises questions concerning the effect on media content (Weaver & Willnat, 2012).

Putting these distinctions aside, there is ample consensus among scholars that the lack of professional autonomy represents an absence of capabilities to work independently knowledge and skills (Waisbord, 2013). This is because to be professional in broader terms is to be able to act and operate according to one's ability and ethics towards the fulfilment of one's duty (Huntington, 1981 [1957]). There is also agreement that key indicators of professional autonomy relate mostly—although not exclusively—to aspects such as freedom of expression, the capacity to exercise authorial control over news that reflects a fact-based independent judgment that provides a critical stance. Hence, one that confers the ability to publish and broadcast content without interference, censorship or retaliation from authorities or other power elites.

These discussions about external pressures and journalistic professional autonomy are often anchored upon Western normative aspirations of what that profession ought to be. In this sense, they reflect other quasi-axiomatic assumptions such as the expected divisions between the private and the public, which has been historically considered to be essential to secure independence and freedom. It is assumed that because the private media is economically independent from government budgetary resources, taxes or public subsidies it can therefore enjoy little or no interference from the state. It considers the pervasive effect of government-funded advertisement upon many local media outlets, questioning the overreliance on official ads and subsidies that can distort the ability of the local news media to confront power in their communities.

This assumption of course is simplistic and problematic. If well is true that states resources and muscle have been used and continue to be deployed to consolidate a state hegemony over the press and the public sphere, it is also the case that other pressures emanate from different sectors in society. For example, there is a long and well-documented history of corporate-media ownership collusion with the state in the context of the industrial–military complex in places such as Australia, Japan, North America and Western Europe.

The contrary is also true, as it is the case with news media outlets such as the BBC in the United Kingdom, YLE in Finland, Fe y Alegría in Venezuela and Al-Jazeera in Qatar. In these last cases, the direct financial link to the state has not been an obstacle for journalistic autonomy in a broader sense (Lugo-Ocando et al., 2010; Maziad, 2021). It is also worth mentioning the examples of the digital-native news outlets, wholly funded by international foreign aid, mostly coming from states. In none of these cases, impartiality has been substantially compromised (Figenschou, 2013; Lugo-Ocando, 2020; Requejo-Alemán & Lugo-Ocando, 2014; Schlesinger, 1978).

Equally important is to highlight that not all limitations to professional autonomy relate to externalities such as political censorship or a weak institutional framework. Other aspects include lack of training and education, absence of spaces to disseminate news stories around science and any other factor that can somehow undermine the ability of journalists to interpret and effectively communicate the subject of their stories. Indeed, what limits reporters to perform according to normative expectations relating to professionalism in areas such as science is widely open for debate. Reasons to explain these limitations are far more complex than just attributing the gaps to the illiberal nature of its political and media systems or to religion and culture.

To be sure, as responded by our interviewees, the lack of training, limited resources, time pressures and the absence of a news audience with the sufficient appetite for this type of content are far more influential as explanatory factors. As one of our interviewees pointed out,

> *I have written several stories on science and technology and not once I have been told to change things or modify the content. Of course, I understand what I can write and what I cannot write. But I was never told not to write something in science. But to be honest, at times I got a press release that I could not understand. The matter was just too complex. In those cases, I just published it as it was.*[1]

These lack of capabilities to cover science in the region and the lack of a robust body of science journalists and specialised media outlets are problematic paradoxes, given the fact that particularly Gulf countries are investing so heavily in science and technology. It also corroborates the view that limitations to professional autonomy does not only come from the ability to produce critical and independent work, which characterises the region. This as it extends also to multiple factors in play that can hinder the ability to report complex issues.

In the chapter, we explore the degree of journalists' professional autonomy in the region while examining how this can create pressures and limitations that can hinder their ability to report science and contribute to the weak state of the profession in the region. In so doing, we look at issues around professional autonomy of journalists in order to examine the nature of these factors and why, despite having more freedom than in other newsbeats, journalists still tend to fail in creating more proactive and

---

[1] Interview with journalists in KSA on June 11, 2021 (identity withheld).

critical news agendas that foster debates in those societies. Consequently, we have undertaken a broad understanding and conceptualisation of the factors that hinder autonomy to include aspects that go beyond state intervention, corporate interference and societal pressures.

## Autonomy in MENA

It should be clear by now that Western analytical frameworks do not necessarily apply to other contexts nor are they a universal threshold. However, these frameworks can be used as a starting point in the assessment of the institutional remit in which many reporters in MENA operate in relation to their ability to be impartial and independent from power elites. In this particular sense, one has to acknowledge that countries in the region lack the type of liberal traditions and strong independent institutions that could potentially safeguard overall professional independence.

The region often scores low—or not free—in the Freedom House index and the World Press Freedom Index of *Reporters Sans Frontières* (García-Marín, 2017). It has also been long established that given the illiberal nature of the political regimes in that part of the world, most of the local media tend to practise non-adversarial forms of journalism. Instead, news reporters rely heavily on protocol news and content supplied by government and corporations (Mellor, 2005, 2010; Reinisch, 2010) and their work is constantly censored externally or self-censored within the newsroom.

This is the institutional framework in which science journalists in MENA have operated over the past few decades. This despite some advances in places such as Kuwait, Tunisia, and to a lesser degree Qatar. All in all, the MENA region still lacks an institutional framework that allows for what could amount to a free press and independent journalistic practices (El Hajj, 2019; García-Marín, 2017). Therefore, the assumption one can make is that this lack of freedom must affect the ability of journalists to produce stories and to be independent in their work. The fundamental question is how much space, ability and independence does a collective group of individuals have to exercise control of what they do and how much of this ability to control their work makes them distinctive from other individuals.

In this sense, Samuel P. Huntington, in his seminal work on civil-military relations in society, *The Soldier and the State* (1981 [1957]), set the basis of professional autonomy by highlighting these criteria in relation to the military. From there, we can argue that a medical doctor is only a medical doctor if they can treat a patient. That is, by having studied and trained sufficiently so as to receive external recognition as a medical doctor, have the skills and knowledge to actually treat the individual, allows the MD to operate while being free from external interference to the point that they can follow their own clinical and ethical criteria to treat another person. This criterion equally applies to most professions that we see in society.

However, the notion of perceived autonomy also targets decisions that must be carried out in the daily work of media organisations and raises questions concerning the effect on media content (Garcés Prettel & Arroyave Cabrera, 2017; Weaver & Willnat, 2012). The degree of journalists' professional autonomy either increases or decreases based on several key factors. To be sure, despite commonly held views that limitations to professional autonomy are mostly imposed by governments, there is ample evidence that financial pressures play a greater role today in Western societies due to the fact that private media companies depend on commercial advertisement revenue and that many media companies are intertwined with, or control by, larger corporations, which are often linked to the so-called industrial–military complex (McChesney, 2015; Usher, 2021).

Journalists' professional autonomy is undermined constantly by all types of pressure, many of which come from political dimensions, the development of the media (because journalists must compete with other types of information on social networks) and from outside sources, including PR industries (Nygren, 2012). But those are not the only ones that can exercise a pervasive effect. Take, as another example, the over-dependency on official sources that we discussed in other chapters, which often contributes to weakening the professional independence of journalists by making them mouthpieces of power.

Hence, it is important to acknowledge that the protection of autonomy is a significant part of 'defending journalism from non-professional outsiders, such as keeping editorial control away from business managers or the influence of government' (Carlson, 2015, p. 12). To be sure, professional autonomy gives journalists professional advantages. Journalists have the right to oppose any threat to their autonomy (McDevitt, 2003). In the case of Arab countries, professional autonomy is limited given all the reasons stated above and aggravated by the context in which they operate where there are illiberal regimes and weak institutional support to secure their ability to produce critical and independent news content.

## Constraints and Censorship

It is clear, from this analysis, that professional autonomy is one of the most important factors influencing the capacity of journalists to produce science news stories in MENA, even if the newsbeat itself is not as politically sensitive as others. There is an ample body of literature around the structural issues that affect the ability of journalists to produce news (McNair, 1998; Schlesinger, 1978; Waisbord, 2013; Weaver & Willnat, 2012). However, in the specific context of the MENA region, one can broadly pinpoint issues such as the political system, religion and culture, economics, media ownership, gender relations and the background, education and training of journalists in that region (Mellor, 2010; Rugh, 2004).

Among the elements that may influence the way the news media produces and disseminates news, it is perhaps politics, religion and culture that are the most mentioned by scholars in relation to professional autonomy in Arab societies. Within these topics, politics is considered the most important factor affecting the media in this region as most scholarly analysis has been performed from the perspective of a secular liberal democracy, in contrast to authoritarian systems (Hamdy, 2013, p. 71). This is because the media has often been closely associated with illiberal regimes, even after the Arab Spring, as governments in the region continue to be, directly and indirectly, the main funders and owners of the mainstream media outlets (Lynch, 2015).

Because of this control, news media outlets tend to operate under official government guidance and follow authorised editorial policy. Journalists have to work in an institutional and legal framework that is not only very restrictive towards freedom of speech, but also highly discretional in how implements censorship. Reporters face possible legal actions from a variety of laws that range from inciting public disturbance and unrest to public offence to those in power and also a situation in which many of these regimes act with almost absolute discretion, making it very difficult for journalists to know exactly where the red lines are drawn.

With limited scope to operate freely, and in the face of not knowing what could provoke a political backlash, journalists are not only censored by the authorities but also widely self-censored within the newsrooms in such a way that reporters have to absorb a culture that swings from prudence to fear, almost on a daily basis and that extends to all newsbeats. Under these circumstances, the main role of journalists becomes one of promoting government politics rather than scrutinising policy or challenging it and therefore trying to have as little intervention as possible in modifying or changing anything that comes as a press release or information package from the authorities.

This behaviour, which extended across MENA, is not surprising as the media systems in the region reflect the state of politics and societies, where the distinctions between the private and public spheres are blurred and, at times, non-existent. In these societies, the control of the media continues to be in the hand of the governments, even after revolutions that brought about a certain degree of change under past movements such as the Pan-Arab Baath party or the current process of economic modernisation where countries such as the UAE, KSA and Qatar have opened up to foreign investors over the years.

This is not to say that there has been no progress at all, and it would be unfair to paint all countries, media outlets and journalists with the same brush. Some countries have opened up spaces for both national and international media (Bebawi, 2016, p. 11). The emergence of international broadcasters such as *Al-Jazeera* in Qatar has redrawn boundaries and makes it much clearer for reporters working in that country where the red lines are, even though strict media control of the local press continues. As one of the interviewees told us,

> *If we see it in Al-Jazeera, we know it can be published. It is good because then we can also ask the Minister about it without being seen as controversial or unpolite towards him. So, topics such as migrant workers' issues, which we never covered before, are now discussed in my newspaper on a regular basis.*[2]

In places such as Egypt, with one of the most comprehensive media systems in the region, the practice of journalism continues to be mostly a mouthpiece of the government (Bebawi, 2016). In that country, successive regimes have continued a long tradition of media control through a variety of institutional mechanisms such as the Supreme Press Council (which licenses newspapers) and the Shura Council's control over the creation of new political parties—in many cases the ones who set up new media outlets—and, more recently, by means of emergency measures and anti-terrorism legislation (Rugh, 2004, pp. 124–125).

Moreover, as recently as July 2021, the Egyptian authorities detained a former leading news editor of its own state-controlled newspaper, Abdel

---

[2] Interview with local journalist in Qatar on March 12, 2021 (identity withheld).

Nasser Salama, who had originally been a supporter of President Abdel Fattah el-Sisi but who later called for him to resign over his role in the 'heavy defeat' related to Ethiopia's Renaissance Dam. Salama was accused of sedition and links to terrorist groups (MEE, 2021). This case shows the nature and limitation of professional autonomy in the largest Arab country.

Things have not improved in other corners. In the aftermath of 9/11, many emergency and anti-terrorism laws were enacted, as well as other vaguely defined pieces of legislation that provided governments with the ability to limit the publication of news and commentary that may be considered a threat to national harmony. Egyptian authorities closed the ethno-religious Coptic weekly newspaper *al-Naba* in 2001 for publishing a personal story about a priest because they considered it could 'undermine public order'. Moreover, journalists can be fined or imprisoned for 'insulting'—a very discretional term—the president, government officials, the leader of a foreign country, the armed forces or even the parliament as an institution.

Even private media outlets remain under strict control of successive governments, which continue to monitor and censor at large the media. This control is not restricted to political-administrative and legal aspects as it also extends to the financial realm. Private newspapers are still largely dependent on governmental funding and there are constant economic pressures on private newspapers via their official agencies and related organisations—such as publicly owned enterprises—that contribute a great deal to these newspapers' revenues, therefore becoming a common form of inducement by proxy. Moreover, as the Egyptian government controls the Supreme Press Council, which also determines advertising distribution, it can easily deprive a particular media outlet of the necessary resources to continue to operate, and therefore can exercise economic pressure on the media (Bebawi, 2016, p. 10). Consequently, private newspapers and other media outlets in the region also avoid controversial issues altogether or pay limited attention to such types of issues.

## SCIENCE REPORTING IN CONTEXT

Overall, science journalists working in MENA have to operate in an institutional context characterised by political rigidity, closeness, lack of transparency and discretionality in the way censorship and self-censorship are imposed. Having said that, for science and technology there is a greater degree of openness and flexibility and, technically speaking, reporters could take advantage of this to develop their own agenda and bring greater debate to, and discussion of, science in the public sphere. After all, MENA states are illiberal regimes but by no means totalitarian as in the former Soviet Union, where just by talking publicly about Mendelian genetics could land someone in a Gulag or to end up dead (Ings, 2016; Rogacheva, 2017).

To be fair, MENA states have progressively opened up to particular areas of journalism despite important setbacks. The increasing presence of both national and international broadcasting networks in the region, the creation of Media Cities in almost all countries to attract investment in the sector and the increasing globalised nature of MENA's economies and political interactions have meant a loosening up of certain restrictions. However, problems relating to censorship persist in MENA due mainly to the general sense of control felt among journalists. As one of our interviewees pointed out,

> *One of our greatest problems is persistent disrectionality. This because it means that I really don't know where I stand. We live in a panopticon state in which the safest position is not to show initiative in regards to the news agenda and to stick with what one is told. This, I think, is more powerful than any state or government telling you what to do.*[3]

## Religion and Autonomy

Following politics, the key aspect often considered central in most analyses about the region relates to the notion of 'religion' and its role in these societies. Religion is, in itself, a category that has been questioned by scholars who see it as a way of 'othering' societies outside the West and that, in the case of Muslims, serves to orientalise the analysis (Asad, 2003; Fitzgerald, 2007). Having said that, there is no questioning that the post-colonial construction of national identity in the Arab countries has been undertaken even before independence, using Islam as a starting point. Even North African countries such as Algeria, Egypt and Tunisia, with a stronger tradition of secularisation, tread carefully around the religious boundaries.

Therefore, in this book, we prefer to speak about a combined notion that includes a syncretic understanding of religion and culture as a

---

[3] Interview with reporter in Egypt on March 12, 2022 (identity withheld).

combined entity. As such, religion and culture continue to play a major role in the Arab region, as Christianity does in Europe and the United States, where faith-based belief systems are crucial in political decisions around abortion or the continues support to apartheid in Israel.

In MENA, the vast majority of its population embrace the Islamic religion and are thus largely influenced by the cultural perspectives and practices that nevertheless have particular characteristics in each society, given their own histories and how Islam was incorporated and embraced into daily life. Having said that, for those who know the region, it is clear that the relation between faith and state and faith and society is deeply complex and varies from community to community.

Nevertheless, despite these variations, any analysis of the professional deontology of journalism in Arab societies ought to consider Islam as a fundamental aspect of truth-seeking. Some scholars have argued that Islam is often portrayed as creating biases (Davey-Quantick, 2020; Mostyn, 2002). Some assumptions among authors are that the prevalent presence of Islam in these societies creates an intrinsic culture that curtails critical and scientific thinking. There is somehow a persistent idea that the professional autonomy is compromised by Islam (Merskin, 2004).

Consequently, it is argued that the solution is to abandon Islamic notions as part of the deontology of journalism and embrace instead the idea of a secular press that safeguards fact-based objectivity (Lind & Danowski, 1998). These arguments are a rehearsal of those broader points presented by scholars such as Bernard Lewis (1980, 1982, 2018) about the need for 'secularisation' of Muslim countries in order to achieve modernisation.

We see these same arguments now been applied to the analysis of journalism as a political institution. It is claimed that news reporters are limited in their actions and constrained in their deontology by the effects of the moral impositions deriving from institutionalised faith. The Kingdom of Saudi Arabia has been consistently cited as newspapers are prone to the pressures from religious leaders when they are disseminating news (Al-Kahtani, 1999).

The problem with this argument is that it assumes that 'religion' is an entity with agency of its own that somehow has power in society at large. If well, as Noha Mellor (2005) has pointed out, Islam plays a fundamental role in defining journalistic practices in Arab countries, it is more about the moral inquiry about how truth is sought rather than shaping the role of professional journalists. Islam does play a key role in influencing journalistic practice but only because of the jurisprudence and institutional framework that derives from it. However, let us not forget that principles of objective truth and quest for knowledge are enshrined in that Islam itself.

Assumptions that the Islamic setting is somehow detrimental in itself to science reporting are plainly wrong. Firstly, because they seem to obviate similar restrictions that are very present in secular societies (Muchtar et al., 2017). They also seem to ignore that several similar societies with shared religious denominations have, nevertheless, very distinctive media systems and exhibit different levels of openness, factual-based reporting and degrees of freedom in their news reporting. Indonesia, Jordan, Kuwait, Malaysia and the Republic of Djibouti share the same faith but not the structure and nature of their respective media systems.

This simplistic assumption about the role of Islam derives from the false notion that it is the separation of church and state that bring about enlightenment into the discussions and debates within the public sphere (Dawkins, 2006; Hitchens, 2008). It is also an assumption that tends to brush aside the very fact that it is not only religion but mostly the illiberal nature of the political and legal systems as well as prevalent hegemonic structures, which in many of the cases were inherited from the former colonial powers, that are at the root cause of lack of freedom of expression in those societies.

Pintak (2014, 2019) points out that instead of religion itself, we should look instead at the role that truth and objectivity occupy in these societies and how they approach communication as a whole. If anything, over the history, interpretations of Islamic values have come to reinforce the quest for objective and factually grounded truth-seeking. The creation of universities and the promotion of natural sciences in the past is a testimony of the later.

At no point are we trying to argue that Islam plays a limited role in shaping journalism. On the contrary, as any other political institution in Arab societies, the ethos and practices around journalism are deeply defined by prevalent cultures in society. We also recognise that in places such as Saudi Arabia, which is not only considered the hub of the Islamic world by many Muslims but also the centre of a particular strand of that religion, religion has been extremely influential in shaping political and societal institutions and practice in that country before and after their independence.

What we reject however are the two reductionist assumptions that (a) the legal institutional framework in society, inspired in Islam, undermines the quest for objective truth in science journalism and (b) the legal and institutional framework is set in the way it is, limiting professional autonomy, mainly because of Islam. For us, instead, religion is just one of the many aspects that have shaped political institutions and news cultures in MENA. There are, in addition, a wider set of historical settings and issues that affect professional autonomy and shape journalism as a political institution. To just ascribe the lack of soundness or accuracy in reporting to religion is, therefore, simplistic.

One particular example that illustrates this point has been cited by El-Feki (2008) and relates to a Sudan-based newspaper, which in 2007 published an article on homosexuality in Khartoum's high schools. The story alleged that half of the students engaging in gay/lesbian activities had contracted HIV/AIDs and quoted a local non-governmental organisation as a source. Consequently, there was a court case involving the Sudanese Ministry of Education, the NGO as well as the media outlet in question. The newspaper's defence was that it was acting in the public interest, but the court saw it as a dishonest effort to spin science into 'scaremongering tactics' against gay/lesbian groups in society. The newspaper was penalised when the NGO in question showed that it had no connection to the story and that it was fabricated by those in the newsroom (Muchtar et al., 2017).

This example shows how the newsroom misconstrued a health issue and linked it to a moral judgement. It also serves to illustrate that it was not the fact that political institutions are shaped by religion but the predominant cultural assumptions in that society. In fact, both the authorities and the courts were quick to demystify the link between HIV/AIDS and homosexuality. While Sudan has a significant HIV/AIDS problem, news stories in the media in that country continue to portray the issue as being confined to the LGTB+ community, making unacceptable and unsubstantiated claims that talk about a higher infection rate among that community.

In these cases, professional autonomy of journalists is not limited by a religious framework but by the fact that journalists often have a poor grasp of medical science and epidemiology (El-Feki, 2008). Indeed, as Mahmood (2008, p. 50) has concluded, scientific reporting in Arab countries is deficient and filled with inaccuracies due to a lack of understanding of the basic fundamentals of science.

This is why the World Federation of Science Journalists (WFSJ, 2015) has deployed efforts to promote the better understanding of science among journalists in Africa. These efforts include providing better education and training for reporters on how to address HIV/AIDS in epidemiological terms, including promoting safe-sex but also the use of condoms, the implementation of cheaper AIDS-testing programmes, fostering debates that take maternal mortality more seriously, promoting collaboration between governments and NGOs and addressing issues around stigma.

## Islam and Autonomy

Overall, assumptions in the West about the professional autonomy of journalists in the Arab are far from subtle and tend to lack the understanding of the deeper and more complex context of history and politics. Consequently, recommendations to improve science reporting in the region often include calls to bring secular-based enlightenment to the Arab world that state that science is rational and religion irrational. Hence, creating a false dichotomy and furthering tensions between faith and secularism.

Western voices tend in many cases to interpret religion in the rest of the world through the lenses of its own secular/religious dichotomy and see the enlightenment in Europe as a revolt against religion, believing that this dichotomy must also be definitive in other societies. This essentialised assumption sees the separation between church and state as fundamental for human rationality (Suran, 2010). Moreover, particular voices among orientalist scholars persist on an image of Muslims as irrationally blinded by faith.

These perceptions and views are in fact a caricature. A historical construct that only presents some of the most extreme and unrepresentative views within that culture. They seem to ignore that the enlightenment as a political project was imposed on the Arab world through colonialism and military interventions in order to establish secular-modernisation (Losurdo, 2014).

Thankfully, many scholars have shed light on the misconstruction of Islam's modern image in relation to science. They have pointed out that is not per se a religion hostile to illuminating and progressive ideas regarding the quest for knowledge (Di-Capua, 2015; Fatih, 2012). Placing responsibility on religion for the issues, challenges and limitations regarding the professional autonomy of journalists is, therefore, an oversimplification of what by all means is a larger problem.

In fact, Islamic scientists and scholars advancing science have been historically reluctant to associate themselves with the state so as not to lose their independence. Paradoxically, a position very similar to that held by scholars and journalists in the West. Moreover, Islam as a religion has had a very strong link to the quest for truth. But in this same tradition, truth is seen as a way of achieving justice. For Muslim scholars such as the Algerian Ahmad al-Tijani (1735–1815), a believer could survive in a place with no faith but not in a place with no justice (Wright, 2020). This is a central idea that explains why Islam stands for independent truth and that highlights that there are historical traditions that underpin this stance. It was the integration of Islamic scholars into the modern state in the twentieth century that made their work more intertwined with and dependent of the state.

We shall also acknowledge that the imposition of modernity was a positive force in many aspects. The enlightenment as such both benefited from Islam's scholars and enriched their thinking at the same time. Al-Tahtawi, a pioneer of 'tradition of Enlightenment' and who was influential in transferring the liberal thought of the French enlightenment to his Egyptian compatriots, believed that Islam does not contradict the values of enlightenment and reform (Najjar, 2004). Modernisation contributed also to a rebirth of scientific engagement, especially after the decline of the Ottoman empire.

Having said that, one must also recognise that it produced tremendous societal damage (Sayyid, 2014; Tharoor, 2018), given the colonial character of this imposition and the levels of brutal force, cruelty and exploitation that it exhibited during that colonial imposition. This is illustrated by the building of the Suez Canal, which provoked over 120,000 registered deaths among its 1.5 million workers during the 11-year excavation project.

This societal damaged that continues to be inflicted up to this day and exemplified by the sustained support of colonial and cleansing practices by Israel in the occupied Palestinian territories. This, in addition to a history of collusion with military and oppressive leaders in the region, has created strong anti-US and anti-Western sentiments that were exacerbated by interventions in Iraq and Afghanistan after 9/11, to name but two. This imposed modernisation not only came from Western colonial powers but also from countries such as the Soviet Union, which paradoxically claimed at some point to be a beacon for post-colonialism. The invasion of Afghanistan in 1979, which took place coincidentally the same year that the Iranian Revolution came to power, proved to be a turning point for many. Moreover, as Muslims were always uneased by the secular nature of the socialist block, despite decolonisation appeals.

The imposition of modernisation by non-Western actors continues today with the massacres perpetrated by Russia in the Chechen Republic since 2009 and its more recent role in sustaining Assad in Syria, where chemical weapons have been used against civilians. Other tensions are generated by actions such as the draconian measures undertaken by Chinese authorities to slash birth rates among Uighurs and other minorities as part of a sweeping campaign to curb its Muslim population (AP, 2020).

However, modernisation is a process that cannot be simply stopped and contrary to medieval Christianity, Islam always encouraged the scientific quest for knowledge (Masood, 2017). The fact remains that today, the MENA region has one of the fastest growing numbers of science, technology, engineering, and mathematics (STEM) graduates in the world and is home of some of the most cutting edge research projects, including experiments in genetics that do not take place even in the United States given faith-based ethical considerations now enshrine in law by Washington legislators.

The MENA region has seen a rise in the investment in science and technology, which covers a diversity of areas. This, in addition to the creation of multiple technological parks, the expansion in the number of universities and an aggressive programme to attract talent from the globe. It is important to clarify that this is something that is happening not only in the wealthiest of the Gulf states in MENA but also in other nations that have also embraced research and development as part of their strategic future.

More importantly, when it comes to gender, an area that is often contested as being problematic for Islam, the fact remains that women achieve more science and maths degrees per capita than their counterparts in the United States and Europe. In fact, up to 57% of all science, technology, engineering and maths graduates in Arab countries are women, according to UNESCO. In specific countries such as the UAE and Qatar, there are now almost twice as many female students enrolled in STEM degrees as males (Margit, 2021).

Overall, there is no strong evidence to claim that religion is the central factor in undermining professional autonomy of science reporters in MENA. On the contrary, the history of Islam teaches us that it has encouraged science and scientists. This because it never had a position on the natural world other that it was created by Allah. Hence, it supported the quest for knowledge and valued scholars and researchers because this did not threaten its centrality in society. In this respect, Muhammad 'Abdu—one of the famous thinkers of the reformist movement—pointed out that Islam and modernity are in fact compatible (Najjar, 2004).

This, because in Islam, the existence of God is already decided. There is no discussion among Muslim scholars and scientists about it. This is why Islam encouraged thinking and exploring beyond religion and did not tie scholars to refer only to the existence of God despite having a similar eschatology to Christianity (Van Engen, 1986). This unlike Christian scholars and scientists of the Middle Ages in Europe, who had to go against a whole explanation of the natural world—that is, that the sun gravitates around the earth—to which the church was fixed to. Science in Europe had to confine itself to Rome's worldview, which meant bowing rationality to religious and political power (Martínez, 2018), something that scientists in Islam did not have to face given the theological nature around the existence of God and that the religion has no centralised structure as the Vatican (Masood, 2017).

Today's limitations of scientific journalism in the Arab world are not, as some orientalists would have us believe, due to religious imposition. Faith has of course played a central part in shaping the institutions of the countries, including the media systems in which science reporters operate. It also plays an important role in justifying policy that limits and constrains free speech. Particularly, as the distinctions between religion and secularism have never occurred in the ways they happened in Europe (Asad, 2003; Fitzgerald, 2003, 2007).

However, the main issues that affect science reporting are mostly the results of history and politics (Fatih, 2012) as the shaping of institutions in those societies owe more to post-coloniality and globalisation than to faith. Let us remember that many of the most oppressive laws and regulations around freedom of expression were directly inherited from the colonial powers.

Overall, one must accept that there is a multiplicity of factors that have combined to undermine not only the ability of science reporters to act independently and find their own voice but also the presence of specialised media platforms to disseminate science to the public. No doubt that religion and culture are part of this equation but by no means they are the only ones. Perhaps more prevalent are the constraints that the political system places upon reporters and newsrooms, the scarcity of skills and capabilities and a widespread culture of self-censorship and lack of initiative to develop original and locally grounded editorial lines and news agendas.

In truth, journalism undertakes multiple grammars and has a diversity of epistemologies. In each society, we will find common and overlapping factors as well as distinctive characteristics. Islamic countries and the way journalists practice news reporting there is no different, and heterogeneity is the norm even among very similar media systems. The point must also be made that there are also important assumptions around the formation of journalism that often links it with the west but that tend to ignore its multiple origins and grammars (Lugo-Ocando, 2020). If, well, Western professional autonomy is often defined by its ability to tell interesting and relevant stories that are truthful, different traditions often provide a different sense of truth. While western journalists are anchored to notions of factual-based objectivity and an impartial stance that differentiates between opinions and facts, other traditions are far more responsive to notions of truth that reflect social justice and equity (Lugo-Ocando, 2020; Wasserman & de Beer, 2010).

Therefore, it is crucial to consider the existing tensions between the history of open and independent engagement with science within the tradition of Islam and, paradoxically, the more conservative tendencies today, which are more closely associated with the legacy of colonialism in many Arab countries since the nineteenth century, the end of the Ottoman empire and the rise of nation-states in the region. As discussed here, religion and culture are problematic categories in itself (Fitzgerald, 2007; Masuzawa, 2005) that need to be comprehensively and critically contextualised in history. Hence, trying to use them to analyse the complexities of news reporting in illiberal political regimes will always carry with them the danger of oversimplification.

It is also important to contrast the richness of the history of science in Islamic countries, which were known for their long and robust tradition of public discussion on science—for example, medieval Islam was more scientifically advanced than European culture (Huff, 2017), and the more modern perceptions about Islam that predominate today. Looking at their histories, one cannot fail to observe that Islamic scientists, especially in astronomy and medicine, managed to reach notable heights of knowledge, even preparing the way for the scientific revolution in the west, something that remains largely unacknowledged in media representations of Islam.

Islamic scholars were drawn to burgeoning libraries and debating salons, and this gathering of intellect produced fruitful Islamic scientists such as ibn-Sina (or Avicenna), who made enormous contributions to philosophy, mathematics, astronomy and medicine. Among his astonishingly varied insights was his view that light and heat were just different forms of energy. These scholars were able to pinpoint to the fact that diseases could spread through water and that nerves transmit pain (Masood, 2017, p. 84).

The tragedy of this is that the imposition of modernity by the West in the form of colonial rule redefined religion as political-institutional and created a framework that proved to be a reaction against the legacy left by the Europeans. As philosopher John Gray has clearly underlined, most, if not all, of the treats that we tend to associate with radical and extremist Islam today are in fact a modern invention in every single way (Gray, 2007, 2015). Many have asked how did the religion of the enlightenment in the Middle Ages that saved the classical world for posterity and made so many important advances in science, when Europe was still in the dark, become one that is perceived by the West as so backward? The answer is, unequivocally, the curse of history and politics, not religion.

## Conclusion

As discussed in this chapter, the degree of professional autonomy that journalists enjoy in a particular society is considered key in understanding their ability to produce news that is sound and independent. However, as we have also discussed, it would be simplistic to try measure it just by benchmarking with other societies. Instead, there is not a unique and universal way of understanding professional autonomy as there isn't a universal deontology. The ethos and practice around news reporting, regardless of the news beat, is complex to study given the distinctive nature in each society, even within the MENA region and the different elements that make up its composition. As some scholars have gone on to highlight, it is difficult to obtain reliable indicators of autonomy, and one's degree of factual professional autonomy changes over time and across various conditions (Nygren et al., 2015, p. 80).

So, what can we expect from science journalists in MENA in terms of their ability to produce content that is critical, independent and sound? The answer is that certainly we could expect much more. That professional autonomy in the region is only a problem in the sense that it has generated a culture of timid intervention, which adopts self-censorship and lack of initiative to set independent agendas and editorial approaches from other news beats and extend it to science and technology. It is neither politics nor religion that is in fact obliging reporters to play it safe.

There is ample space to exercise professional independence in science across the region, regardless of the degree of liberality in its regimes. This is despite the fact that no matter how non-sensitive science is, professional autonomy among journalists in the region will always be conditioned by the political, cultural and religious context. Can we expect to benchmark the deontology in MENA countries with western normative aspirations for journalism? Certainly not at the moment as the current political contexts are too dissimilar. Therefore, there may be a need to reassess professionalism for scientific journalism in a way that allows reporters in these countries to produce true, engaging, and critical news stories, while taking into consideration the fact that they will be operating within their own constraints and limitations.

Our own normative aspirations cannot be the guiding principle in examining science news and professional autonomy of journalists in the region. Instead, we should focus on the need for specialisation when it comes to covering science, the skills that can contribute to the development of this news beat and the knowledge to be able to produce more accurate, appealing and relevant science content; something that is applicable not only to MENA but to the whole of the Global South (Mbarga et al., 2012).

Not that we are by any means insinuating that professionalism, independence and criticality are not needed, which they are. However, these cannot be the centre of our analysis or efforts to improve science reporting in the region because it continues to be the setting by default in that part of the world.

Instead, the critical questions relate to cultures of fear and inaction and to the lack of knowledge and skill-related capabilities, including the lack of financial support and resources and important gaps in the understanding from both journalists and their audiences. The mandate for reporters in MENA is very different to that of their counterparts in the West, despite shared normative aspirations. In the case of science journalism in MENA, the primary goal is to promote and transfer scientific knowledge to the public and raise awareness among every one of the need to engage with science as a way of dealing with present and future challenges, as some scholars have already suggested (El-Awady, 2009).

## Bibliography

Al-Kahtani, A. M. (1999). *The performance of the Saudi Arabian press during the Gulf Conflict, 1990–1991*. University of Leeds.

AP. (2020). China cuts Uighur births with IUDs, abortion, sterilization. *The Associated Press*. Retrieved June 1, 2022, from https://apnews.com/article/ap-top-news-international-news-weekend-reads-china-health-269b3de1af34e17c1941a514f78d764c

Asad, T. (2003). *Formations of the secular: Christianity, Islam, modernity*. Stanford University Press.

Bebawi, S. (2016). *Investigative Journalism in the Arab World: Issues and Challenges*. Springer.

Benson, R., & Neveu, E. (2005). *Bourdieu and the journalistic field*. Polity Press.

Carlson, M. (2015). Introduction: The many boundaries of journalism. In M. Carlson & S. Lewis (Eds.), *Boundaries of Journalism: Professionalism, Practices and Participation* (pp. 1–18). Routledge.

Davey-Quantick, J. (2020, March 24). *Censorship in the Islamic World, Through the Eyes of Journalist Jessica Davey-Quantick* [Recording]. Spotify. https://open.spotify.com/episode/2FA1XVGFixhntNAlua5PJl

Dawkins, R. (2006). *The God delusion*. Bantam Books.

Dennis, E., Martin, J., & Allagui, I. (2020). Media Use in the Middle East. Northwestern University in Qatar. https://www.mideastmedia.org/survey/2019/ [Accessed on January 18, 2022]

Di-Capua, Y. (2015). Nahda: The Arab project of enlightenment. In *The Cambridge Companion to Modern Arab Culture* (pp. 54–74). Cambridge University Press.

El Hajj, M. C. (2019). Digital media and freedom of expression: Experiences, challenges, resolutions. *Global Media Journal, 17*(32), 185.

El-Awady, N. (2009). Science journalism: The Arab boom. *Nature, 459*, 1057.

El-Feki, S. (2008). *Strong medicine*.

Fatih, Z. (2012). Peering into the Mosque: Enlightenment views of Islam. *The French Review*, 1070–1082.

Figenschou, T. U. (2013). *Al Jazeera and the global media landscape: The South is talking back*. Routledge.

Fitzgerald, T. (2003). *The ideology of religious studies*. Oxford University Press.

Fitzgerald, T. (2007). *Discourse on civility and barbarity*. Oxford University Press.

Garcés Prettel, M. E., & Arroyave Cabrera, J. (2017). Autonomía profesional y riesgos de seguridad de los periodistas en Colombia. *Perfiles Latinoamericanos, 25*(49), 35–53.

García-Marín, J. (2017). Media and media freedom. In *Political change in the Middle East and North Africa: After the Arab Spring* (pp. 231–251). Edinburgh University Press.

Gray, J. (2007). *Black Mass: Apocalyptic religion and the death of Utopia*. Macmillan.
Gray, J. (2015). *Al Qaeda and what it means to be modern* (Vol. 2). Faber & Faber.
Hamdy, N. (2013). Arab investigative journalism practice. *Journal of Arab & Muslim Media Research, 6*(1), 67–93.
Hitchens, C. (2008). *God is not great: How religion poisons everything*. McClelland & Stewart.
Huff, T. (2017). *The rise of early modern science: Islam, China, and the West*. Cambridge University Press.
Huntington, S. P. (1981). *The soldier and the state: The theory and politics of civil–military relations*. Harvard University Press.
Ings, S. (2016). *Stalin and the scientists: A history of triumph and tragedy 1905–1953*. Faber & Faber.
Lewis, B. (1980). The Ottoman Empire and its aftermath. *Journal of Contemporary History, 15*(1), 27–36.
Lewis, B. (1982). The question of Orientalism. *New York Review of Books, 24*(6) https://www.nybooks.com/articles/1982/06/24/the question-of-orientalism/
Lewis, B. (2018). *The political language of Islam*. University of Chicago Press.
Lind, R., & Danowski, J. (1998). The representation of Arabs in US electronic media. In R. Yahya & C. Theresa (Eds.), *Cultural diversity and the US media* (pp. 157–168). State University of New York Press.
Losurdo, D. (2014). *Liberalism: A counter-history*. Verso.
Lugo-Ocando, J. (2020). *Foreign aid and journalism in the global south: A mouthpiece for truth*. Lexington Books.
Lugo-Ocando, J., Cañizales, A., & Lohmeier, C. (2010). When PSB is delivered by the hand of God: The case of Roman Catholic broadcast networks in Venezuela. *International Journal of Media & Cultural Politics, 6*(2), 149–167.
Lynch, M. (2015). How the media trashed the transitions. *Journal of Democracy, 26*(4), 90–99.
Mahmood, S. (2008). *Scientific media*. Alfagar Publishing.
Margit, M. (2021). Women changing the face of Science in the middle east and north Africa. *The Media Line*. https://themedialine.org/top-stories/women-changing-the-face-of-science-in-the-middle-east-and-north-africa/
Martínez, A. A. (2018). *Burned Alive: Bruno, Galileo and the Inquisition*. Reaktion Books.
Masood, E. (2017). *Science and Islam (Icon Science): A History*. Icon Books.
Masuzawa, T. (2005). *The invention of world religions: Or, how European universalism was preserved in the language of pluralism*. University of Chicago Press.
Matter. (2017). Science and sports news most trusted by British public. https://www.techmezine.com/top-10-news/science-sports-news-trusted-british-public/ [Accessed on March 12, 2022]
Maziad, M. (2021). Qatar in Egypt: The politics of Al Jazeera. *Journalism, 22*(4), 1067–1087.

Mbarga, G., Lublinski, J., & Fleury, J.-M. (2012). New perspectives on strengthening science journalism in developing countries: Approach and first results of the 'SjCOOP' mentoring project. *Journal of African Media Studies*, 4(2), 157–172.

McChesney, R. W. (2015). *Rich media, poor democracy: Communication politics in dubious times*. New Press.

McDevitt, M. (2003). In defense of autonomy: A critique of the public journalism critique. *Journal of Communication*, 53(1), 155–164.

McNair, B. (1998). *The sociology of journalism*. Oxford University Press.

MEE. (2021). Egypt detains former al-Ahram editor after he called on Sisi to step down [News]. *Middle East Eye*. https://www.middleeasteye.net/news/egypt-ahram-nasser-salama-sisi-criticism-ethiopia-dam-detained

Mellado, C., & Humanes, M. L. (2012). Modeling perceived professional autonomy in Chilean journalism. *Journalism*, 13(8), 985–1003.

Mellor, N. (2005). *The making of Arab news*. Rowman & Littlefield Publishers.

Mellor, N. (2010). More than a parrot The case of Saudi women journalists. *Journal of Arab & Muslim Media Research*, 3(3), 207–222.

Merskin, D. (2004). The construction of Arabs as enemies: Post-September 11 discourse of George W. Bush. *Mass Communication & Society*, 7(2), 157–175.

Mostyn, T. (2002). *Censorship in Islamic Societies*. Saqi Books.

Muchtar, N., Hamada, B., Hanitzsch, T., Galal, A., & Masduki, & Ullah, M. (2017). Journalism and the Islamic worldview: Journalistic roles in Muslim-majority countries. *Journalism Studies*, 18(5), 555–575.

Najjar, F. (2004). Lbn Rushd (Averroes) and the Egyptian Enlightenment Movement. *British Journal of Middle Eastern Studies*, 31(2), 195–213.

Nygren, G. (2012). Autonomy—A crucial element of professionalization. In G. Nygren & B. Dobek-Ostrowska (Eds.), *Journalism in Russia, Poland and Sweden—Traditions, cultures and research* (pp. 73–95). Peter Lang.

Nygren, G. (2015). Media development and professional autonomy. *Journalism in Change. Journalistic Culture in Poland, Russia and Sweden*, 119–152.

Nygren, G., Dobek-Ostrowska, B., & Anikina, M. (2015). Professional autonomy. *Nordicom Review*, 36(2), 79–95.

Pintak, L. (2014). Islam, identity and professional values: A study of journalists in three Muslim-majority regions. *Journalism*, 15(4), 482–503.

Pintak, L. (2019). Middle Eastern and North African Journalism. In *The International Encyclopedia of Journalism Studies* (pp. 1–12). John Wiley & Sons.

Reinisch, L. (2010). Environmental journalism in UAE. *Arab Media & Society*, 11, 1–19.

Requejo-Alemán, J. L., & Lugo-Ocando, J. (2014). Assessing the sustainability of Latin American Investigative Non-profit Journalism. *Journalism Studies*, 15(5), 522–532.

Rogacheva, M. (2017). *The private world of Soviet scientists from Stalin to Gorbachev*. Cambridge University Press.
Rugh, W. (2004). *Arab mass media: Newspapers, radio, and television in Arab politics*. Greenwood Publishing Group.
Sayyid, S. (2014). *Recalling the Caliphate: Decolonisation and world order*. Oxford University Press.
Schlesinger, P. (1978). *Putting 'Reality' together: BBC News. Series: Communication and society*. Constable.
Sjøvaag, H. (2013). Journalistic autonomy. *Nordicom Review, 34*, 155–166.
Suran, M. (2010). The separation of church and science: Science and religion offer different worldviews, but are they opposite or complementary? *EMBO Reports, 11*(8), 586–589.
Tharoor, S. (2018). *Inglorious Empire: What the British did to India*. Penguin.
Usher, N. (2021). *News for the Rich, White, and Blue: How Place and Power Distort American Journalism*. Columbia University Press.
Van Engen, J. (1986). The Christian Middle Ages as an historiographical problem. *The American Historical Review, 91*(3), 519–552.
Waisbord, S. (2013). *Reinventing professionalism: Journalism and news in global perspective*. John Wiley & Sons.
Wasserman, H., & de Beer, A. S. (2010). Journalism in the global South: South Africa and Brazil., *36*(2), 143–147.
Weaver, D., & Willnat, L. (2012). *The global journalist in the 21st century*. Routledge New York.
WFSJ. (2015). *Impact of African and Arab science journalists*.
Wright, Z. V. (2020). *Realizing Islam: The Tijaniyya in North Africa and the Eighteenth-century Muslim World*. The University of North Carolina Press.

CHAPTER 6

# News Sources and Access in Science

Over the previous chapters, when discussing a series of issues related to the news coverage of journalism, we have touched upon the relationship between science journalists and their news sources. In this sense, it is possible already to see that the nature and characteristics of this relationship in the MENA region present many similitudes with other parts of the world as well as distinctive features that are somehow unique. To explore these overlaps and divergences, it is important to examine the different dynamics that take place in the interaction between journalists, scientists, communication professionals and government officials during the process of gathering and production of science news.

This chapter, therefore, assesses how journalists in these countries access and engage with the multiple news sources in their daily newsbeats while studying the nature and function of news sources in science reporting. It does so by exploring the way reporters in the region link to, and use, the news sources to articulate science stories. The section describes frequent practices in the use of sources and how dependent journalists are in relation to specific official organisations and institutions to provide 'expert voices' in the construction of news.

We look at how access to these news sources is restricted but at the same time how these restrictions are not only political but rather structural. By this, we mean how access to sources is not only determined by aspects such as political and religious censorship but also determined by

© The Author(s), under exclusive license to Springer Nature Switzerland AG 2023
A. Alhuntushi, J. Lugo-Ocando, *Science Journalism in the Arab World*, Palgrave Studies in Journalism and the Global South, https://doi.org/10.1007/978-3-031-14252-9_6

the inability to understand or even engage at a deeper level with the technical aspects of the content provided. These structural factors play a greater role in limiting the ability to produce more rounded and comprehensive news stories.

The section draws from the existing theoretical frameworks used by scholars to analyse the types of exchanges and nature of relationship between journalists and their sources (Berkowitz & Beach, 1993; Dimitrova & Strömbäck, 2009; Manning, 2000) and argues that a more fully developed explanation needs to explore the ways in which a distribution of political and symbolic power shape the relationships between science correspondents, news agencies and the key information flows between the scientific community and the news media in MENA.

Perhaps we should start by clarifying that, contrary to common perceptions which assume that locally produced science reporting is almost non-existent, there is enough evidence to affirm the contrary. Our own sample showed that reporters working for the local-national newspapers in MENA produced 687 articles out of a total of 932 science articles from a selected sample. That is more than three times what the international agencies provided, which came in second with only 193 articles. Put another way, over 70% of news stories on science are produced locally. This is an interesting finding given the fact that it is often thought that in this region science news is mostly provided by international external agents (e.g., news agencies) or simply lifted from other news outlets abroad.

Instead, our own findings indicate that most science news is produced by journalists working in the newsrooms of the MENA countries. These same results also indicate that the national news agencies of Saudi Arabia and Kuwait, to give two examples, produced just 41 science articles from a total of 932, while only 11 science news stories came from unknown content providers. This suggests that the news on science is produced mostly by those in the newsroom and not by external agents within or outside the country.

This initial exploration suggests that most STEM news stories are gathered and produced by people working in the newsroom. Secondly, that national news agencies—which are government controlled—pay lip service to science despite figuring as a strong priority in all national 2030 visions across the region, as we can see in Table 6.1.

The fact that almost two-thirds of science news that includes science published in Arab newspapers were locally produced by Arab journalists is truly remarkable and to some extent unforeseen in our original thesis.

**Table 6.1** Science news producers

|  |  | Frequency | Per cent | Valid per cent | Cumulative per cent |
|---|---|---|---|---|---|
| Valid | The newspapers | 687 | 73.7 | 73.7 | 73.7 |
|  | Nation agency | 41 | 4.4 | 4.4 | 78.1 |
|  | International agency | 193 | 20.7 | 20.7 | 98.8 |
|  | Unknown | 11 | 1.2 | 1.2 | 100.0 |
|  | Total | 932 | 100.0 | 100.0 |  |

Source: Authors' data

This, because it means that there is a great deal of added value to the collective public knowledge of science in the region being produced by local journalists. At least much more than we were originally envisaging.

However, these results can also be interpreted in other ways, particularly when one pays a closer look to the evidence in hand. For example, a close reading of 25 selected pieces showed that journalists tend to draw the content of their news stories from official or institutional materials handed to them, which includes information packages and press releases. By cross-comparing 25 news stories, one can see not only a close degree of similarity in the same stories in different newspapers but also similarities with the original press releases from the government or institutions that issued the story in the first place. These results indicate heavy dependency upon either a small group of people to act as expert voices or on press releases and materials produced by the scientific community, research centres and government officials that produced the press releases.

They are similar to those found by research in other countries when analysing a variety of newsbeats such as in the United Kingdom, where researchers found similar trends regarding journalists' increasing dependency on public relations materials (Davies, 2011; Lewis et al., 2008). If we are referring to newsbeats such as politics and economics, the main difference is that while in the United Kingdom this is due to the need to fill the information deficit in the newsroom, in MENA this issue can be mostly ascribed to the culture of political dependency and lack of professional autonomy, which lead to self-censorship, reproduction of official agenda and lack of an independent news agenda formulated within the newsroom.

Science journalism in MENA faces similar challenges to those we find in other societies. These include lack of expertise to engage comprehensively and critically enough with the news sources, opportune and non-mediated access to scientists and expert sources, ability to apply critical interpretation and produce original content around what the sources say, and limitations imposed by the lack of resources (e.g., few newsrooms can access academic journals unless they are under open-source agreements) and pressing deadlines.

It also includes the type of tensions that arise between reporters and their sources when the dynamics of news gathering and production take place. This, because there is a clash of professional cultures that characterise distinctively both news people and the scientific community. Scientists, for example, are concerned about making sure that the results and knowledge derived from their research and experimentation are an accurate reflection of that work. Scientists often point to the news media as the prime reason for the public's presumed knowledge deficit and irrational beliefs (Besley et al., 2013).

Among the scientific community there is not necessarily a commitment to telling the world out there that they 'discovered' this or that. In fact, more often than not, scientists communicate—through journals—that 'nothing was found' as in science this is equally important to actual findings. The fact that some lab tests provided negative results can mean a lot to the development of theory but also—and as is mostly the case—that the pursuit of a particular avenue of enquiry is a dead end. For scientists, admitting uncertainty is normal.

Journalists instead do not tend to communicate 'negative' (or an absence of) results as this goes to the criterion of what news is. In news reporting, where audiences search for answers and certainty, it is almost unacceptable to acknowledge uncertainty. While scientists accept that complexity is part of nature, journalists look for simplicity and clarity. News media thrive on dichotomy and confrontation that suggest rights and wrongs. Within the scientific narratives, 'incomprehensibility' (Radford, 2007, p. 96) is what characterises the way in which researchers communicate the knowledge derived from their work. This, because scientists tend to speak within their own terms of reference as they write for a very small and selective audience of their peers. They do so in their own way and by their own channels such as specialised peer-review journals, scientific conferences, events and meetings.

Journalists, on the other hand, must reach the wider public and therefore need to translate scientific results and conclusions into accessible language that can be grasped by audiences who are not necessarily aware of the themes, nor are able to manage the concepts and ideas referred to in that particular science work. They do so also in a context in which there is a struggle for space in which their content can be published and in which they compete for an audience market that is increasingly more fragmented and less interested in serious news (Borges, 2017; Lugo-Ocando, 2015). According to one of the journalists interviewed in Qatar,

> *On occasions, I have had to deal with scientists and at times it is difficult to understand what they are trying to say. Particularly if the story is complex. The scientists are often very nice and try to explain their work. They speak with pride. However, it is still very hard to grasp what they are trying to say. They try hard and once, the person even gave me copies of their journal articles, but frankly it was of little help. I could just not get what they were trying to say. I could just not see the news angle. I finally published something that I know neither the scientists liked nor did I.*[1]

Several studies, both in MENA and in other regions of the world, have acknowledged that most scientists do not prioritise media and public attention for their work (Hunter, 2016; Marcinkowski & Steiner, 2014; Suleski & Ibaraki, 2010). This, even after years of heavy investment and focus in promoting science communication projects and sustained efforts to make the scientific community aware of the need to reach out to the wider public (Dajani et al., 2020; Wiseman et al., 2016; Zahlan, 2012).

Nevertheless, many of the key and most relevant aspects of the work of scientists are lost in translation from the science language to the common spoken word. At times this is due to lack of general and media interest in the subject and sometimes because the communication between scientists and journalists is difficult. Not only because of the language but also due to different perspectives as to how science should be presented to the public. For example, scientists are against speculating because they understand that science is about uncertainty. For example, they are reluctant to say if a new drug has the potential to cure a particular disease. Journalists and PR officers are instead prone to the speculative element because they know this awakes the public's imagination and gains their attention. Equally, scientists avoid conflict in the way they present their findings, and controversy is therefore exposed in rational and reasoned manners. Journalists and PR officers thrive on conflict as they know this brings ratings and news engagement.

[1] Interview in Doha on October 20, 2021.

Another important difference between journalists and scientists relates to the way they understand key concepts such as truth, knowledge and research. However, both sets of professionals have very similar aspirations around achieving truth. For scientists, truth is objective and rational as explained by Peter Atkins when stating,

> *[A] major achievement [of science] is the demonstration that the world is a rational place, and although it may be too complex globally to be subject to much prediction, science continually reaffirms the view that structures and events can be explicated.* (1995, p. 97)

Journalists have wanted to emulate science in how they go about producing knowledge and normative claims around truth; being objective and rational are also central to their work. Walter Lippmann (Lippmann, 2018 [1920]) made a strong emphasis on that point by calling for journalism to be objective and scientific in the pursuit of truth. In more recent years, other authors have stated that journalists should apply the 'scientific method' more often in their work (Anderson, 2018; Meyer, 2002). However, in their daily practices, journalists and scientists differ in relation to notions of knowledge and truth.

In science, knowledge is accumulated by systematic study and organised by general principles. These scientific principles of inquiry have been developed within a set of assumptions that allow scientist to interpret these as part of a larger theory of the field. Hence, a physicist may interpret certain facts in a way that is distinctive from a zoologist while also conducting experimentation around the same phenomenon in a very different manner (Khun, 2012 [1962]). The scientist will act as a community that would acknowledge and subscribe to these interpretations in terms of larger paradigms that tend to be 'objectively true' in the physical world but that is tested over and over again to confirm how much it holds up in time (Popper, 2005 [1959]). However, they accept that nothing is static and that these facts and interpretations can be revisited at any moment if new facts and circumstances are uncovered.

On the other hand, journalists are of an 'interpretative community' (Zelizer, 1993) that seeks to establish certainty and consensus around particular issues and topics. Collectively, reporters construct social reality and shape public perceptions around key issues in society based on broad assumptions. Those who are part of this professional community claim that truth is what they can see and fact-check. However, those 'facts' are dependent upon the words and ideas provided by their news sources. Take, for example, the fact that most statistics disseminated by journalists are almost always produced and provided by government officials and when they are published in news stories this happens with little to no questioning of their validity (Alhuntushi & Lugo-Ocando, 2020; Brandao, 2016). These prevalent assumptions are far more powerful within news cultures because they define the discursive regimes that later frame narratives. Contrary to scientists, journalists tend to take at face value what their sources say because it is not the reporter who is the expert. Reporters do occasionally question the validity of what their sources say, which is the basis of the notion of objectivity and impartiality in journalism. However, in news beats such as science, the expert voices—the sources—are rarely questioned/challenged in what they say, except to complement details or further explain the issue in question.

In MENA, the relationship between journalists and their sources is further complicated by a news culture that is non-adversarial and at times deferential. These attitudes among journalists in the region are associated with a news culture characterised by compliance, censorship and self-censorship. However, these restrictions cannot explain the gaps and deficiencies observed in the news coverage of science and technology. Instead, as we have discussed already, they can be attributed rather to the lack of training and skills, which hinders journalists' ability to interact in more engaging and comprehensive ways with their sources.

In this sense, reporters in the Arab media face persistent difficulties in obtaining information as access to news sources and government data is more tightly controlled and restricted. In addition, many journalists covering science have little or no access to news sources because they simply do not exist. As Mahmood (2008) pointed out some years ago, finding science sources in that region has proved to be one of the most difficult tasks faced by journalists. If we look at the sources of science news in that part of the world, we quickly learn that they usually come from western media, despite the stories being locally produced. There are several reasons for this including the fact that a lot of the content is not created but rather 'processed' or 'ensembled' in MENA. Lugo-Ocando (2008) has called this phenomenon the Maquilas of Power, referring to how the news media in the global media captures content from the centre and reproduces it for the periphery by making it appear original. Other reasons include the fact that in many cases journalists are unable to find a suitable local source that can help explain, clarify or critically analyse a particular issue in science and technology. In addition, we can mention the scarcity of specialised science journalists who lack the basic understanding of science and therefore have not built up a portfolio of sources and who also find it extremely difficult to identify experts and engage with them.

In addition, as is the case in other countries, news media outlets in MENA also face decreasing resources in the newsroom and rising workloads, which have come to compromise the ability to actually engage with primary sources and spend the time necessary to explore their work. As a result, journalists tend to rely on sources that are keen to disseminate official versions and promote particular media campaigns. In these cases, reporters tend to reproduce what official sources say in their press briefing and information packages. At least five of our interviewees confessed to having published stories that cited journalists to whom they never spoke in person.

## Sources and Findings

Overall, our findings suggest three main characteristics regarding how science journalists engage with their sources. The first element involves normative aspirations/claims of professional autonomy against reality on the ground. Rather than relying entirely on official sources, many journalists working in media cite unofficial statistical sources in their science news reporting. Nevertheless, the broad picture that we can draw from the findings is one of an over-reliance by journalists rather than their ability to challenge prevalent narratives. The fact that there are cases in which reporters seek out authoritative sources beyond the state suggests a desirable degree of professional autonomy and gives some hope for the future (although not without setbacks).

The second element involves transparency and accessibility to the sources used to produce news context. In this sense, the findings suggest that overwhelmingly, journalists in MENA use a single source, they all too often allow the sources to go unmentioned, employ anonymous sources and rarely truly question statistical data or the sources. In fact, as we saw here, statistical sources are either double-checked or triangulated with other sources and that provides an account of events that tends to reproduce prevalent official accounts.

The final element is the ability to provide a meaningful and comprehensive context for each story so that audiences may interpret the information and engage with the subject properly. However, the fact that most science news in Arab newspapers is presented in the form of 'hard news' has limited the scope of interpreting science and has made it difficult to contextualise and elaborate each story. Therefore, in these cases, the presence of the news sources is limited to announcements and descriptions of issues rather than debating or explaining, which is what is needed more in the region if we wish to raise the levels of awareness and engagement with STEM.

Most Arab news media outlets tend to behave as mouthpieces of their own governments, and this can be observed by the over-reliance upon official sources (Harb, 2019; Mellor, 2011). Nevertheless, our sample does indicate that many Arab journalists reporting science quote repeatedly from unofficial rather than official sources. This practice, in our view, reflects an increasing degree of autonomy, despite important setbacks in the past few years for journalism in general in the region. Nevertheless, the norm continues to be, as we can see in the data below, accessing official sources (Table 6.2).

In a sample of 879 health stories, a news beat dominated by government, the majority (58%) used official sources. However, in a sample of 53 technology news stories, official sources were only used in 22.6% of the

**Table 6.2** Types of science news cross-tabulated with the sources

|  |  |  | Official source | Non-official source | Unknown |
|---|---|---|---|---|---|
| The type of science news | Health | Count | 509 | 153 | 217 |
|  |  | % within the type of science news | 57.9% | 17.4% | 24.7% |
|  |  | % within source 1: the main source of statistics | 97.7% | 86.0% | 93.1% |
|  | Technology | Count | 12 | 25 | 16 |
|  |  | % within the type of science news | 22.6% | 47.2% | 30.2% |
|  |  | % within source 1: the main source of statistics | 2.3% | 14.0% | 6.9% |
| Total |  | Count | 521 | 178 | 233 |
|  |  | % within the type of science news | 55.9% | 19.1% | 25.0% |
|  |  | % within source 1: the main source of statistics | 100.0% | 100.0% | 100.0% |

Source: Authors' data

cases due to the fact that this is a news beat dominated by the private sector. Non-official sources were used more in technology with 47.2% of technology stories relying upon them compared to just 17.4% in the case of health. Having said that, the use of non-official sources cannot be interpreted as having greater autonomy because technology is dominated by corporate interests and voices, which are supplied by the private sector through either companies or private corporate guilds.

Another important aspect we can observe that 'original' scientific sources—produced and mediated by scientists themselves—were first in this category, representing more than one-third of the sources of statistics in science news. This is an interesting result because content coming from scientific sources (as opposed to government institutions or officials), such as universities and journals, is perceived to be more legitimate as they are produced—one might assume—with the intervention of the scientist and/or the scrutiny of a peer-review process. Though Bucchi and Mazzolini (2003) suggested a while ago that there is a lack of direct participation by the scientific community, our findings in the Arab world show that in this part of the world there is an 'indirect' participation by scientists in the production and dissemination of scientific statistical data (Table 6.3).

On the other hand, sources which were not mentioned in the story came in second place, occurring in nearly a quarter of the articles. This suggests not only an over-reliance on press releases but also a lack of critical engagement with this data on the part of the journalist who fails to fact-check the statistics. Meanwhile, only 22.5% of the content came from sources in organisations that have an official relationship with science, such as the World Health Organization.

Another important aspect in assessing the use of—and engagement with—news sources in MENA relates to the number of sources accessed

Table 6.3 Provenance

|       |                            | Frequency | Per cent | Valid per cent | Cumulative per cent |
|-------|----------------------------|-----------|----------|----------------|---------------------|
| Valid | government source          | 199       | 21.4     | 21.4           | 21.4                |
|       | Original scientific source | 293       | 31.4     | 31.4           | 52.8                |
|       | Organisations and others   | 210       | 22.5     | 22.5           | 75.3                |
|       | Not mentioned              | 230       | 24.7     | 24.7           | 100.0               |
|       | Total                      | 932       | 100.0    | 100.0          |                     |

Source: Authors' data

to produce a story. This, because triangulating to check content, assess data and contrast versions of events from different sources is considered to be part of the vital routines so as to achieve transparency (Berkowitz & Beach, 1993; Manning, 2000). As Howell and Prevenier have pointed out, journalists are expected not to rely on only one source but on many. In this way, they can construct their own interpretations about the past by means of comparison among sources by sifting information contained in many sources, by listening to many voices (2001, p. 69).

Scholars and practitioners have argued that having multiple sources allows for critical comparisons of sources' views and perspectives while offering a more comprehensive picture of what is being reported. Moreover, triangulating more than one source is considered to be helpful in underpinning fairness and providing different perspectives. This is not to say that a high percentage of single-sourced stories should be dismissed (Franklin & Carlson, 2010; Nölleke et al., 2017). Reliable and accurate science news content can be present in stories with only one source too, particularly if that source is a competent one with sufficient expertise and weight in the area.

Nevertheless, when just 6 science articles out of 932 in our sample having two or more sources, one needs to acknowledge that there is a systemic problem that is affecting science reporting and that affects transparency and criticality in the reporting of this newsbeat in MENA. Indeed, in our sample we only saw 4.4% of the news articles with just two or more sources, something that goes against widely accepted editorial conventions that require journalists, editors and producers to test 'the information against known facts or other sources' (Frost, 2015, p. 69).

It is worth reminding, however, that this problem is not circumscribed to Arab science journalists and findings from other research projects allowed us to reach similar conclusions in other parts of the world, where journalists in considerable numbers tend to rely upon one single source when reporting scientific or technical issues (Lugo-Ocando & Brandão, 2016), something that suggests they take the information provided by these expert sources on their face value (Table 6.4).

It is also important to examine what happens with those stories that use two or more sources as this can shed light upon approaches and practices in the MENA newsrooms. Not all topics covered showcased an equal number of sources. Different areas of STEM reporting present variations around the number of expert sources used. To illustrate this point, we compared two areas in STEM, such as health and technology, although

**Table 6.4** The numbers of sources, when mentioned

| | | Frequency | Per cent | Cumulative per cent |
|---|---|---|---|---|
| Valid | One source | 885 | 95.0 | 95.0 |
| | Two sources | 41 | 4.4 | 99.4 |
| | More than two sources | 6 | 0.6 | 100.0 |
| | Total | 932 | 100.0 | |

Source: Authors' data

**Table 6.5** The type of science news and number of sources mentioned

| | | One source | Two sources | More than two sources | Total |
|---|---|---|---|---|---|
| Type of science news | Health | 834 | 39 | 6 | 879 |
| | Technology | 51 | 2 | 0 | 53 |
| Total | | 885 | 41 | 6 | 932 |

Source: Authors' data

both subjects were very close to each other. However, only health had stories with three or more sources, while we were unable to find in our sample a single news story in technology with more than one (Table 6.5).

Overall, the great majority of stories in STEM in the MENSA region tend to use one source. We have already provided several possible factors that might help us understand why this happens. These reasons include contexts, practices and approaches that account for the over-dependency on one source. Some of these factors correspond to rationales around news cultures—for example, the deference to official and expert sources—but others seem to be more mundane. For example, the fact that health stories tend to be awarded more space by editors could be explained by the use of additional sources, given the possibility and necessity of filling out that space.

Table 6.6 shows an association between the number of sources and the size of the article. The expectation might be that the longer a science article is, the more sources it uses. However, this study suggests instead that there is only a minor correlation between the size of the article and the number of sources that provide statistical data (so size in this case almost does not matter).

**Table 6.6** Correlation between the numbers of sources

|  |  | The number of sources mentioned | Number of words |
|---|---|---|---|
| Source 3: the number of sources mentioned | Pearson Correlation | 1 | 0.173** |
|  | Sig. (2-tailed) |  | 0.000 |
|  | N | 932 | 932 |
| Number of words | Pearson Correlation | 0.173** | 1 |
|  | Sig. (2-tailed) | 0.000 |  |
|  | N | 932 | 932 |

Source: Authors' data

In other words, size does not matter, and it is not the length or airtime given to a piece that will determine the number of news sources that a reporter will use. Instead, based on the interviews with journalists, it is rather the ability to gain access, and the time that reporters have to prepare their work, that has a greater impact on this.

One key aspect to highlight is that scientists in MENA do not seem to talk directly to journalists but rather through a mediated process in which the intermediaries are professional communication specialists from areas such as public relations and strategic communication. Further research in the field will need to look at the role and practices of communication professionals in the realm of science and technology. Particularly regarding the mediation between reporters and scientists or research institutions. Interviewees all said that only on a few occasions did they take the initiative to search for a scientist and added that either they met them at organised events—such as press conferences—or they received the information from press releases or information packages sent to them.

This is not only the case for journalists operating in the MENA region. Most literatures on news sources in science reporting indicate that journalists do not tend to talk directly to scientists but nevertheless they appear quoted in the news stories as primary sources. This is either because journalists add their names based on the journal articles which they use to develop their stories or because their quotes come in the press releases or information packages provided to journalists by public relations teams from the universities, research centres or organisations in which scientists work. Even when scientists talk to journalists, many interviews are arranged by communication professionals who set up press conferences or interviews under controlled conditions where they are briefed and coached to say particular things and how to manage reporters and their questions (Bennato, 2017; Carver, 2014; Shipman, 2014).

Of course, there is still a great deal of interaction between scientists and reporters, particularly when it is journalists and not organisations or corporations who take the initiative to seek information. These individual, one-to-one exchanges tend to be more open and fluid but nevertheless only in very rare circumstances in well-resourced media do we see these news people sufficiently prepared so as to conduct robust and comprehensive interviews. In the majority of cases, reporters have to deal with so many stories that they have to fit an interview in to a heavily compacted day of work. Consequently, many of these interviews are rushed and improvised to the extent that a journalist has not had any time to prepare and read about the topic beyond very basic pointers.

## Conclusion

Over the years, the relationship between scientists and journalists has been characterised by the tensions that arise during the process of news gathering, and production that takes place. This because, as we have seen here, there is a clash of professional cultures that characterise distinctively both news people and the scientific community. According to existing research, these tensions are present in most societies, and also found that attitudes and patterns of behaviour are similar across countries (Bauer, 2013; Nguyen & McIlwaine, 2011; Nguyen & Tran, 2019). Although in many countries these tensions have been dramatically reduced over the years, in many others—such as those in the MENA region—they continue to persist and at times even intensify.

On the one hand, scientists seem to be concerned with making sure that any media representation of their work is an accurate reflection of what they believe to be important and relevant. Scientists insist that details of their work are not spared and that reporters do not hype or exaggerate the facts on the ground. On top of this, these experts are not necessarily committed to accessible language or to explain sufficiently their process of inquiry and findings. More often than not, many scientists remain reluctant to speak directly to reporters given past experiences with the media and their fear of being misquoted or misrepresented in the public eye (Dunwoody & Ryan, 1983; Massarani & Peters, 2016).

Several studies, both in MENA and other regions of the world, have acknowledged that most scientists do not prioritise media and public attention for their work (Hunter, 2016; Marcinkowski & Steiner, 2014; Suleski & Ibaraki, 2010). This is the case even after years of heavy investment in, and focus on, promoting science communication projects and sustained efforts to make the scientific community aware of the need to reach out to the wider public. Moreover, many scientists have taken a step back and allowed professional communication departments from universities and research centres to mediate between them and the public while they continue to focus instead on communicating via peer-review journals and at specialist scientific conferences. Scientists from all corners continue to point to the news media in general, and reporters in particular, as the prime reason for the public's presumed knowledge deficit and irrational beliefs (Besley et al., 2013).

Journalists, on the other hand, see their primary function as having to reach out to the wider public, even if this means at times stretching aspects of the story or oversimplifying key and critical issues. They assume that their function is to translate complex scientific results and conclusions, which at times they themselves do not sufficiently understand, into accessible language that can be grasped by audiences who are not necessarily aware of the themes, nor are able to manage the concepts and ideas referred to in that particular science work. Reporters do so in a context in which there is a struggle and competition for space and air time in which their content can be published and in which they compete for an audience market that is increasingly more fragmented and less interested in serious news (Borges, 2017). All this is in a context defined by tight deadlines and decreasing resources and capabilities to carry out these tasks.

Consequently, many of the key and most relevant aspects of the work of scientists is often distorted or lost in the translation from the scientific language to the common spoken word of the news audiences. At times this is due to lack of general and media understanding of the subject and others because the communication between scientists and journalists is difficult. Not only because of the language and functions each use and play, but also due to different perspectives each have about how science should be presented to the public.

For example, scientists are against speculating and reluctant to say if a new drug has the potential to cure a particular disease. Journalists and PR officers are instead prone to the speculative element because they know this awakes the public's imagination and gains their attention. Equally, scientists avoid conflict in the way they present their findings and treat controversy in rational and reasoned ways. All this while journalists and PR officers thrive on conflict as they know this brings ratings up and expanded news engagement.

These tensions are problematised in the case of MENA given the context in which both scientists and journalists work. It is not only because this regional setting is characterised by the presence of theocracies and military dictatorships in many of these countries and the limitations of freedom of speech that this signifies, but also because the Arab news media suffers deficiencies in several aspects. To start with, the volume of scientific information that appears in the Arab media is slight, if not negligible, when compared to the reporting of scientific information worldwide, and when considered against the size of the Arab media establishment (El-Awady, 2009).

In addition to this, the region lacks enough specialised journalists who can comprehensively and critically engage scientists and expert sources. Equally detrimental is the fact that scientific media outlets in MENA either do not exist or are so few that they have very limited reach. For example, though Egypt is one of the largest countries in the Arab world, the space its daily newspapers, weekly and monthly magazines allocate to science is few and far between (Mehran, 2018, p. 101). There simply does not seem to be a sufficiently developed science journalism news culture in that region.

In MENA, the relationship between journalists and their sources is further complicated by a news culture that is non-adversarial and at times deferential (Al-Suaid, 2016; Awad, 2010; Mellor, 2010). These attitudes among journalists in the region are associated with a news culture characterised by compliance, censorship and self-censorship. However, as this thesis aims to discuss, these restrictions cannot explain all the gaps and deficiencies observed in the news coverage of science and technology. Other aspects should also be considered, such as the lack of training and skills, which also hinders journalists' ability to interact in more engaging and comprehensive ways with their sources.

In this sense, reporters in the Arab media face persistent difficulties in obtaining information and accessing news sources and government data. In addition, many news reporters covering science have little or no access to news sources because in many cases they simply do not exist. As Mahmood (2008) pointed out some years ago, finding science sources in that region has proved to be one of the most difficult tasks faced by journalists. If we look at the sources of science news in that part of the world, we quickly learn that they usually come from western media, despite the stories being locally produced.

There are several reasons for that, including the fact that a lot of the content is not created but rather 'processed' or 'ensembled' in MENA. That is, journalists use news pieces from foreign news agencies or simply reproduce press releases provided to them by officials or press officers. Other reasons include the fact that in many cases journalists are unable to find a suitable local source that can help explain, clarify or critically analyse a particular issue in science and technology. In addition, we can mention the scarcity of specialised science journalists who lack the basic understanding of science and therefore have not built up a portfolio of sources and who also find it extremely difficult to identify experts and engage with them.

News media outlets in MENA also face decreasing resources in the newsroom and rising workloads, which compromise their ability to engage with primary sources and spend the necessary time to sufficiently explore issues and aspects of science. As a result, journalists tend to rely rather on sources that have their own agenda and are all too keen to disseminate official versions or promote corporate products (Hallin & Briggs, 2015). In these cases, reporters tend to reproduce what official sources say in their press briefings and information packages.

This last point explains why a direct link between journalists and scientists is central for a sound, comprehensive and critical engagement between the news media and the scientific community. Science journalism cannot be just about reproducing and translating science information so as to fill the deficit gap. It is also about the ability of society to scrutinise its own science. This by reporters being able and capable of asking relevant and pertinent questions that help to integrate scientific knowledge into our daily lives. This can only happen if there is a fluent and critical relationship between journalists and scientists. For this, we need capabilities and proper accessible channels that can make this happen. Exploring this last point is central in improving science journalism in the region.

## Bibliography

Alhuntushi, A., & Lugo-Ocando, J. (2020). Articulating statistics in science news in Arab newspapers: Cases of Egypt, Kuwait and Saudi Arabia. *Journalism Practice*. https://doi.org/10.1080/17512786.2020.1808857

Al-Suaid, I. M. (2016). Emirati media: Its origin and development. *The Scientific Journal of Public Relations and Advertising Research, 2016*(8), 437–467.

Anderson, C. (2018). *Apostles of certainty: Data journalism and the politics of doubt*. Oxford University Press.

Atkins, P. (1995). Science as truth. *History of the Human Sciences, 8*(2), 97–102.

Awad, T. (2010). *The Saudi press and the Internet: How Saudi journalists and media decision makers at the Ministry of Culture and Information evaluate censorship in the presence of the Internet as a news and information medium*. The University of Sheffield.

Bauer, M. W. (2013). The knowledge society favours science communication, but puts science journalism into a clinch. *Science Communication Today, Paris, CNRS*, 145–166.

Bennato, D. (2017). The shift from public science communication to public relations. The Vaxxed case. *Journal of Science Communication, 16*(2), C02.

Berkowitz, D., & Beach, D. W. (1993). News sources and news context: The effect of routine news, conflict and proximity. *Journalism & Mass Communication Quarterly, 70*(1), 4–12.

Besley, J. C., Oh, S. H., & Nisbet, M. (2013). Predicting scientists' participation in public life. *Public Understanding of Science, 22*(8), 971–987.

Borges, R. E. (2017). Towards an epistemology of data journalism in the devolved nations of the UK: Changes and continuities in materiality, performativity and reflexivity. *Journalism*. https://doi.org/10.1177/1464884917693864

Brandao, R. (2016). *Study shows: How statistics are used to articulate and shape discourses of science in the newsroom*. University of Sheffield.

Bucchi, M., & Mazzolini, R. (2003). Big science, little news: Science coverage in the Italian daily press, 1946–1997. *Public Understanding of Science, 12*(1), 7–24.

Carver, R. B. (2014). Public communication from research institutes: Is it science communication or public relations? *Journal of Science Communication, 13*(3), C01.

Dajani, R., Dhawan, S., & Awad, S. M. (2020). The increasing prevalence of girls in stem education in the Arab World: What can we learn? *Sociology of Islam, 8*(2), 159–174.

Davies, N. (2011). *Flat earth news: An award-winning reporter exposes falsehood, distortion and propaganda in the global media*. Random House.

Dimitrova, D. V., & Strömbäck, J. (2009). Look who's talking: Use of sources in newspaper coverage in Sweden and the United States. *Journalism Practice, 3*(1), 75–91.

Dunwoody, S., & Ryan, M. (1983). Public information persons as mediators between scientists and journalists. *Journalism Quarterly, 60*(4), 647–656.

El-Awady, N. (2009). Science journalism: The Arab boom. *Nature, 459*, 1057.

Franklin, B., & Carlson, M. (2010). *Journalists, sources, and credibility: New perspectives*. Routledge.

Frost, C. (2015). *Journalism ethics and regulation*. Routledge.

Hallin, D. C., & Briggs, C. L. (2015). Transcending the medical/media opposition in research on news coverage of health and medicine. *Media, Culture & Society, 37*(1), 85–100.

Harb, Z. (2019). Challenges facing Arab journalism, freedom, safety and economic security. *Journalism, 20*(1), 110–113.

Howell, M., & Prevenier, W. (2001). *From reliable sources: An introduction to historical methods.* Cornell University Press.

Hunter, P. (2016). The communications gap between scientists and public: More scientists and their institutions feel a need to communicate the results and nature of research with the public. *EMBO Reports, 17*(11), 1513–1515.

Khun, T. (2012). *The structure of scientific revolutions.* University of Chicago Press.

Lewis, J. M. W., Williams, A., Franklin, R. A., Thomas, J., & Mosdell, N. A. (2008). *The quality and independence of British journalism.* Cardiff School of Journalism, Media and Cultural Studies.

Lippmann, W. (2018). *Liberty and the news.* Routledge.

Lugo-Ocando, J. (2008). *The Media in Latin America.* McGraw-Hill Education (UK).

Lugo-Ocando, J. (2015). Journalists do live in a parallel universe: A response to practitioner critiques of journalism academics. *Journal of Applied Journalism & Media Studies, 4*(3), 369–379.

Lugo-Ocando, J., & Brandão, R. (2016). STABBING NEWS: Articulating crime statistics in the newsroom. *Journalism Practice, 10*(6), 715–729.

Mahmood, S. (2008). *Scientific media.* Alfagar Publishing.

Manning, P. (2000). *News and news sources: A critical introduction.* Sage.

Marcinkowski, F., & Steiner, A. (2014). Mediatization and political autonomy: A systems approach. In H. Kriesi (Ed.), *Mediatization of politics: Understanding the transformation of western democracies* (pp. 74–89). Palgrave Macmillan.

Massarani, L., & Peters, H. P. (2016). Scientists in the public sphere: Interactions of scientists and journalists in Brazil. *Anais Da Academia Brasileira de Ciências, 88*, 1165–1175.

Mehran, Z. (2018). *How to introduce science to the Arab child.* Academic Library.

Mellor, N. (2010). More than a parrot The case of Saudi women journalists. *Journal of Arab & Muslim Media Research, 3*(3), 207–222.

Mellor, N. (2011). *Arab media: Globalization and emerging media industries* (Vol. 1). Polity.

Meyer, P. (2002). *Precision journalism: A reporter's introduction to social science methods.* Rowman & Littlefield.

Nguyen, A., & McIlwaine, S. (2011). Who wants a voice in Science issues—And why? A survey of European citizens and its implications for science journalism. *Journalism Practice, 5*(2), 210–226.

Nguyen, A., & Tran, M. (2019). Science journalism for development in the Global South: A systematic literature review of issues and challenges. *Public Understanding of Science, 28*(8), 973–990.

Nölleke, D., Grimmer, C. G., & Horky, T. (2017). News sources and follow-up communication: Facets of complementarity between sports journalism and social media. *Journalism Practice, 11*(4), 509–526.

Popper, K. (2005). *The logic of scientific discovery*. Routledge.

Radford, T. (2007). Scheherazade: Telling stories, not educating people. In M. W. Bauer & M. Bucchi (Eds.), *Journalism, Science and Society* (pp. 95–100). Routledge.

Shipman, M. (2014). Public relations as science communication. *Journal of Science Communication, 13*(3), C05.

Suleski, J., & Ibaraki, M. (2010). Scientists are talking, but mostly to each other: A quantitative analysis of research represented in mass media. *Public Understanding of Science, 19*(1), 115–125.

Wiseman, A. W., Abdelfattah, F. A., & Almassaad, A. (2016). The intersection of citizenship status, STEM education, and expected labor market participation in Gulf Cooperation Council Countries. *Digest of Middle East Studies, 25*(2), 362–392.

Zahlan, A. (2012). *Science, development, and sovereignty in the Arab World*. Palgrave Macmillan.

Zelizer, B. (1993). Journalists as interpretive communities. *Critical Studies in Mass Communication, 10*(3), 219–237. https://doi.org/10.1080/15295039309366865

CHAPTER 7

# Gender and Science News in the Arab World

In most discussions referring to the modern Arab world, gender is considered a central issue. Indeed, gender in the Arab world has been a central dimension of any type of analysis in media and journalism studies (Al-Malki et al., 2012; Sreberny, 2000). This, because general perceptions and views on Islam and in particular relation to the MENA region take the view that women are considered and treated as second-class citizens while persistently highlighting how they have fewer opportunities than men in those societies (Kandiyoti, 1991; Mir-Hosseini, 2006; Ong, 1999). The default views have portrayed women in MENA societies at a disadvantage, who have limited access to power and decision-making despite being guaranteed ample rights in Islam.

There has been a prolific body of research that has produced a robust and comprehensive theoretical explanatory framework around the role of women in these societies. These works explore prevalent assumptions about this secondary status and underline instead the different degrees of complexity and diversity across the region in relation to women's role and access to power (Al-Malki et al., 2012; Byerly, 2016; Fargues, 2005; Khamis, 2013). Across different countries, research has found that there are significant differences in relation to status, political rights, cultural attitudes, and access to professional roles.

Some go on to point out that women in MENA—for example—play a very active role in science and technology that in cases is greater than that

© The Author(s), under exclusive license to Springer Nature Switzerland AG 2023
A. Alhuntushi, J. Lugo-Ocando, *Science Journalism in the Arab World*, Palgrave Studies in Journalism and the Global South, https://doi.org/10.1007/978-3-031-14252-9_7

of their peers in the west (Abdallah, 2021; Islam, 2017; Koblitz, 2016). In places such as Saudi Arabia, there has been some progress in relation to the professional empowerment of women, where we can now observe more engagement with the media and science. Over the years, there have been an increasing number of women studying university degrees in media and science-related areas, although there are still very few females in science journalism in general. At the same time, we do see a growing number of women work in other news beats, such as political and economic news as well as more female journalists now entering the coverage of sports news (Aljuaid, 2020).

Having said all that, and acknowledging that there has been a significant improvement in women's engagement with the media industry (Ross & Carter, 2011), they still lag behind in terms of participation, accessing editorial responsibilities in the media and pay gaps (Khamis, 2013; Skalli, 2006). The findings in our own sample indicate that across all Arab news media in Egypt, Saudi Arabia and Kuwait, few female journalists produce science and technology news as part of their regular beat, leaving those areas to their male counterparts.

Our work suggests that not only are there fewer women in science journalism but that they also face greater difficulties than their male counterparts when dealing with STEM-related news sources. This includes stereotyping and even discrimination by some male officials and scientists who act as sources. This happens in terms of restricted access to datasets and interviews, limited or regulated participation in press conferences and they are often not invited to particular events because of assumptions around gender participation.

Indeed, according to some authors, there is the factor of 'gender', which in Arab countries is a central issue in explaining challenges for journalism as a political institution in society (Abdulrahman, 2008; Abu Samra, 1995; Al-Mutairi, 2009). Having said that, not all countries in MENA are the same and women journalists face different levels of restrictions and access when performing their jobs. Some authors have highlighted how women confront very different levels of exclusion in Saudi Arabia than their counterparts in Kuwait and Egypt (Mellor, 2011). Most observers agree that overall women face structural, institutional and cultural obstacles in the Arab region (Al-Rawi, 2010; J. Melki & Hitti, 2021; J. Melki & Mallat, 2018; J. P. Melki & Mallat, 2016).

Despite continuous developments and some progress, women journalists continue to struggle in the professional arena. These challenges also include discrimination by official sources when providing information or responding to requests. This has led some women journalists to rely on the Internet to obtain figures, regardless of the validity of those sources. As one of our interviewees pointed out,

> *My job depends a great deal upon me been able to speak directly to my sources. I find this at times difficult because there is simply not a culture of talking directly to the people in some areas. It is always in larger meetings, press conferences or events that I find the time to speak to scientists or experts. Then I find myself at the back of the queue as most journalists there are men and they ask their questions first. [INT17]*

In the MENA region, women still get fewer opportunities than men in regard to facilities that help journalists improve their skills, as well as having less access in the hierarchies of the media and continue to be discriminated at large across the region's newsrooms (J. P. Melki & Mallat, 2016). Many female journalists continue to be treated differently and to be seen, by many men in position of editorial power, as not capable of producing work of as high a quality as men do. Furthermore, some news sources avoid giving information to female journalists because they do not believe in their journalistic abilities, especially when the woman mentions her name on the news (Abdulrahman, 2008; J. P. Melki & Mallat, 2016).

Although there are calls for equality by a number of organisations, the state of women's role in journalism in the region continues to be dire. This is why gender is a key element in understanding the dynamics and cultures around the gathering, production and dissemination of science and technology stories in the region. This, not only because women represent half of the population of those societies but also because they have played a significant historical role in different fields of public life and especially in journalism, which regrettably has largely remained unrecognised (Byerly, 2016; J. P. Melki & Mallat, 2016; Sakr & De Burgh, 2005). Women's position in Arab journalism practice is far from equal in terms of the workplace, opportunities, and access to opportunities. However, the greatest issue faced by women in MENA is perhaps the lack of sufficient professional journalistic skills as a result of not having equal access to training and education provision, internship and supportive working environments that foster better professionals.

This of course is a paradox, given that both Arab culture and Islamic tradition normatively claim to recognise the role of women in society. It also happens despite a historical tradition in Islam of empowering women. This paradox, however, can be understood if one situates these discriminatory practices in the larger context of local cultures and post-coloniality. As John Gray (2007) has pointed out, a lot of the radicalisation and conservatism in Islam is a direct backlash to the forceful imposition of modernity in the nineteenth and twentieth centuries. Therefore, some of these very same issues that we question in the west about Islam are problems associated with the imposition of the enlightenment as a political project in Arab countries, which started during and after the Napoleonic wars (Losurdo, 2014).

In fact, social stratifications of opportunities for women were particularly exacerbated in the past 200 years in particular regions of the world such as the Arab world (Hasso, 2000; Stearns, 2015). In these societies, the situation has persisted despite the fact that women have increasingly assumed greater roles and accepted more challenges. In the media industry, there has been a significant improvement in women's empowerment (Ross & Carter, 2011), but they still lag behind in terms of participation and assuming editorial responsibilities (Khamis, 2013; Skalli, 2006). Even in countries where women have played a more visible role in public life, their experiences and expertise continue to be regarded by news industries as less important than those of men.

General treatment of women in the Arab world has been a subject of focus by western scholars and observers alike, who have often underlined the predominant conservatism in cultural practices (El Saadawi & Saʿdāwī, 2007; Golley, 2004; Lewis, 2009; Minces, 1982). However, not too many of these scholars go out of their way to remind their readers that Islam was one of the first cultures to provide rights to women in areas such as property ownership, childcare and others, way before nations such as the United Kingdom had similar rights (Cole, 1981; Moaddel, 1998).

If well, it is true that for a long time Ottoman Muslim women had had to endure desertion and/or maltreatment by their husbands, with almost no recourse through the law since the Hanafi had been made the official imperial school of law in the sixteenth century, the final decades of the empire not only saw a series of reforms that gave them ample rights, but that also society witnessed an ever-growing and stronger women's rights movement. One that had become important and influential with women writing and producing their own magazines, journals and newspapers, which became widely read by both women and men (Cole, 1981; Moaddel, 1998). Scholars studying the history of the Ottoman empire do acknowledge the rigid patriarchal structures under which women had to live in those times. However, they also acknowledge the rich and dynamic levels of participation they had in the public sphere, including their writing and engagement with journalism in general, particularly by the end of the empire.

These reforms, as well as many progressive aspects undertaken in that empire, which reached many of its corners, were abruptly disrupted by the war and the collapse of the Ottomans, which in turn led to European colonial powers re-imposing restrictions. If well, the anti-colonial insurgencies of the 1920s and 1930s have passed into history as the formative expressions of new nations (Provence, 2011), it is no less true that it would take many decades for those states to fully form. What came after the Ottomans was a complex system where European powers asserted their hegemonic power by conceding to arrangements with local leaders. Something that translated into reinterpretations of the law that were more attuned to particular versions of Islam and, mostly, with local customs (Kuehn, 2011; Mikhail & Philliou, 2012; Močnik, 2019). These European alliances with local leaders of the new protectorates and colonies that were no longer part of the Ottoman empire (Çakır, 2007; Zilfi, 1997) became spaces for regressive reforms in terms of women's rights and their participation in journalism. In part, because the new leaders were no longer bound by the cosmopolitanism that had flourished in the last part of the Ottoman rule (Şentürk & Bilal, 2020) but also because the Europeans became, at least at the start of their rule, oppressive masters that were not interested in fostering public debates that could upset the balance of power in their newly gained territories (R. Miller, 2010; Paris, 2004; Quataert, 2005). It will take many decades for women's participation in journalism to recover and even today, the MENA region experiences very different levels of engagement in each one of its countries. Therefore, the role of women in science reporting in these countries needs to be appreciated as a set of inter-gender issues that are intertwined with power relations in these societies.

That is not say that there are no serious challenges for women in MENA, but to highlight that it is a more complex picture than is normally assumed. It is also to underline that Islam as a truly global culture provides a variety of interpretations in its relations with women and to explain how many of these issues are problems that persist as a result of post-colonial realities inherited since the First and Second World Wars and the fall of the Ottoman empire. To be sure, many codes, laws and attitudes that undermine the capabilities and abilities of women to fully participate in society are in fact a reaction and an expression of resistance to political and cultural imposition on many societies. Many western observers, perhaps obsessed with Islam as the only seemingly explanatory framework, tend to forget that while the United States has never had a woman president, Islamic countries such as Bangladesh, Indonesia, Malaysia, Pakistan and Senegal are among those that have elected women prime ministers and state leaders.

We do, however, need to acknowledge that women in MENA today face a series of barriers at the entry point in the workplace, which include not only traditional male-dominated hierarchies but also important cultural expectations around the role of women in society and, perhaps, more importantly, the lack of accommodation or special arrangements to allow them to face the demands of daily professional life while balancing family expectations. With economies increasingly globalised in MENA, women have grown in numbers in the workplaces (Khan, 2019; Saviano et al., 2017). However, without flexible working conditions they face tremendous pressures on their own families given the societal expectations placed upon them. In addition to that, many countries in the region have seen wages in real terms stagnate or decline, while hours worked outside the home have risen in the face of family leave policies that are not sufficiently attractive or supportive of women (K. Miller et al., 2017; Moghadam, 2015).

In the past decades, most countries in MENA have made progress in relation to women's rights, although to different degrees. The law of the Kingdom of Saudi Arabia, to explore an example that has often been the centre of attention by western media, has now incorporated the notion of 'complementary equality' between men and women, 'taking into account the characteristics of both sexes, to achieve ultimate justice' (UNP, 2020). Although there is still a path to cross between legislation and practice on the ground, there are already visible changes taking place.

In this sense, the new language on official websites refers to 'the integration of the relationship between the sexes is an ideal way to promote and protect human rights and to guarantee the equality between men and women, such as the rights to work, education, health, economic rights and others'. The KSA has established reforms 'dedicated to the promotion of women's engagement in economic development by setting an equal age for both genders, preventing gender discrimination in terms of wages, occupation, work field and hours, and enabling women to incorporate and practice commercial business without obtaining prior consent' (UNP,

2020). These reforms include equality in workplaces and wage and other measures to address discrimination in the workplace.

Other countries in MENA too have delivered similar reforms and some, perhaps, far more reaching. In some cases, these changes have been in place for a long time as is the case of Egypt, Jordan, Morocco and Tunisia (Amrane-Minne & Abu-Haidar, 1999; Charrad, 2001), although in all of these cases, there is a considerable gap between law and practice. However, progress is been made and the 2020 World Bank report titled 'Women, Business and the Law' (2020) highlights that over the last few years, authorities in countries such as the United Arab Emirates have shown a commitment to removing legal barriers to women's work. These reforms include prohibiting discrimination based on gender in employment, introducing penalties for sexual harassment and lifting restrictions on women's work at night and in certain industries. The UAE now also allows cohabitation and has de-penalised a series of issues that before were, under the law, the subject of fines or even jail.

Bahrain has also reportedly made progress with its Supreme Council for Women recently adopting a second National Plan for the Advancement of Bahraini Women for 2013–2022, which focuses on supporting women's entrepreneurship and enhancing their physical and psychological wellbeing and protection from domestic violence. That country also adopted provisions regarding sexual harassment in employment, including criminal penalties for perpetrators (AW, 2021). Other places in the Gulf Cooperation Council, where steady progress has been made over the years, include Kuwait, Oman and Qatar, where women have for years enjoyed an important degree of autonomy and rights in their workplaces and the progressive erosion of the institutions of classic patriarchy (Alzougool et al., 2021; Kirat, 2018; Salem & Yount, 2019). Other countries such as Iraq, Jordan, Lebanon, and Palestine, to name a few, have had a longer tradition of making the workplace accessible for women and the integration of gender.

This, however, does not mean that this progress is sufficient enough so as to claim any sense of equality comparable to, let us say, Australia, Europe or North America. On the contrary, non-profit organisations such as Human Rights Watch have emphatically argued that there is still a very long way to go for women's rights in the region (Ng, 2021). Furthermore, discriminatory labour practices against women continue to be prevalent in the region and it is still common practice in many workplaces to treat women as second-class citizens and employees. More important, the constant trend in all of these places is the gap between what the law says and daily practices and organisational cultures in which one can still observe a great deal of discrimination.

In addition to existing discriminatory practices against women, it is important to mention that in the case of journalists working in MENA, many female reporters are not nationals of that country, which further complicates their status. This is not only the case of GCC countries, where few nationals work as reporters, but also refers to large groups such as Palestinians who have lived in a variety of countries for generations but remain stateless. In the case of GCC, we found in our own sample only a few individual reporters who had the citizenship status of the countries in which they were practising journalism. This means that these women have a double vulnerability when it comes to working rights. On the one hand, they face limitations and obstacles as women and secondly, their status as non-citizens—even if they are of a third generation born in that country— means that they are subject to deportation if found guilty of violating censorship-related or defamation laws.

## Arab Female Science Journalists

Women practising journalism do so in the context in which they also face additional challenges and problems relating specifically to the activities they carry out when reporting STEM news. Overall, the empowerment of women in journalism in Arab countries still faces important challenges that range from lack of professional autonomy, limited access to sources, absence of appropriate training and education towards specialisation and lack of economic incentives (Mellor, 2010, p. 219). There are undoubtedly common issues that one can observe across the region in which issues such as culture and politics play a central role.

To explore these and other issues, we carried out semi-structured interviews with a total of 17 female journalists across the region working in news media outlets and who have covered the news beat of science and technology at least three times in the year. This sample is by no means representative, but we use it to open our discussion in relation to gender and science reporting by means of qualitative analysis. Needless to say, more comprehensive and larger studies that look at the characteristics and background of women news reporters in MENA have been conducted by a variety of scholars (Al-Malki et al., 2012; Bebawi, 2016; Kirat, 2018; Mellor, 2010, 2019). We refer to those and other studies to contextualise our own findings and to provide an explanatory theoretical framework for the discussion.

At first glance, this initial profile of women who have covered STEM news proved to be insightful and illustrative. For example, one of the first things we noticed is that all of these journalists have a bachelor's degree in disciplines as diverse as law, cardiology, media and social sciences. In most of these countries, female journalists tend to have better qualifications than their male counterparts, who in some cases, we found, have no degree at all. The fact that many Arab men have no university degree, but still managed to get into media outlets, can be explained by the fact that they have accessed the newsroom by means of occupational pathways (e.g., trainees or informal connections). Instead, women without a degree face impossible obstacles to enter the newsroom and even when they have one they are, nevertheless, often subjected to additional requirements. As one of the interviewees pointed out,

> *To get my first gig in a newsroom, I had to jump so many hoops. It was very hard. I had to prove myself all the time. For me it was very difficult to work in this field as we do not receive any training to deal with science and instead are expected to be able to produce stories straight away. As a woman, you do not really feel that you can go to a mentor. [INT16]*

In most news media outlets, formal and informal systems of mentoring are central to integrating newcomers into the daily routine and practices. To be sure, the notion of a formal mentoring scheme cuts across the informality of newsrooms. Where 'coaching' may once have meant little more than a few gruff words hurled at a junior who made a mistake, today there are elaborate systems that prepare the recently arrived individual to adapt and perform better at their jobs and integrate into their organisations (Lublinski et al., 2014; Walker & Clokie, 2013).

In this sense, we spoke to human resources (HR) officials in three newspapers in the region. They all assured us that in all cases there are formal mechanisms that apply to all employees regarding health and safety, general codes of conduct of the company and more general procedures about their contracts in the sense of obligations. In none of these cases, however, are there any resources or procedures allocated to allow reporters to specialise in a particular newsbeat, such as science. All three HR officials were emphatic when stating that their organisations expected their newly hired reporters to be fully prepared and functional on their arrival to cover stories, although they do have specialised support for internships which they have created with universities and editors in the newsroom.

Having said that, the challenges may vary in each country as laws, organisational dynamics and professional normative expectations are shaped by local histories, cultures and politics. Indeed, our study suggests that difficulties in the engagement with, and access to, science news among women can be different in each country despite broad common issues. For example, Saudi women journalists reported that they encountered particular difficulties around accessing male sources individually or sharing working spaces with their male counterparts. However, female reporters interviewed in Egypt and Kuwait said they had no such problems and instead highlighted low salaries, long working hours and lack of resources as their key problems.

## Gender Balance

Female journalists from the Kingdom of Saudi Arabia said in the interviews that they encountered challenges that negatively influenced their ability to report science news effectively. These issues mostly related to external influences and organisational cultures within the newsrooms of that country. These include accessing official sources, ability to attend events and other obstacles relating to being assigned to specific news beats. All these journalists, [INT07], [INT08] and [INT10], agreed that there were several other difficulties which, in their views, are linked to cultural factors and prevalent male-dominated views about the role of women in the newsroom. As one of the interviewees said,

> *At times, I face a wall when trying to speak to some sources. They would just not talk to me. My editor knows this so the newspaper will send a man instead to cover a story. There are events at which women are not expected to attend. I mean, it is not said like that, but we all know that it is an all-male event. [INT10]*

Journalists [INT07] and [INT10] underlined that there has been progress made and things are changing for the better. They both agreed that the number of obstacles that women have encountered in the past have become less present. Nevertheless, they are both quick to point out that there is still a long way to go,

*In the past, there were many barriers for women journalists to get the numbers and information in general. These barriers have shrunk and become simpler, but they still exist. [INT07]*

*In the past it was difficult, but now it seems to be a lot easier. I see how I started myself, and what new female reporters have to go through now and definitively it is much better now. Having said that, I feel that we [women] all still struggle. [INT10]*

Additional issues faced by women relate to accessing sources. A closer analysis of the findings indicated that male journalists used official sources in 64% of the 448 articles they wrote, which was more than female journalists, who used official sources in nearly 56% of their 86 articles. There might be a gender dimension determining 'trust in' and 'engagement with' official sources (which in these countries tend also to be male) by journalists but further research is needed in order to explore this argument further (Table 7.1).

Non-official sources were also used by male journalists five times more than female journalists (19.9% compared to 3.5%), who tended to rely more on the use of unknown sources more often than male journalists (40.7% compared to 16%). From this data, it might seem that male journalists tend to engage more in fact-checking than their female counterparts when dealing with science news. However, we must highlight the fact that female journalists in Arab societies face greater challenges in accessing sources in general, something that is easier for men in these societies. In the interviews, it is clear that female journalists are well aware of the routines and practices necessary to undertake fact-checking. They also feel prepared to do so. However, all of the interviewees concurred that they felt limited in being able to access a variety of sources to

**Table 7.1** The main source and gender

|  |  | *Male* | *Female* | *Total* |
|---|---|---|---|---|
| Source 1: The main source | Official | 287 | 48 | 335 |
|  | Non-official | 89 | 3 | 92 |
|  | Unknown | 72 | 35 | 107 |
| Total |  | 448 | 86 | 534 |

Source: Authors' data

cross-reference a story. They agreed that the greatest difficulty faced by Saudi female journalists related to accessing official sources,

> *The source may deliberately delay giving journalists information and sometimes ignores the journalists. Although in Saudi Arabia there is currently an increasing openness and growing awareness of the concept of journalism, there is still a big delay in providing us [women] with the information that we request. [INT10]*

Another female journalist complained about the lack of co-operation from science sources in universities and research centres,

> *The sources said sometimes do not co-operate with us and do not give me the information I seek. Instead, they give her information that is old and no longer newsworthy. [INT07]*

There are several reasons as to why a news source might refrain from giving journalists the information needed. For instance, traditional practices in the region dictate that their own public relations department will prepare the press release to ensure that the story is published in the terms set by their own institutions or organisation. In this sense, by not providing the information, the officials can withhold the authorial control over the story and avoid mistakes on the part of journalists in what is published. Nevertheless, there might be more to this. Some years ago, Abdulrahman (2008) explained how sources in the Arab world are not convinced of the ability of women to cover the news well. It could also be the case that it is not the unwillingness of official sources to work with women and providing female journalists with the information requested, but rather the fact that communication professionals and PR officials cannot handle the specialised information themselves. This last point might be the case as some male journalists expressed similar frustrations when interviewed about this topic.

Having said that, the broader comments from female journalists do suggest that some official sources treat men and women unequally. Although difficulties in obtaining science information are common for both male and female journalists, that female journalists seem to perceive having more difficulties than their male counterparts to secure interviews or access to data. This was something upon which all the interviewees agreed. This may be related to culture, especially in Saudi Arabia and other Gulf countries, as gender has been in itself a long-standing issue (Abdulrahman, 2008; Abu Samra, 1995; Al-Mutairi, 2009).

One of the journalists pointed out that she always tends to use a handful of sources that facilitate her access to the required information rather than those that put obstacles in front of her. She explains that for other female reporters it might not be as easy,

> As they do not have many choices. I know that as a fact because many of my [female] colleagues cannot access some sources, that leads them to accept the information from other sources, even if it is not reliable, accurate or even the proper source who is supposed to speak to you. [INT08]

The content analysis reinforces these perceptions by confirming that female Arabic journalists used unknown sources more often than male journalists (40.7% compared to 16%). This result might reflect the greater difficulties faced by female journalists than male journalists in the Arab world in relation to their position, external recognition, and ability to reassert their role in front of the sources.

Overall, the amount of STEM news stories produced by female journalists in the region is minimal compared to their male counterparts as only a small percentage of the news stories have a female byline. The sample also suggests that female reporters focus on particular areas such as health rather than technology or other STEM areas. In our findings from the content analysis, we noticed that no female reporter worked in technology news. Further triangulation with the qualitative data by means of semi-structured interviews suggests several reasons for this. This includes the fact that technology news does not attract female journalists' interest and that it is seen as a male topic. Second, but deeply interwoven with the first reason mentioned above, editors and producers do not provide any specific guidance to cover technology news to female journalists and instead tend to direct their male counterparts to do so. Third, there is simply not the expertise among women reporters in the newsrooms to cover these types of stories. In MENA, technology is seen as an all-male dominated area despite the growing numbers of female engineers and experts,

> We simply do not have female journalists in Saudi Arabia who specialize in a particular subject. Women tend to work temporarily in a field and then move to another area, depending on the kinds of stories the paper needs. If you were to ask most journalists in the Kingdom, they would say that they have worked in every area—political, social, health, economy; the journalist covers whatever news the editors want them too. [INT07]

Female journalists interviewed highlighted that technology is a newsbeat in which they find it hard to relate to the topics in question and in which they encounter difficulties in accessing the news sources. There is a scarcity of female journalists who specialise in technology, as our own content analysis suggests that only a few bylines were attributed to women. The rest of the stories that covered technology either had no byline or mostly male names.

The correlation between the type of science news and the gender of the journalist is notable as well; female journalists are overall far less likely than their male counterparts to cover technology news and more likely to have their bylines in stories about biology and health science. In fact, just over 16% of all health news stories were written by female journalists, which is much higher than the average they get in other STEM subjects. Having said that, while this percentage is better than that of technology news, it is still comparatively low (Table 7.2).

One aspect that comes to light in this analysis is how journalists, men and women, conceptualise what is science and technology. Technology seems to associate with areas that are not of particular interest to women. As one female reporter put it,

*I prefer not to cover it. Technology does not attract me very much. Health is possibly my second choice, but my first preference is the social news that deals with citizens' problems, because I consider the press an amplifier through which the voice of the public is conveyed to the government. [INT08]*

The problem does not seem to be their professional background or ability to engage with the topic. On the contrary, the educational qualifications of female Arab journalists are in general better than those of their

**Table 7.2** Gender cross-tabulated by type of science news

|  |  | The type of science news | | Total |
|---|---|---|---|---|
|  |  | Health | Technology |  |
| The gender of the journalist | Unknown | 355 | 43 | 398 |
|  | Male | 438 | 10 | 448 |
|  | Female | 86 | 0 | 86 |
| Total |  | 879 | 53 | 932 |

Source: Authors' data

male counterparts. Instead, we need to explore factors such as culture and, overall, prevalent attitudes as they seem to offer a better explanation for the lack of engagement with technology.

Attitudes and traditional cultural dynamics play a central role in determining access of female journalists to sources and establishing the boundaries of what should be covered. Despite progress, obtuse attitudes towards women persist in the region and have also been internalised by women themselves. One anecdote relating to this study is revealing and which relates to the difficulties in interviewing women journalists. Many interviews had to be done over the phone, even though we were at times in same city and many were conducted before COVID-19 hit. This suggests that local customs and practices derived from cultural backgrounds—which include religion—continue to be not only an issue, but also still a powerful factor defining the ability of female reporters to do their job.

## Health News

Regarding the news coverage of health science, there is also a gap between women and men, with women making up just a fraction of those who are awarded a byline in heal. In Arab newspapers, the situation is similar, as the findings shows that only 16% of newspaper articles in this news beat were written by female journalists. For us, these findings speak loud and clear about organisational cultures in the newsrooms, which, for a number of reasons discussed here, tends to favour men over women.

As to the question of which newspaper featured more science news produced by female journalists, the findings suggest that the *Al-Ahram* newspaper was in first place as women wrote 54 science articles for that paper, compared to 40 by men. *Al-Ahram* was in fact the only newspaper for which female journalists wrote more science articles than male journalists. This might be due to greater social openness in Egypt, where women have been able to practise journalism for a longer time compared to other Arab countries and where there is no gender segregation in the newsrooms. *Al-Qabascame* came in second place, with 26.4% of the science news written by women, followed by *Oqaz* with 6.2%. The percentages were close at *Al-Riyadh*, *Al-Rai* and *Al-Masry Al-Yuom*, with 3.7%, 3.65% and 3.1%, respectively.

Despite contemporary developments in Saudi society, specifically in regard to women's rights, the percentage of female-published science news compared to male-published news was very low: 3.7% in *Al-Riyadh* and 6.2% in *Oqaz*. This disparity is consistent with similar research about gender participation in Arab newspapers (Mellor, 2010, p. 207). Despite new opportunities for female Saudi journalists, it is still superficial rather than a reflection of genuine change in women's status inside the Kingdom.

Most scholars agree with the need for a much larger discussion around modernity and gender in the Arab world and to what extent is it possible for women to push against the boundaries and challenge traditional roles assigned to them in these societies. To be sure, women in Arab societies face many difficulties and limitations, especially in the field of journalism, even as some have started to fade away. For example, until relatively recently, Saudi Arabia's media schools in universities were restricted to men but in the past few years this has started to change. Many women have joined J-schools in Saudi universities, although there continues to be gender segregation in terms of common spaces, as in other countries in the Gulf. Regardless of this relative progress, the need to empower women in journalism in Saudi Arabia and other Arab countries still faces crucial challenges. One of them is the lack of adequate economic incentives, such as maternity leave pay, and support for childcare, for women in the media industry but which are in effect also challenges faced by many poor women in the West (Mellor, 2010, p. 219). Having said that, countries such as the UAE have very recently decreed new legislation to address some of these issues and hopefully others will follow suit.

Overall, the participation of reporters in the creation of scientific news within Arabic newspapers is low; the exception to this trend is the Egyptian newspaper *Al-Ahram*. This may confirm the cultural impact on gender in the region (Table 7.3).

**Table 7.3** Gender of the journalist cross-tabulation

|  |  | *Male* | *Female* | *Total* |
|---|---|---|---|---|
| Newspaper's name | *Al-Qabas* | 39 | 14 | 53 |
|  | *Oqaz* | 30 | 2 | 32 |
|  | *Al-Riyadh* | 169 | 10 | 179 |
|  | *Al-Rai* | 108 | 4 | 112 |
|  | *Al-Ahram* | 40 | 54 | 94 |
|  | *Al-Masry Al-Yuom* | 62 | 2 | 64 |
| Total |  | 448 | 86 | 534 |

Source: Authors' data

Even among newspapers in Egypt, which is more liberal in terms of women's rights, there is no homogeneity between the number of female journalists and male journalists. For example, at *Al-Ahram*, over 57% of the journalists who produced science news were women, while at *Al-Masry Al-Yuom*, only 3% of science news was produced by women. Nevertheless, as we know from other countries, increasing the number of women in the newsroom helps to address the issue but does not solve it. To achieve that a change in the organisational culture and work ethics would be necessary.

## Conclusion

What we see in this chapter is that gender is a central issue when trying to examine science journalism practices in the MENA region. There are distinctive conditions and outcomes as well as a different entry barrier for both women and men. The data suggest that women lag behind and that there is an urgent need to create a critical mass of female reporters who can investigate and produce news stories relating to science and technologies. However, as we have argued here, simply fostering a critical mass in terms of numbers will not be enough. There are quantitative and qualitative issues to be addressed, such as the prevalent attitudes and lack of support and training for women who want to report science as a news beat.

The good news is that this is a region that is starting to liberalise and embrace a more active and participatory role for women in the media. There are today far more opportunities to improve the practice of science reporting as a whole by incorporating larger numbers of women. The reason for doing that is simple: Diversity in the newsroom brings about new perspectives for inquiry and a more comprehensive and holistic understanding of the natural world. Also, having a newsroom that is more representative of society can help to create stronger links between audiences and news media organisations.

This is a crucial task to undertake in a time of fragmented and declining audiences and is essential if the media industry wants to survive and thrive in a digital and interactive environment in which almost anyone can create content or simply click on a hyperlink to explore other alternatives. More women producing science news means that there can be a stronger link with the audiences as the agenda of what is covered sets a wider net.

However, it is equally important to remember that gender in terms of the cultural and social distinctions predicated on biological sex, is only one side of the coin. The other being the issues relating to gender and personal identity. This remains largely a taboo in most MENA societies despite important lessons from the past in which gender discrimination, stereotyping and criminalisation led to the misunderstanding of important challenges such as the misreporting of the HIV/AIDS crisis of the 1980s and 1990s, which continues to kill many in the region as it continues to be stigmatised.

It seems that some lessons in this respect have been learnt. As some scholars have pointed out, some countries in the region exhibit a significant attitudinal shift of the media's portrayal of health issues such as HIV/AIDS with the gradual disappearance of the negative attributes. The mainstream media in the region no longer calls this the 'plague of our time', a term which sadly was used extensively in the earlier stages of HIV/AIDS and that referred to the sexual orientation of the people living with it (Anema et al., 2010; Hamdan, 2011). Instead, journalists, editors and producers today in most of MENA tend to be much more careful and at times show the necessary compassion for those who suffer, as mandated by faith. This is a promising development, despite prevalent attitudes and important challenges ahead.

## Bibliography

Abdallah, H. (2021). Qatari women 'outnumber men' at local universities [News]. *Doha News*. Retrieved May 12, 2022, from https://www.dohanews.co/qatari-women-outnumber-men-at-local-universities/

Abdulrahman, A. (2008). *Arab women journalists' concerns and challenges: Realistic testimonies*. Al-Arabi.

Abu Samra, N. (1995). *Media performance obstacles of female Egyptian journalists*. Assiut University.

Aljuaid, K. (2020). *Media in Saudi Arabia: The challenge for female journalists*. PhD Thesis, University of Bedfordshire.

Al-Malki, A., Kaufer, D., Ishizaki, S., & Dreher, K. (2012). *Arab women in Arab news: Old stereotypes and new media*. A&C Black.

Al-Mutairi, R. (2009). *Job satisfaction among Saudi female journalists and influencing factors*. Imam University.

Al-Rawi, A. K. (2010). Iraqi women journalists' challenges and predicaments. *Journal of Arab & Muslim Media Research, 3*(3), 223–236.

Alzougool, B., AlMansour, J., & AlAjmi, M. (2021). Women leadership styles in the public sector in Kuwait: The perspective of their subordinates. *Management Science Letters, 11*(2), 465–472.

Amrane-Minne, D. D., & Abu-Haidar, F. (1999). Women and politics in Algeria from the War of Independence to our day. *Research in African Literatures, 30*(3), 62–77.

Anema, A., Freifeld, C. C., Druyts, E., Montaner, J. S. G., Hogg, R. S., & Brownstein, J. S. (2010). An assessment of global Internet-based HIV/AIDS media coverage: Implications for United Nations Programme on HIV/AIDS'Global Media HIV/AIDS Initiative. *International Journal of STD & AIDs, 21*(1), 26–29.

AW. (2021). GCC sees women's rights progress in wake of reforms. *The Arab Weekly.* https://thearabweekly.com/gcc-sees-womens-rights-progress-wake-reforms

Bebawi, S. (2016). *Investigative Journalism in the Arab World: Issues and Challenges.* Springer.

Byerly, C. (2016). Jordan: Towards Gender Balance in the Newsroom. In C. Byerly (Ed.), *The Palgrave International Handbook of Women and Journalism.* Palgrave Macmillan.

Çakır, S. (2007). Feminism and feminist history-writing in Turkey: The discovery of Ottoman feminism. *Aspasia, 1*(1), 61–83.

Charrad, M. (2001). *States and women's rights: The making of postcolonial Tunisia, Algeria, and Morocco.* University of California Press.

Cole, J. R. (1981). Feminism, class, and Islam in turn-of-the-century Egypt. *International Journal of Middle East Studies, 13*(4), 387–407.

El Saadawi, N., & Saʻdāwī, N. (2007). *The hidden face of Eve: Women in the Arab world.* Zed Books.

Fargues, P. (2005). Women in Arab countries: Challenging the patriarchal system? *Reproductive Health Matters, 13*(25), 43–48.

Golley, N. A. (2004). Is feminism relevant to Arab women? *Third World Quarterly, 25*(3), 521–536.

Gray, J. (2007). *Black Mass: Apocalyptic religion and the death of Utopia.* Macmillan.

Hamdan, J. M. (2011). Newspaper stories on HIV/AIDS in Jordan: A look into the Lexicon. *International Journal of Arabic-English Studies (IJAES), 12.*

Hasso, F. (2000). Modernity and gender in Arab accounts of the 1948 and 1967 defeats. *International Journal of Middle East Studies, 32*(4), 491–510.

Islam, S. I. (2017). Arab women in Science, Technology, Engineering and Mathematics fields: The way forward. *World Journal of Education, 7*(6), 12–20.

Kandiyoti, D. (1991). *Women, Islam and the state* (Vol. 105). Temple University Press.

Khamis, S. (2013). Gendering the Arab Spring: Arab women journalists/activists, 'cyberfeminism,' and the sociopolitical revolution. In C. Cynthia, S. Linda, & M. Lisa (Eds.), *The Routledge companion to media & gender* (pp. 583–594). Routledge.

Khan, M. A. I. A. A. (2019). Dynamics encouraging women towards embracing entrepreneurship: Case study of Mena countries. *International Journal of Gender and Entrepreneurship, 11*(4), 379–389. https://pustaka-sarawak.com/eknowbase/attachments/1584599252.pdf

Kirat, M. (2018). The world of women public relations practitioners in Qatar. *International Journal of Business and Social Science*, 9(9), 81–94.

Koblitz, A. H. (2016). Life in the fast lane: Arab women in science and technology. *Bulletin of Science, Technology & Society*, 36(2), 107–117.

Kuehn, T. (2011). *Empire, Islam, and politics of difference: Ottoman rule in Yemen, 1849–1919*. Brill.

Lewis, B. (2009). Free at last-the Arab world in the twenty-first century. *Foreign Affairs*, 88, 77.

Losurdo, D. (2014). *Liberalism: A counter-history*. Verso.

Lublinski, J., Reichert, I., Denis, A., Fleury, J., Labassi, O., & Spurk, C. (2014). Advances in African and Arab science journalism: Capacity building and new newsroom structures through digital peer-to-peer support. *Ecquid Novi: African Journalism Studies*, 35(2), 4–22.

Melki, J., & Hitti, E. (2021). The domestic tethering of Lebanese and Arab women journalists and news managers. *Journalism Practice*, 15(3), 288–307.

Melki, J., & Mallat, S. E. (2018). When Arab women (and men) speak: Struggles of women journalists in a gendered news industry. In Steiner L, Carter C, & S. Allan (Eds.), *Journalism, Gender and Power* (pp. 33–48). Routledge.

Melki, J. P., & Mallat, S. E. (2016). Block her entry, keep her down and push her out: Gender discrimination and women journalists in the Arab world. *Journalism Studies*, 17(1), 57–79.

Mellor, N. (2010). More than a parrot The case of Saudi women journalists. *Journal of Arab & Muslim Media Research*, 3(3), 207–222.

Mellor, N. (2011). *Arab media: Globalization and emerging media industries* (Vol. 1). Polity.

Mellor, N. (2019). The (in) visibility of Arab women in political journalism. In L. Steiner, C. Carter, & S. Allan (Eds.), *Journalism, Gender and Power*. Routledge.

Mikhail, A., & Philliou, C. M. (2012). The Ottoman empire and the imperial turn. *Comparative Studies in Society and History*, 54(4), 721–745.

Miller, K., Kyriazi, T., & Paris, C. M. (2017). Arab women employment in the UAE: Exploring opportunities, motivations and challenges. *International Journal of Sustainable Society*, 9(1), 20–40.

Miller, R. (2010). *Britain*. Ashgate Surrey.

Minces, J. (1982). *The house of obedience: Women in Arab society*. Palgrave Macmillan.

Mir-Hosseini, Z. (2006). Muslim women's quest for equality: Between Islamic law and feminism. *Critical Inquiry*, 32(4), 629–645.

Moaddel, M. (1998). Religion and women: Islamic modernism versus fundamentalism. *Journal for the Scientific Study of Religion*, 108–130.

Močnik, N. (2019). Occupying the Land, Grabbing the Body: The Female Body as a Disposable Place of Colonialization in Post-Ottoman Bosnia-Herzegovina. *Southeastern Europe*, 43(2), 93–110.

Moghadam, V. M. (2015). Women, work and family in the Arab region: Toward economic citizenship. *DIFI Fam Res Proc, 7*, 1–20.
Ng, A. (2021). Saudi Arabia sees a spike in women joining the workforce, Brookings study shows. *CNBC News*. https://www.cnbc.com/2021/04/29/saudi-arabia-sees-a-spike-in-women-joining-the-workforce-study-says.html
Ong, A. (1999). Muslim Feminism: Citizenship in the shelter of corporatist Islam. *Citizenship Studies, 3*(3), 355–371.
Paris, T. J. (2004). *Britain, the Hashemites and Arab rule: The sherifian solution.* Routledge.
Provence, M. (2011). Ottoman modernity, colonialism, and insurgency in the interwar Arab East. *International Journal of Middle East Studies, 43*(2), 205–225.
Quataert, D. (2005). *The Ottoman Empire, 1700–1922.* Cambridge University Press.
Ross, K., & Carter, C. (2011). Women and news: A long and winding road. *Media, Culture & Society, 33*(8), 1148–1165.
Sakr, N., & De Burgh, H. (2005). The changing dynamics of Arab journalism. In *Making journalists: Diverse models, global issues* (pp. 142–157). Routledge.
Salem, R., & Yount, K. M. (2019). Structural accommodations of patriarchy: Women and workplace gender segregation in Qatar. *Gender, Work & Organization, 26*(4), 501–519.
Saviano, M., Nenci, L., & Caputo, F. (2017). The financial gap for women in the MENA region: A systemic perspective. *Gender in Management: An International Journal, 32*(3), 203–217.
Şentürk, R., & Bilal, M. S. (2020). *Human rights in the Ottoman reform: Foundations, motivations and formations.* İbn Haldun Üniversitesi Yayınları.
Skalli, L. (2006). Communicating gender in the public sphere: Women and information technologies in the MENA. *Journal of Middle East Women's Studies, 2*(2), 35–59.
Sreberny, A. (2000). Television, gender, and democratization in the Middle East. *De-Westernizing Media Studies*, 63–78.
Stearns, P. (2015). *Gender in world history.* Routledge.
UNP. (2020). Women Empowerment in the KSA. https://www.my.gov.sa/wps/portal/snp/careaboutyou/womenempowering
Walker, R., & Clokie, T. (2013). *Mentoring for the modern newsroom.* The Age of Mobile News/Jeanz 2013 Conference. http://researcharchive.wintec.ac.nz/3007/
Zilfi, M. C. (1997). *Women in the Ottoman Empire: Middle Eastern women in the early modern era* (Vol. 10). Brill.

CHAPTER 8

# Data and Statistics in Science News Reporting in the Arab World

People often say that a picture is worth a thousand words. This adage, used in multiple languages, refers to the idea that when looking at a photograph, the person not only sees the exact picture of a story, but also sees that the picture itself becomes unquestionable proof of the veracity of what has been said. For decades, reporters and staff writers in newspapers and magazines undertook their beats accompanied by photographers who over time became known as photojournalists. Their work was considered to be as important as that of those who wrote the story because they brought insightfulness and corroboration to the story (Silva & Eldridge, 2020).

With the emergence of videos and immediate news coverage, thanks to satellite television, the idea of the legitimising function of pictures became even more powerful in the public imagination and in the newsrooms. For decades, visual culture dominated the news agenda and awarded truthfulness to the millions of news stories in the world (Hamilton, 2020; Jenks, 2002). The screens of television networks reigned, together with the front pages of main newspapers and very graphic magazines such as LIFE, in setting the agenda and telling people what to talk and think about.

However, in the past few years, images have become less influential despite their growing presence on social media platforms. They simply do not have the same power, or at least the same capacity, to influence people as they once did. Yes, the world was still shocked by the gruesome and

© The Author(s), under exclusive license to Springer Nature Switzerland AG 2023
A. Alhuntushi, J. Lugo-Ocando, *Science Journalism in the Arab World*, Palgrave Studies in Journalism and the Global South, https://doi.org/10.1007/978-3-031-14252-9_8

tragic picture of Alan Kurdi, the three-year-old Syrian boy of Kurdish ethnic background, whose image made global headlines after he drowned on September 2, 2015, in the Mediterranean Sea, along with his mother and brother (Adler-Nissen et al., 2020; Mortensen & Trenz, 2016). However, beyond the initial shock and outrage, very little happened, and Europe continues to allow people looking for safety to die on its doorstep.

Today, what moves the world instead is something very different and, paradoxically, far more abstract: numbers, in the form of data. Indeed, from statistics that tell people about a particular issue or event to complex algorithms that define what news we read and what videos we watch, data is now at the centre of modern life and currently sets not only the agenda, but also the tone for what is being reported. Never has the news media been so attentive to what audiences want, or think they want, as now more than ever numbers have played such as important role in our daily lives (Anderson, 2018; Martinisi & Lugo-Ocando, 2020; O'Neil, 2016).

Indeed, as Eddy Borges-Rey (2016, 2017) has pointed out, the centrality of data in modern society is such that it has prompted a need to examine the increasingly powerful role of data brokers and their efforts to quantify the world. These brokers are journalist themselves, who in the quest for authorial control and efforts to award truthfulness and legitimacy to their accounts of the events and people they cover, are keen in using numbers (Martinisi & Lugo-Ocando, 2020). For journalists today, one number can be worth a million words.

On the other hand, statistics are important in science because that is how scientists quantify the relative probability that a statement is true. Statistics are needed because of the inductive nature of scientific reasoning. We use statistics to express the relative confidence that a particular idea is correct and also to constantly test the results of experiments and wider research efforts. That is also the reason why science tries to quantify things. The more the data, the better the reliability (Otto, 2016). It is inconceivable in this day and age that science could operate without numbers, nor could it communicate its ideas and results.

Therefore, for science journalists, numbers are central in substantiating the claims made by scientists and are also crucial in helping to explain the world to their audiences (Borges-Rey, 2016; Lugo-Ocando & Faria Brandão, 2016; Lugo-Ocando & Lawson, 2017). Numbers can be complex and abstract, but it is this data that captures context and meaning and summarises this in accessible data. It is numbers around probabilistic averages and frequency that tell people their potential health risks and infinite

## 8 DATA AND STATISTICS IN SCIENCE NEWS REPORTING IN THE ARAB WORLD

aggregates that remind all of us how big the universe is. Despite often being caricaturised as 'bland', 'cold' and 'boring' (Randall, 2000 [1996]), numbers are instead beautiful and comprehensive metaphors for things and trends that happen around us. They have become a key feature in journalism in general, and science reporting in particular, which is why this chapter discusses how those in the newsroom engage and use these numbers to report science news.

Therefore, this chapter examines the use of data and statistics in articulating science news by journalists in the Arab world. In so doing, it explores why and how data and statistics have become a significant part of journalism practice and particularly important in science journalism in the Arab world and the state it is in at the moment. The section assesses the current capabilities of journalism to identify key knowledge gaps in the area, while examining the nature of the news sources that provide this data and how journalists handle these sources in relation to the outputs that they produce.

The chapter, overall, suggests similarities in the existing gaps and causes of these deficits in the west but also some important distinctive contextual features. With regard to journalists' use of statistics to produce scientific news, we argue that the background and training of journalists play a crucial role in allowing reporters to examine and validate claims made on the basis of statistical information in the press. The chapter highlights that there is a lack of ability in terms of critically understanding and using these numbers to produce news stories. This trait was displayed by more than half of the Arab journalist interviewees. Several factors contribute to this lack of understanding, such as educational background and the scarcity of training courses. This also suggests a possible lack of interest in scientific stories by the newspapers as they tend to prioritise other news beats.

This section explores the relationship between journalism and information in relation to how statistics are used by news reporters to articulate their stories about science in terms of accessibility, engagement, accuracy and rigour. Consequently, this study involves looking at how journalists engage with, use and manage statistical data when gathering and producing science news. The study also aims to assess the current capabilities of journalism and to identify key knowledge gaps in the area. In addition, and in order to better understand how reporters engage with statistics, the research examines the nature of the news sources that provide this data and how journalists handle these sources in relation to the outputs that they produce.

It attempts to offer an explanatory theoretical framework and to set a design model that allows for the analysis of both process and outputs around uses and engagement with statistics in the production of science news, while permitting a more comprehensive understanding of the rationale, dynamics and interactions between journalists and data. The study adapted an interdisciplinary approach that triangulates a variety of methods in order to facilitate a much clearer and critical picture of this area.

## Studying News and Numbers

Let us start by highlighting that despite being a relatively recent area of study, the use of statistics by journalists has already received important attention from several scholars and experts (Alhumood et al., 2016; Al-Qafari, 2009; Brand, 2008; Curtin & Maier, 2001; Cushion & Lewis, 2017; Genis, 2001; Koetsenruijter, 2011; Lugo-Ocando & Lawson, 2017; Mahmood, 2008; Maier, 2002; Martinisi & Lugo-Ocando, 2020; Nguyen, 2017; Porlezza et al., 2012; Utts, 2010). The research agenda in this field has increasingly engaged with how reporters interact, embrace and use statistics and data and has also explored for what purpose they are often utilised by reporters in the articulation of news (Lawson, 2021; Tasseron & Lawson, 2020). However, these studies have mostly concentrated in the United States and Western Europe, where most of the studies have been carried out. Important gaps in relation to the so-called Global South remain unfulfilled, particularly around journalistic practices and numbers in illiberal societies in the Arab world.

Most researchers tend to agree that numbers are used fundamentally to produce, contextualise and/or substantiate the facts and context in a news story (Brand, 2008; Lawson, 2021; Lugo-Ocando & Lawson, 2017). These authors also suggest that reporters tend to be over-reliant on official sources to produce news stories while lacking the capabilities to engage critically with these numbers, which tend to remain uncontested. Their work shows that the background and training of journalists play a crucial role in allowing reporters to examine and validate claims made on the basis of statistical information in the press.

Robert Brand's (2008) own study in South Africa concluded that journalists in general have inadequate skills in arithmetic when dealing with quantitative elements in news reports, which translates into a high rate of numerical errors. In other words, the lack of training and skills is a global issue in this field and in places such as the United States only a fifth of the journalism educational programmes actually require their students to undertake statistics, despite being a mandatory subject by the accreditation awarded by the Association for Education in Journalism and Mass Communication to colleges that teach journalism (Martin, 2016). The situation is similar in other countries, where only a few university media and journalism programmes have academic courses in statistics and almost none of them meet the traditional standards for such courses or are actually tailored to the specific needs of news reporting.

Education and training, or the lack of it, is in fact one of the most pressing issues in relation to the limitations and problems that reporters face when engaging and using numbers in their daily work. Central to this problem is a generalised animadversion among professional reporters and journalism students to dealing with numbers and maths. Curtin and Maier (2001), who have examined how journalists deal with numbers in the news, pointed out in their own study how maths anxiety, in its different forms, causes many journalists to have considerable dissimilarities when dealing with numbers, making some more likely than others to critically engage with them. Maier highlights the failure of many journalists to pay attention to, and exercise care with, numbers that they regularly employ in different sections of their work (2002, p. 58). Others suggest that journalists need direction and assistance in how to understand and illustrate statistics, so they can refrain from making mistakes in calculating numbers (Utts, 2010).

Another important observation, this time made by Genis in a study about the important ability of journalists to work with numbers, pinpoints the significance of the ability of journalists to change and simplify numbers in their news stories to make them understood by their readers (2001, p. 32). This author also pointed out the general worry concerning journalists' poor skills, by stating that experienced journalists, academics in the communications field, mathematicians and statisticians are either 'taken aback' by the inability of journalists to do even the most basic calculations or 'horrified' by the 'amount of numeric incompetence' in newsrooms. In this sense, Frank Swain, National Coordinator for Science Training for Journalists, pointed out in his final report for the Royal Statistical Society that a lack of understanding of numbers and statistics is key to many of the common errors in reporting science (Harrison, 2014, p. 2). This view is not an isolated one and there is rather a wide and sustained concern among many scientific institutions around the limited capabilities within professional mainstream journalism to engage with statistics.

The other area singled out by the body of scholarly research is in relation to the use itself that journalists make of statistics. In her study, Brandao (2016) found that journalists lean towards using statistics mostly to preserve the objectivity and reinforce the legitimacy and autonomy/authority of their own work; something that Tuchman (1972) addressed when referring to professional values associated with news people such as 'objectivity', which are used as mechanisms to achieve legitimacy in the newsroom. Her research suggests that statistics are often used as a legitimising tool, although few reporters are familiar with scientific mathematical language.

Despite all these contributions, the studies centred on this issue are still limited, while those focusing on Arab journalism and science statistics are almost non-existent. Hence, it is possible to identify an important knowledge gap regarding how Arab journalists engage with statistics when producing science news. It is this particular sense of 'newness' of this data-driven epistemology of journalism that offers us the opportunity to produce a more comprehensive and de-westernised understanding of journalism. This, by means of an innovative journalism studies research agenda that examines how reporters interact, embrace and use data in general (Borges-Rey, 2016; S. C. Lewis & Westlund, 2015; Nguyen & Lugo-Ocando, 2016) within different contexts and cultures.

Numbers continue to be, in science and public discourse, the most indivisible and pure element of absolute and universal truth as it is anchored to mathematical reasoning. No other branch of science can make this claim. So far, most studies around the use of statistics and data in journalism have concentrated in the United States and Western Europe, where most of the fieldwork has been carried out. This, despite significant and emerging contributions in relation to exploring the work of news reporters in relation to data in many places of the so-called Global South (Borges-Rey et al., 2018; N. P. Lewis & Nashmi, 2019; Mutsvairo, 2019). Nevertheless, there continue to be important gaps in relation to the so-called Global South. Particularly around non-liberal societies where journalism is also practised, such as the Arab world at large and specifically in relation to science journalism where there is very little-to-no advanced research around these topics.

All in all, statistics have become an important part of the world and a universal feature of daily life (Nguyen & Lugo-Ocando, 2016). They play a significant role in delivering information in a way that helps the public to understand social issues (Dorling & Simpson, 1999; Fioramonti, 2013,

2014) while facilitating scrutiny and critical examination of public policy and governance in general. Many decisions in the world today are based on, underpinned by and/or justified with statistics, including individual and collective issues that affect our lives, such as equality, governance and policymaking, among others (Spirer & Spirer, 1998, p. 3).

Statistics have become a key component of daily news and they are particularly relevant to science news. This is even more the case at a time when the so-called big data society is becoming widespread. According to Zillmann and Brosius (2012), at least 44% of news includes some sort of numbers. In news beats such as science, news reporters rely on statistics to produce, contextualise and/or substantiate their stories and they play a fundamental role in reinforcing the accuracy of science stories; something that is directly related to the quality of the news.

## Objective Numbers

In science news, numbers also underpin the notion of objectivity in the making of news as they summarise and contextualise reality in qualitative terms. This is of particular importance at times in which we increasingly face a mathematised understanding of society in which one has to 'travel mathematical roads in order to arrive at objectivity in the real world' (Davis & Hersh, 2005, p. 276). Those who embrace this view have argued that an understanding of statistics can account for more reliable and trustworthy news because numbers have an important role in making news more credible and evidence based (Koetsenruijter, 2011; Livingston & Voakes, 2011).

Having said that, most research so far has suggested that an inappropriate use or misinterpretation of these numbers often occurs in the news, something that has received ample attention from scholars. According to statistics professor at the University of California, Irvine, Jessica Utts (2010), misleading science reporting of statistical results can easily be found, and in fact tends to be widespread. She refers as an example in the 2008 study, titled 'You Are What Your Mother Eats', which asserted that pregnant mothers who eat cereal for breakfast are more likely to have boys than pregnant mothers who do not. This was refuted by a group of experts the following year in their own analysis, which showed that this result was almost certainly a false positive. However, she added, this did not stop the study from gaining widespread media attention and people making badly substantiated assumptions.

This is not a new problem and was observed early in the twentieth century by people such as Walter Lippman and H.G. Wells who argued for journalists to engage more comprehensively with statistical sciences (Lugo-Ocando, 2017; Riccio, 1994; R. Seyb, 2015; R. P. Seyb, 2015). Lippmann was particularly keen in advocating for journalists to engage more with statistics as a means of making news reporting more scientific. However, it was perhaps Philip Meyer (1989, 2002) who would arguably make the strongest call for reporters to embrace numbers with his efforts to introduce social science methods and computer-assisted reporting into journalism classrooms and newsrooms.

Meyer has emphasised that journalists should be aware of the importance of understanding numbers: 'write with words, but we must learn to read in numbers' (Meyer, 2002, p. 145). For him, numerical competence is a necessary quality of journalism. Indeed, according to the Poynter Institute in the United States, numeracy is one of ten fundamental abilities for journalists, and on goes to point out that 'without math skills, journalists are certain to fall short in their quest for accuracy. And if they keep their jobs, their numerical incompetence will only undermine the already shaky credibility of the news organizations for which they work' (Maier, 2003, p. 921).

Hough observed that many journalists did not understand the meaning of numbers as 'too many people today, including journalists, are innumerate—they lack an understanding of what numbers mean', a situation that generally persists today (Hough, 1995, p. 377). To explore this issue, Kilpatrick (1999) collected a wide range of examples of errors containing particularly mathematical errors that were published in newspapers. He found several cases in which the misuse or mistake was so basic that one could easily conclude that many journalists cannot even deal with school-grade elemental mathematics.

In addition, it has been suggested that 'many journalists have difficulties with interpreting the statistics' and that they did not understand 'all of the statistical tests presented and whether they were appropriately applied' (Genis, 2001, p. 13). Several scholars have pointed to three main aspects in which most mistakes are made in the newsroom. These include validity, reliability and interpretation (Lugo-Ocando, 2017; Martinisi & Lugo-Ocando, 2020), which are described as the key problems of statistical engagement in journalism practice. In the first instance, journalists often are unable to discern when the information contained in a number is truly representative of the phenomenon observed. A classic example is when reporters refer to numbers that highlight the association between marriage and poverty and assume that this means that being married reduces poverty, which of course is not the case. The second instance has to do with being unable to determine when a particular statistical test, or the conditions in which it was performed, confer the necessary rigour. Countless times, reporters have included surveys or polls in which the sample does not have adequate parameters or is unrepresentative of the larger universe. The third is perhaps the most common, in which reporters simply misinterpreted a particular dataset or meaning of a number.

Having said that, that majority of journalists are in fact capable of handling the kinds of elementary calculations demanded for most day-to-day reporting, even though in one study about one-in-six news editorial staff failed to answer most of the mathematical questions in a test-survey (Curtin & Maier, 2001). As Cohn (1989) pointed out almost three decades ago, journalists' misunderstanding and misuse of statistics continues to lead them to repeatedly provide poor reports, as they do not consider some statistics or 'get bamboozled by phoney or unreliable numbers'.

It is very clear that the future of journalism will depend increasingly in the ability of a world dominated by data and numbers (Anderson, 2018; Martinisi & Lugo-Ocando, 2020). In this respect, Shirky (2014) advises journalists that in order to save their jobs and their profession, they should 'get good with numbers':

> The old 'story accompanied by a chart' was merely data next to journalism; increasingly, the data is the journalism [...] Learning to code is the gold standard, but even taking an online class in statistics and getting good at Google spreadsheets will help. Anything you can do to make yourself more familiar with finding, understanding, and presenting data will set you apart from people you'll be competing with, whether to keep your current job or get a new one.

The journalist's job is not to learn and calculate complex things but instead to deal with already processed data from other sources. Thus, they need a basic level of statistical reasoning to enable them to constantly understand and be able to question the data. According to Potter (2010), 'you don't need to be a nerd to improve your reporting of news with numbers, you just need to remember one basic journalistic question: does this make sense?'. Journalists do not need a set of skills to create or calculate their own data, 'they need instead to use logical, valid reasoning and journalistic scepticism to (a) find and acquire data, (b) explore and evaluate their real meaning in context, (c) investigate non-numerical factors shaping them, and (d) report them in a balanced, fair, accurate, accessible and engaging manner, none of which requires any special mathematical skills' (Nguyen & Lugo-Ocando, 2015, p. 5).

Journalists reporting science must learn and use statistics comprehensively for two reasons. The first is the emergence of the big data community, which means that daily news work itself is increasingly dependent on 'number-crunching'. The second is that journalism is operating in an increasingly chaotic world of 'lies, damn lies and statistics' (Nguyen & Lugo-Ocando, 2015, p. 6). However, to do so they also need education and training as it could help them acquire basic statistics and statistics-related capabilities. Although it is difficult to find journalism programmes in universities that have statistics courses, institutions in some countries do make their journalism students engage with statistics in a comprehensive manner (Nguyen & Lugo-Ocando, 2015; Wilby, 2007).

One example is the Indiana University Bloomington, which in 1999 realised that their students were not using numbers in their reporting, even though they were required to include statistics. Following on from that concern, the Department of Mathematics and the National Science Foundation created a mathematics course specifically for journalism (Livingston & Voakes, 2011). In the United Kingdom, numeracy is a suggested skill of the professional accreditation bodies such as the Broadcast Journalism Training Council and the National Council for the Training of Journalists (Harrison, 2014), but only a handful of HE institutions in that country actually make any provision to fulfil this requirement. In the United States, statistical training in journalism education is less common. The Accreditation Council on Education in Journalism and Mass Communication has for some time required affiliated journalism schools to 'apply basic numerical and statistical concepts' in its 13 essential values and capabilities. However, as a study has shown, there are few provisions across the United States that actually do so (Martin, 2016; Nguyen & Lugo-Ocando, 2015).

In the case of the Arab region, the lack of statistics education among journalists has also been noted by scholars (F. Alaqil & Lugo-Ocando, 2021; Alhumood et al., 2016; Ibnrubbian, 2016). For instance, Alheezan (2007) conducted a study on media education in Saudi Arabia and found that statistics is taught in just one media school, which can help explain the lack of skills in dealing with statistical information within the profession. Furthermore, the importance of statistics is often ignored among journalists themselves, who did not see it as a priority in their work. According to El-Nawawy (2007), news practitioners and educators do not consider the ability to deal with statistics important, and they do not see it as part of their main job.

All this happens despite efforts to raise the awareness of the importance of teaching statistics in media schools in places such as Saudi Arabia, which have started to teach statistics as part of their journalism and media programmes (F. A. Alaqil & Lugo-Ocando, 2019; F. Alaqil & Lugo-Ocando, 2021). These efforts come from both an increasing awareness of, and curricular review debates taking place, within national HE institutions and thanks to external demands placed by many universities in the Arab world looking for international accreditation. Indeed, the decision of the Department of Mass Communication of the College of Arts and Sciences at Qatar University, led by then Professor Saadia Izzeldin Malik to seek accreditation of the Association for Education in Journalism and Mass Communication, meant complying with its requirements. Among them, to dedicate a portion of the teaching to liberal arts and include statistics and numeracy as part of the curriculum. Once this was achieved, other institutions in the region followed suit, including University of Sharjah, Zayed University and the American University in Dubai, all three based in the United Arabs Emirates. Having said that, the lack of more comprehensive provision for the teaching of statistics in the region persists.

The knowledge deficit among reporters in their ability to engage with and use statistics can be linked not only to the inability of journalists to deal with numbers, but also to the generally poor state of statistics and mathematical literacy education in the Arab region in general. In 2015, the Programme for International Student Assessment (2015) carried out a study about the mathematical skills of 15-year-olds around the world. Some Arab countries—such as Qatar, Lebanon, United Arab Emirates, Tunisia, Algeria and Jordan—were found to be at the bottom of the list in terms of mathematics performance (out of 70 Organisation for Economic Co-operation and Development [OECD] countries) (Table 8.1).

The same assessment found that all these Arab countries performed below the OECD average, ranking between 427 and 367 points (scored). They also performed below the average for science (between 437 and 386 points (scored)) and reading (between 434 and 361 points (scored)). Moreover, the situation is deteriorating, as the PISA assessment showed that the mathematics performance of Arab students in 2015 was worse than in 2012, with most Arab countries obtaining lower rankings than

**Table 8.1** Mathematics performance among 15-year-olds in some Arab countries in 2015

| Country | Rank | Score |
|---|---|---|
| Tunisia | 67 | 367 |
| Jordan | 64 | 380 |
| Lebanon | 60 | 396 |
| Qatar | 58 | 402 |
| United Arab Emirates | 47 | 427 |

before—only Qatar scored better. A lower numeracy skill is a problem that is also linked to other challenges in relation to science journalism. As most studies have shown, low numeracy skills are linked to lower scores in natural sciences at the schooling levels. This in turn has an impact on the degree of awareness with STEM subjects in general among the public and, as the research shows, this correlates with the level of engagement with science news across national audiences (Brossard & Scheufele, 2013; Majetic & Pellegrino, 2014; McCallie et al., 2009).

## SCIENCE AND STATISTICS IN THE NEWS

There are three main problems relating to the use of statistics that we can find when analysing news coverage of science. These issues faced by reporters can be summarised in problems relating to the validity, reliability and interpretation of the numbers. In addition, Arab journalists confront other challenges that emerge from factors linked to political and sociological contexts in which science is communicated. The prevalent news cultures in Arab countries and the way in which journalists are trained and prepared to deal with statistics, are, in many cases, an obstacle to a more comprehensive debate around science.

To this we can also add the distinctive technical languages and organisational dynamics in which scientists and reporters operate. Scientists and journalists speak different languages, not only because they have a different educational and professional background but also because they perform within organisational cultures that have different objectives. Hence, when dealing with numbers the interpretation serves different goals. For example, while a scientist describing findings as 'significant' is referring to its statistical significance, a journalist—on the other hand—might assume the result is significant for the population out there (Genis, 2001, p. 13).

In exploring our own data, we found some additional issues relating to science news reporting and numbers. Our data indicate, for example, that nearly 26% of the sources which provide statistical data were unknown. This suggests that some statistical data cited in science news are lifted and pasted without further scrutiny from the press releases of web pages. This ratio also threatens the credibility of statistics in the public mind as previous research has shown that anonymous sources tend to have a negative impact on readers' perceptions of credibility. To be sure, Sternadori and Thorson suggest that 'it is also possible that the use of anonymous sources without sufficient explanation is interpreted by readers as a sign of journalistic incompetence, which in source credibility theory is another reason to assign lower credibility to a source' (Sternadori & Thorson, 2009, p. 63).

## On Anonymous Sources

However, in the MENA region, the use of anonymous sources is rare given the levels of external editorial control over the press, which makes access to publication subject to scrutiny. One assumes therefore that if a source identity or origin is not disclosed in the story it is because the information originates from the government itself. In other parts of the world, reporters tend to be reluctant nowadays to include an anonymous source unless there is a reason for it that is not necessarily linked to disclosing a wrongdoing—as was the case of the Watergate scandal in the United States. Instead, it is much more likely that if and when reporters publish stories containing numbers without a clearly identified source, it would be more likely to do with the fact that the story emanated from a press release from an official department.

Our interviewees explained that, in addition, they may fail to cite the sources of number for several reasons, including a simple matter of forgetfulness,

> *I cannot recall a specific case where I have done this but it is very likely that at one point, I forgot to cite the source of a particular statistics. It might have been because I forgot to do it or simply because it was such an obvious number (…) I mean why would you source the number of people living in a country?* [INT11]

Other journalists did highlight that sometimes the number 'came in a press release and they just published it without the source because the story itself came in that press release' [INT14].

The reason we are highlighting this is because it denotes the fact that journalists, who see these numbers as facts, use them in their stories without proper scrutiny. At times, this happens because they accept them without examining the origin, history and context of the data.

Having said that, it is equally important to highlight that there is a fair degree of good practices across the region. In our sample of newspapers, 74% of the sources of statistics were wholly transparent in the sense that they clearly specified from where the data originated. This is a fairly good percentage considering the limitations of access to sources and the scarcity of scientific journalists in Arab newspapers (Table 8.2).

Another important aspect that was highlighted by observing the sample is the nature and type of statistics used in science journalism. Accordingly, inferential statistics were used more often than descriptive statistics—with 450 and 242 articles, respectively—in the stories reporting science. This marks a contrast to other studies in areas such as crime, which found that in that newsbeat, descriptive statistics were more predominant (Lugo-Ocando, 2017; Martinisi & Lugo-Ocando, 2020). There are a series of reasons for this, including the nature of the data that is managed in science and the fact that health sciences are, in general, the most frequent stories covered in the news media.

It is important to highlight this, as the nature of the statistics used reflects the nature itself of the stories and also the way audiences might relate to them. In stories about health, which by far are the most present in science coverage in MENA, inferential statistics will mostly refer to probability, while descriptive data will signal frequency. Hence, a story about cancer is really about what are the chances that the reader or a close relative will suffer from it while a story about astronomy would more likely be about the number of exoplanets in a galaxy.

The findings also underpin that there is a relation between the reliability of sources and geographical coverage (international versus national

**Table 8.2** Reliability of cited sources

|  |  | *Frequency* | *Per cent* | *Valid per cent* | *Cumulative per cent* |
|---|---|---|---|---|---|
| Valid | Yes | 692 | 74.2 | 74.2 | 74.2 |
|  | No | 240 | 25.8 | 25.8 | 100.0 |
|  | Total | 932 | 100.0 | 100.0 |  |

Source: Authors' data

stories). It showed that the sources of statistics were identified more often in covering international news science stories than in covering national news (with 370 articles compared to 322, respectively). On the other hand, there was a negative correlation between the reliability of an article and its geographical coverage (corr = -0.169); this indicated that reliable sources for statistics were used more frequently in the coverage of international science news (one can assume produced by international news agencies) than in national science news (mostly produced by local journalists and derived from press releases). That the use of statistical sources in international science news is presented more transparently than in local science news suggests the difficulty journalists in Arab countries face in accessing the best quality of statistical data.

In light of this, we carried out a closer reading of news articles in several newspapers in the region and found that many of the local stories lag behind in terms of incorporating numbers and data in relation to news stories produced by international news agencies. In other words, it is far more likely to find statistics well sourced in a news piece produced by AFP or Reuters—two of the most used news agencies in the region—than in news stories produced by local journalists in the MENA region. The reasons for this vary from country to country and from newsroom to newsroom, but it is sufficient to say that it comes down to pressures of time, existing capabilities among journalists and access to sources.

## CONCLUSION

In this chapter, we have tried to make the point that journalists in the MENA region engage with and use statistics to articulate science news in the Arab media in ways that are both similar to other parts of the world and at the same time distinctive in some ways. In fact, the data indicate that, contrary to common assumptions that claim exceptionalism in the MENA region in terms of challenges and issues faced by reporters when using data and statistics to report science—due to assumptions around culture, politics and religion—these are not necessarily true in the cases examined here. Instead, what we found is that the flaws and issues are similar to those faced by practitioners in other parts of the world and that they come down to the lack of ability to engage effectively and comprehensively with data and statistics. This lack of capabilities is concerning on the one hand but promising on the other. It is concerning because this means that there are important gaps that need to be urgently filled. It is promising because underpinning and improving capabilities is a variable that can be controlled and addressed in the region.

From the evidence presented here, we can also reiterate that there is, however, a long road ahead. Particularly as we see that the lack of capabilities relates not only to education and training but also to the need for the news media to allow the creation of spaces and time for reporters to specialise in science while providing opportunities to engage properly with data. This last point, of course, does not depend uniquely upon the news media outlets, but also on a change in the MENA countries in ways that access to data and statistics becomes more feasible for reporters. The good news is that the organisational culture of research centres and universities where science takes place is much more open and transparent than in other institutions in MENA. There is already a culture in the scientific world that requires results and experiments to be accountable and that researchers are expected to publish in peer-reviewed international journals that demand access to the quantitative data in order to guarantee replicability of the results.

What can the reporters do with that data? That is another completely different matter. Yes, their work has to have rigour and be accurate in representing the work and outcomes of scientists. However, beyond that, journalists need to use this data to construct stories that contain narratives that are appealing and relevant to audiences. They also need to ensure their job is not only about disseminating science but also bringing science into the public debate. This translates in recognising that numbers and data have a meaning in the context of society, even when they are reflecting the natural world. Here, journalists have lots of agency because they can contextualise science in the daily lives of people. In so doing, the numbers became a powerful tool to highlight issues in society such as cancer, pollution, mental health and others and the risk for the whole of the community.

Numbers themselves are to a degree neutral and objective, despite being human objects that reflect socially constructed reality. The problem instead is about who produces and disseminates the numbers for the public. Journalists ought to present statistics in an accessible manner and clearly explained within a context to increase the public's understanding, especially as 'the public is susceptible to political and commercial manipulation of their anxieties and hopes, which undermines the goals of informed consent and shared decision-making' (Gigerenzer et al., 2007, p. 53).

The challenge in MENA is even bigger now because of the fact that society is becoming datafied. In the past few years, the numbers have become bigger. Data are now everywhere and have a powerful presence in the way the natural world today is described to us. As Beer argues, 'big data has the effect of making up data and as such, is powerful in framing our understanding of those data and the possibilities that they afford' (2016, p. 1). In science, data can be small, such as the number of patients who suffer from a very rare disease or very big data, such as the numbers of galaxies in the universe. However, in the end, it is not size that matters but the ability of reporters to understand it, and be able to explain it to their audiences in a way that makes sense and helps bring accountability to science while making it interesting and relevant to all.

## Bibliography

Adler-Nissen, R., Andersen, K. E., & Hansen, L. (2020). Images, emotions, and international politics: The death of Alan Kurdi. *Review of International Studies, 46*(1), 75–95.

Alaqil, F., & Lugo-Ocando, J. (2021). Using statistics in business and financial news in the Arabian Gulf: Between normative journalistic professional aspirations and 'real' practice. *Journalism Practice*, 1–24. https://doi.org/10.1080/17512786.2021.1930572

Alaqil, F. A., & Lugo-Ocando, J. (2019). Challenges and opportunities for teaching data and statistics within journalism education in Saudi Arabia: Fostering new capabilities in the region. *Journalism Education, 8*(2), 55–66.

Alheezan, M. (2007). Teaching media in the Saudi and American universities. *Arabic Journal for Media and Communication, 2*, 187–230.

Alhumood, A., Shami, A., & Safia, A. (2016). *Media framing of the national economic projects in the Arab World.* Seventh Annual Forum of the Saudi Association for Media and Communication: The Media and the Economy—Integration Roles in the Service of Development, 11–12 April 2016, Riyadh.

Al-Qafari, A. (2009). *Science media in Saudi journalism.* King Abdul-Aziz City for Science and Technology (KACST).

Anderson, C. (2018). *Apostles of certainty: Data journalism and the politics of doubt.* Oxford University Press.

Beer, D. G. (2016). How should we do the history of big data? *Big Data & Society, 3*(1), 1–10.

Borges-Rey, E. (2016). Unravelling Data Journalism: A study of data journalism practice in British newsrooms. *Journalism Practice, 10*(7), 833–843.

Borges-Rey, Eddy L. (2017). Data literacy and citizenship: Understanding 'big Data' to boost teaching and learning in science and mathematics." In Handbook of research on driving STEM learning with educational technologies, pp. 65–79. Hershey, Pennsylvania: IGI Global.

Borges-Rey, E., Heravi, B., & Uskali, T. (2018). Periodismo de datos iberoamericano: Desarrollo, contestación y cambio social. Presentación. *La Revista ICONO 14: Revista de Comuncacion y Tecnologias Emergentes, 16*(2), 1–13.

Brand, R. (2008). The numbers game: A case study of mathematical literacy at a South African newspaper. *Communication: South African Journal for Communication Theory and Research, 34*(2), 210–221.

Brandao, R. (2016). *Study shows: How statistics are used to articulate and shape discourses of science in the newsroom.* University of Sheffield.

Brossard, D., & Scheufele, D. A. (2013). Science, new media, and the public. *Science, 339*(6115), 40–41.

Cohn, V. (1989). *News & numbers: A guide to reporting statistical claims and controversies in health and other fields.* Iowa State University Press.

Curtin, P. A., & Maier, S. R. (2001). Numbers in the newsroom: A qualitative examination of a quantitative challenge. *Journalism & Mass Communication Quarterly, 78*(4), 720–738.

Cushion, S., & Lewis, J. (2017). Impartiality, statistical tit-for-tats and the construction of balance: UK television news reporting of the 2016 EU referendum campaign. *European Journal of Communication, 32*(3), 208–223. https://doi.org/10.1177/0267323117695736

Davis, P., & Hersh, R. (2005). *Descartes' dream: The world according to mathematics.* Courier Corporation.

Dorling, D., & Simpson, S. (1999). *Statistics in society: The arithmetic of politics.* .

El-Nawawy, M. (2007). Between the newsroom and the classroom: Education standards and practices for print journalism in Egypt and Jordan. *International Communication Gazette, 69*(1), 69–90.

Fioramonti, L. (2013). *Gross domestic problem: The politics behind the world's most powerful number.* Zed Books Ltd.

Fioramonti, L. (2014). *How numbers rule the world: The use and abuse of statistics in global politics.* Zed Books Ltd.

Genis, A. (2001). *Numbers count: The importance of numeracy for journalists.* Stellenbosch University.

Gigerenzer, G., Gaissmaier, W., Kurz-Milcke, E., Schwartz, L., & Woloshin, S. (2007). Helping doctors and patients make sense of health statistics. *Psychological Science in the Public Interest, 8*(2), 53–96.

Hamilton, J. F. (2020). Drone journalism as visual aggregation: Toward a critical history. *Media and Communication, 8*(3), 64–74.

Harrison, S. (2014). History of numeracy education and training for print journalists in England. *Numeracy: Advancing Education in Quantitative Literacy, 7*(2), 2.

Hough, G. (1995). *News writing* (Vol. 5, 5th ed.). Houghton Mifflin.

Ibnrubbian, A. (2016). *Economic media in the Kingdom of Saudi Arabia: The reality and development opportunities.* Seventh Annual Forum of the Saudi Association for Media and Communication: The Media and the Economy—Integration Roles in the Service of Development, 11–12 April 2016, Riyadh.

Jenks, C. (2002). *Visual culture.* Routledge.

Kilpatrick, J. (1999). *Números e escritores não somam.* Barganca: Fundação Calouste Gulbenkian.

Koetsenruijter, A. W. M. (2011). Using numbers in news increases story credibility. *Newspaper Research Journal, 32*(2), 74–82.

Lawson, B. (2021). Hiding behind databases, institutions and actors: How journalists use statistics in reporting humanitarian crises. *Journalism Practice,* 1–21.

Lewis, N. P., & Nashmi, E. A. (2019). Data journalism in the Arab region: Role conflict exposed. *Digital Journalism, 7*(9), 1200–1214.

Lewis, S. C., & Westlund, O. (2015). Big data and journalism: Epistemology, expertise, economics, and ethics. *Digital Journalism, 3*(3), 447–466.

Livingston, C., & Voakes, P. (2011). *Working with numbers and statistics: A handbook for journalists.* Routledge.

Lugo-Ocando, J. (2017). *Crime statistics in the news: Journalism, numbers and social deviation.* Palgrave Macmillan.

Lugo-Ocando, J., & Faria Brandão, R. (2016). STABBING NEWS: Articulating crime statistics in the newsroom. *Journalism Practice, 10*(6), 715–729.

Lugo-Ocando, J., & Lawson, B. (2017). Poor numbers, poor news: The ideology of poverty statistics in the media. In A. Nguyen (Ed.), *News, Numbers and Public Opinion in a Data-Driven World.* Bloomsbury Publishing Inc.

Mahmood, S. (2008). *Scientific media.* Alfagar Publishing.

Maier, S. (2002). Numbers in the news: A mathematics audit of a daily newspaper. *Journalism Studies, 3*(4), 507–519.

Maier, S. (2003). Numeracy in the newsroom: A case study of mathematical competence and confidence. *Journalism & Mass Communication Quarterly, 80*(4), 921–936.

Majetic, C., & Pellegrino, C. (2014). When science and information literacy meet: An approach to exploring the sources of science news with non-science majors. *College Teaching, 62*(3), 107–112.

Martin, J. (2016). A census of statistics requirements at US journalism programs and a model for a 'statistics for journalism' course. *Journalism & Mass Communication Educator, 72*(4), 461–479.

Martinisi, A., & Lugo-Ocando, J. A. (2020). *Statistics and the quest for quality journalism: A study in quantitative reporting.* Anthem Press.

McCallie, E., Bell, L., Lohwater, T., Falk, J. H., Lehr, J. L., Lewenstein, B. V., Needham, C., & Wiehe, B. (2009). *Many experts, many audiences: Public engagement with science and informal science education.* A CAISE Inquiry

Group Report. https://digitalcommons.calpoly.edu/cgi/viewcontent.cgi?article=1011&context=eth_fac

Meyer, P. (1989). Precision journalism and the 1988 US elections. *International Journal of Public Opinion Research, 1*(3), 195–205.

Meyer, P. (2002). *Precision journalism: A reporter's introduction to social science methods.* Rowman & Littlefield.

Mortensen, M., & Trenz, H.-J. (2016). Media morality and visual icons in the age of social media: Alan Kurdi and the emergence of an impromptu public of moral spectatorship. *Javnost-The Public, 23*(4), 343–362.

Mutsvairo, B. (2019). Challenges facing development of data journalism in non-western societies. *Digital Journalism, 7*(9), 1289–1294.

Nguyen, A. (2017). *News, numbers and public opinion in a data-driven world.* Bloomsbury Publishing.

Nguyen, A., & Lugo-Ocando, J. (2015). Introduction: The state of statistics in journalism and journalism education–issues and debates. *Journalism, 1*(14), 1464884915593234.

Nguyen, A., & Lugo-Ocando, J. (2016). The state of data and statistics in journalism and journalism education: Issues and debates. *Journalism, 17*(1), 3–17.

O'Neil, C. (2016). *Weapons of math destruction: How big data increases inequality and threatens democracy.* Broadway Books.

Otto, S. L. (2016). *The war on Science: Who's waging it, why it matters, what we can do about it.* .

Porlezza, C., Maier, S., & Russ-Mohl, S. (2012). News accuracy in Switzerland and Italy: A transatlantic comparison with the US press. *Journalism Practice, 6*(4), 530–546.

Potter, D. (2010). *News with numbers.*

Randall, D. (2000). *The universal journalist.* Pluto Press.

Riccio, B. D. (1994). *Walter Lippmann: Odyssey of a liberal.* Transaction Publishers.

Seyb, R. (2015). Trouble with the statistical curve: Walter Lippmann's Blending of History and Social Science during Franklin Roosevelt's First Term. *American Journalism, 32*(2), 138–160.

Seyb, R. P. (2015). What Walter Saw: Walter Lippmann, The New York world, and scientific advocacy as an alternative to the news-opinion dichotomy. *Journalism History, 41*(2), 58.

Shirky, C. (2014). Last call: The end of the printed newspaper. *Medium. Com,* August, 21.

Silva, M. F., & Eldridge, S. A. (2020). *The ethics of photojournalism in the digital age.* Routledge.

Spirer, H., & Spirer, L. (1998). *Misused statistics.* CRC Press.

Sternadori, M., & Thorson, E. (2009). Anonymous sources harm credibility of all stories. *Newspaper Research Journal*, *30*(4), 54–66.

Tasseron, M., & Lawson, B. T. (2020). Legitimizing military action through statistics and discourse in the 2014 IDF assault on Gaza. *Media, War & Conflict*, 1750635220917692.

Tuchman, G. (1972). Objectivity as strategic ritual: An examination of newsmen's notions of objectivity. *American Journal of Sociology*, *77*(4), 660–679.

Utts, J. (2010). *Unintentional lies in the media: Don't blame journalists for what we don't teach*. Proceedings of the Eighth International Conference on Teaching Statistics.

Wilby, P. (2007). Damn journalists and statistics. *The Guardian*.

Zillmann, D., & Brosius, H.-B. (2012). *Exemplification in communication: The influence of case reports on the perception of issues*. Routledge.

CHAPTER 9

# Science News Audiences in the Middle East

Communicating science to the general public has always been a challenge because of a variety of reasons (Ashwell, 2016; Humm et al., 2020; Shapin, 2020). However, paramount among them is the ability (or inability) to connect to a public that in many cases lacks the knowledge to understand basic principles of science or is simply not interested enough in science itself so as to engage routinely with these types of news stories. Many cannot seem to find a direct link to what is being said about science in the news and their daily lives (Nguyen & McIlwaine, 2011), while scientists tend to use professional and technical language that people find at times inexpugnable and convoluted (Cook et al., 2004; Humm et al., 2020; Rakedzon et al., 2017).

Consequently, and despite tremendous efforts by officials and the scientific community, it has been a bumpy and difficult ride for those trying to deliver science to the public. This was made painfully evident during the COVID-19 pandemic as science became increasingly more politicised and under attack in many ways because people found it difficult to relate to. Central to this problem are the different conceptions that scientists and journalists have in relation to what aspects of and how science needs to be communicated to the public. For scientists, rigour and accuracy are paramount and therefore what is said to the public needs to be a mirror-image version of the process they undertake in the lab and an exact account of the results that led to the discovery or identifying the issue. For

© The Author(s), under exclusive license to Springer Nature Switzerland AG 2023
A. Alhuntushi, J. Lugo-Ocando, *Science Journalism in the Arab World*, Palgrave Studies in Journalism and the Global South, https://doi.org/10.1007/978-3-031-14252-9_9

journalists, instead, it is about storytelling derived from facts in which science is narrativised to make it appealing, relevant and fundamentally engaging.

It is also the case that journalists and scientists, in many instances, do not understand each other's motives and aims, nor do they understand the dynamics that determine what they do or how they do it. Scientists work in terms of months, years and even decades while for journalists their time frames are often the very same day—if not coming hours—especially if they want to avoid an impossible deadline. Many scientists still do not see it as a priority for them to communicate their work to the general public and instead restrict themselves to publishing in peer-review journals or presenting academic papers to their peers at conferences. Their source of income, ability to get promoted and access to resources derives not from the general public but from very small and selected groups of experts who determine who can get a research grant and funding, who gets hired, promoted and secures tenure and, ultimately, who is dismissed.

For journalists, on the other hand, the public is the leitmotif of their daily routines. Without an audience, there is no reason to write or produce a story. Consequently, journalists and scientists seem to live in separate worlds. Their commitment and level of engagement with the public is very different and has been so for most of the history of modern news reporting and science. It is only recently, perhaps in the past few decades, that there has been a truly coordinated effort to professionalise science communication and some real attempts made to bring both worldviews closer (Dunwoody, 2014; Friedman et al., 1986; Maillé et al., 2010; Ransohoff & Ransohoff, 2001).

## Normative Aspiration

These efforts have not been homogenous or have always steered towards the same direction. This is because the science community has broadly assumed that because there is a knowledge gap, what is really needed is science and experts able to speak to the public clearly and with accuracy. Journalists, on the other hand, have other priorities including reaching the widest audience possible so as to make their own workplaces economically viable. All this combined with a normative aspiration of being a watchdog to those in power, including scientists. Accordingly, most reporters understand that the public needs news not only to make science appealing and relevant but also accountable to the public.

All these challenges have suddenly become even harder to sort out as additional complexity has been added in the field while the media and societal landscapes evolved into uncharted territories. In this respect, two very important transformations need to be highlighted that, although intertwined, are nevertheless distinctive. One relates to technology and the disruptive impact that this has had on the way we all produce and consume media content (Nee, 2013; Russell, 2019). The other is mostly political and profoundly marked by a modern globalisation process in ways that have altered how we engage and use knowledge and how we now socialise with each other (Lugo-Ocando, 2013; Ruddock, 2007). In this last sense, the notion of 'polis' that Aristotle once described as a well-defined geographical space of connection with others, is now, in many cases, boundaryless and remote.

In the first case, disruptive digital technologies have brought with them profound changes in the manner in which audiences consume and use media content (Pavlik et al., 2018; Picard, 2003). The power of these technologies also means that everyone's personal and professional time has literally been colonised by the media. 'Gone are the days when one would rush home to watch their favourite soap opera and so are the days when one would just watch. Now consumers get to interact with content creators and other consumers, and even create their own content' (Dennis et al., 2020). We live in an age of such information abundance that we constantly see ourselves overwhelmed and even paralysed by the exorbitant amount of data at our disposal (P. Boczkowski, 2021; P. J. Boczkowski & Mitchelstein, 2017).

These technologies have been powerful instruments characterised by moral duality. On the one hand, they have facilitated change and decentralised access to information while, on the other, they have also enabled surveillance and control over society (Fuchs et al., 2013; Stoycheff, 2016). These technologies have made us all perennial consumers and, at the same time, producers of content. They have made mobility, interactivity and velocity central issues of our lives in ways that a great segment of the planet is interconnected 24/7 while people know when others are asleep, lovers exchange texts and satellites send the exact location of an individual so they can be assassinated by a drone that comes literally out of the blue (Ahmad, 2015; Loukinas, 2017).

In the second case, political attitudes and levels of civic engagement have also suffered a profound shift. The erosion of public trust, increasing apathy and depoliticisation, particularly among the young, threatens the very foundations of the political culture (Jones, 2004; Splendore & Curini, 2020). It is important to understand that political culture is not a theory but rather refers to a set of variables, which may be used in the construction of theories (Almond & Verba, 1989, p. 26) and that can help us describe the sociological and anthropological aesthetics that characterise the way we engage with others and how we all engage with scientific knowledge as a community.

## On News Consumption

In fact, news consumption does not happen in a vacuum but rather occurs within societal and political contexts, which in turn are both defined by political culture. If the political culture changes, so does the way people engage and consume news. The formation of political culture is defined by the way we socialise our political actions, which includes accessing and consuming the news. For example, reading the newspaper is no longer as common as it used to be and, according to the most available data today, in many regions of the world social media has instead become the entry point for most people accessing news (Dennis et al., 2020; Pavlik et al., 2018; Pentina & Tarafdar, 2014). The traditional process of news consumption and 'socialization', where families sat down in front of the television to watch the 7 o'clock news—having read the newspapers earlier—to share, comment and contextualise news within each family, simply no longer takes place. Family members consume media content in different spaces, and on different devices and platforms, thereby creating more connections with external participants than with members of their own family or their traditional opinion leaders.

The Arab world has lived both strands of this transformation, even as many of their political systems remain closed and restricted (Pavlik et al., 2018). The globalisation of their economies, their interaction with the outside world and generational changes have meant the amplification of available information and the shift from traditional media to the digital and interactive platforms (Dennis et al., 2020). Today, there are very high youth rates in Arab populations, which in turn means higher consumption of mobile media. In GCC countries, to give a case, people now enjoy high standards of life, access to education, regular interaction with the rest of the world and a very modern telecommunication infrastructure that provides Internet access, to the extent that these countries showcase some of the highest levels of Internet and mobile phone penetration in the world (Dennis et al., 2020).

However, we should not forget either that the MENA region continues to present profound inequalities and differences (Lassoued, 2021; Neaime & Gaysset, 2018). As the annual study conducted by Northwestern University in Qatar, designed and implemented by Professor Everette Dennis (2020) for the past five years, reminds us, while many of these countries have by now reached almost full saturation among nationals, in other less-developed Arab countries, Internet access is still by far a luxury to those who have no access even to electricity, who continue to struggle to feed their families and who still cannot read or write.

This study, perhaps the only one in the region with such a comprehensive intake, has accounted for the changes that have taken place in MENA, highlighting the shifts and trends across seven countries. In countries such as Qatar and the UAE, for example, there has been a significant decline of traditional newspaper readership which follows a more general global trend in Europe and the United States. However, as others have noticed, this is not only because of technological disruptions but also due to the fact that an important segment of local and national news media in these countries has not evolved much in the past few years and continues to present the information to their readers in formats, genres and styles that are almost archaic (El Oifi, 2019; Mellor, 2005).

## Changing Landscape

These studies also indicate that despite the technological disruptions and societal changes, television networks remain very present and have been able to keep a good hold among Middle East audiences. Having said that, it is clear that in the next few years, television on-demand will completely take over all audiences, something that is already happening among millennials (18–24-year-olds) who tend to watch videos mostly online and on-demand. The newer generations like to decide when to watch what they want and on which platform and have grown accustomed to having those choices (Khalil & Zayani, 2021; Sakr, 2022). This last trend also signifies an important change in the nature of media content consumption in which the newer audiences do not follow schedules or a particular channel but rather follow content itself. Indeed, the newer generations consume content differently as they jump from platform to platform, watching longer content posted on social media platforms (Dennis et al., 2020; Pavlik et al., 2018).

In the face of this changing landscape, but also as a consequence of traditional settings, we need to acknowledge the extreme difficulties for new media outlets and journalists in general to establish links with the audience and gain their interest and trust. This is a particularly important point for science journalists who struggle in the region to reach wider audiences. If, well, people in the region do pay a fair degree of attention to news, this does not happen equally across the board. Levels of trust in the traditional media vary between legacy and digital-native among different segments of the public (Douai, 2019). This is because each media outlet has its own history in the region where most of the legacy media outlets in the MENA region are associated with the existing regimes and political systems in place (Fandy, 2000; Miladi & Mellor, 2020). People still read newspapers, but as our focus groups signalled, they are suspicious of what they read and assume that it is rather the voice of those in power.

These complexities and the nature of the changes affect all news beats, including science. Some evidence suggests that suspicion and scepticism regarding science flies high in the region, at least among segments of the population (Essam & Abdo, 2021; Gray, 2010). Not because of religion or culture, but because science is often associated in the public imagination with the west and often treated with suspicion around its motives. Drugs, vaccinations and treatments are seen by important segments of the population as a way to impose power over the Arab world. It is important to emphasise that post-colonialism plays an important role in the widespread acceptance of conspiracy theories in the region.

However, contrary to those in the West, the general public in MENA cannot avoid or resist the implementation of policies such as mandatory vaccination against COVID-19 or the use of masks, as these types of policies are ingrained into the wider apparatus of political control. The upturn of this draconian imposition of health policies is perhaps that MENA not only exhibits some of the highest levels of vaccination but also some of the lowest levels of sexually transmitted diseases including HIV/AIDS (Gökengin et al., 2016; Madani, 2018). The downturn is that it is very likely that in time this will translate in rejection of many of these measures and over time a further erosion on those who predicate these policies and measures, including journalists and their new media outlets.

To understand these complexities, we need to explore the characteristics of the audiences for science news in the Middle East. In so doing, we ask how people in the region access, consume, engage and understand science in the news. We have tried to answer this and other related questions based on grounded research in this area, but we must also acknowledge the limitations around this task given current restrictions around fieldwork in some countries. We refer to data produced by mostly third parties over the past few years plus some additional data gathered by ourselves. Therefore, the section provides an analysis about how people on the ground read science news, what they use it for and to what degree it affects their worldview in more general terms. We do not claim, however, that this is all representative data and we accept instead that some of our conclusions and suggestions remain as useful insight on the matter.

We explore here how theories such as that of 'uses and gratifications approach' (Lee, 2013) can help us better understand science news audiences and explain the ways in which news consumption in the Middle East happens. This audience-based chapter seeks to understand why and how people in that region use news to fill science information gaps and the motivations that define the different types of media consumption choices when it comes to accessing scientific knowledge. If, well, it is evidently clear as to why most people engage with health news instead of mathematics, no less true is that events such as the passing by of the 'Oumuamua'—the first known interstellar object detected passing through the solar system, which was formally designated 1I/2017 U1—are able to create a profound effect on the public imagination thanks to the narratives that surround it. We know this by observing peaks in thematic discussion in social media, from which we make that assumption.

In this chapter, we argue that science news audiences in the Arab world are active consumers of media. We also highlight that their consumption of science news is driven by specific reasons and motivations, within a wide range of gratifications that vary across individuals and groups to the point that communication processes are somehow both similar and distinctive to those in the west. However, as we also discuss here, the overall consumption of science news in MENA remains comparatively low in relation to other parts of the world.

It is also important to clarify that contrary to misconceptions around the assumed 'homogeneity' of the Arab world, the evidence here suggests instead that the audiences in these countries are diverse in all senses, including culture, level of political engagement and socio-economic status. These differences can be appreciated both across the region as well as intra-nationally. The so-called Middle East and North Africa (MENA) region shows a highly populated and culturally diverse society spanning different continents. The population of some 580 million people come from a diversity of backgrounds although it's overwhelmingly of Arab-speaking descent. Most of these societies are considered to be religious and most of its peoples identify with one form of Islam. Despite this, every single country is in reality a kaleidoscope that shows galvanising trends in which the only common factor is historical and cultural syncretism. Believers in the Christian religion, for example, now make up the second most common religion in the Arab region that includes an estimated 12 million Arabs, and so large segments of the population respond to a diversity of denominations, or not at all. If, well, the MENA region is mostly divided between Asia and Africa, it is often assumed to be the 'Arab world', this, despite the fact that in countries such as Bahrain, Qatar and the UAE the actual Arab population makes up a smaller part of the population (Mirkin, 2013).

If, well, the region presents similarities in terms of religion, language, tradition and overall culture the notion of 'Middle East' is in fact an orientalist construction in the public imaginary that encompasses people, geography and histories (Said, 2008). Wave after wave of immigration, displacement and globalisation has reconfigured these societies in ways that would appear unrecognisable to previous generations. Today, many religions co-exist as well side by side with a thriving secular world that seeks to integrate to a global economy. In very recent times, for example, the United Arab Emirates changed its own working week to adapt it to western markets so as to go from Monday to Friday rather than starting on a Sunday (Treisman, 2021).

The region is mostly governed by 'closed regimes' but nevertheless presents diverse and at times conflicting worldviews around politics and culture, including the role of Islam in society (Al-Sayegh, 1999; Kalathil & Boas, 2010; Masoud, 2015). Far from being monolithic, it is a region of contrasts and, to a certain degree, of great plurality (Abdulmajid, 2018). This diversity of positions reflects the tensions between tradition and globalisation but also the inner dynamics within the region that ride on the fact that neither culture nor public attitudes are static or fixed in time. Hence, it is crucial to understand the region as an amalgamation of factors that have shaped and defined its news audiences. These audiences respond to different interests and are not bound by a single identity as commonly assumed in the west.

Having said that, there seems to be common and overlapping aspects across the region. For example, in none of the countries does there seem to be a robust enough audience to sustain science news, at least not on a scale that would make science publications financially sustainable. As we suggested in an earlier section, without listeners the tree of science will make no sound if it falls in an empty forest full of indifferent deafness or simply ignorance. Few media investors will take the risk of creating commercial enterprises dedicated to science news in the region if the market is not there. Unless there is a potential market or enough support from governments or organisations, there is little chance for news outlets dedicated to science (Gamal, 2020). This is because without an audience, science news is neither feasible nor sustainable in time. Indeed, as we will also discuss here, the main challenge to science journalism in MENA does not emanate from religion, political oppression or censorship, but from the apathy of the many towards science in general.

## Understanding Audiences

The other challenge in understanding current trends and nature of media consumption in the MENA region is that of the disruptive nature of media technologies that have emerged in the past decades. The technologies have been embraced by news audiences in their daily lives and consequently have altered the ways people relate to media content. In this context, different publics develop distinctive relationships with news and adopt a variety of formats and platforms to access stories. This is because these technologies offer a new level of choice never seen before. Consequently, people can combine different media forms into a comprehensive setting that feeds their daily intake of news (Deuze, 2011; Livingstone, 2019).

This in turn leads, for better or for worse, to a variety of patterns of exposure and repertoires of consumption. Yet there is a limited understanding of the reasons behind this and the long-term implications for journalism. This article has argued for a more comprehensive, temporal approach; a process-based set of analytical prisms; and a flexible methodological agenda to advance an integrated framework that moves a research agenda on news repertoires forward.

The move to a digital, social and mobile news landscape has created a number of paradoxes, chief among them being that, while some marshal technology to take advantage of a more diverse, networked and participatory news landscape, these exact same tools lead others to filter bubbles, passivity or full-scale avoidance (Peters & Christian Schrøder, 2018).

In the MENA region, people's media consumption habits differ greatly. Selection of social media platforms, media formats and even nature of the content vary both from country to country as well as intra-nationally. Consumers buy different products, have different hobbies and use the media differently in their lives. They also differ in their interest in, attitudes on, and behaviour towards specific issues. These variations are distributed across the different populations who also show distinctive attitudes, ways of appropriation and final cognitive and behavioural effects around the way they engage with the media.

This is not surprising if one takes into account that as stipulated by the Uses and Gratifications Theory (UGT), people actively seek out specific media to satisfy their particular needs (Katz et al., 1974; Ruggiero, 2000). As is the case in the West, news audiences in MENA are not passive consumers of media content, nor do they simply assume truthfulness or legitimacy of the media outlets mostly controlled by governments in the region. Instead, there is some evidence to suggest that people assume an active role in interpreting and integrating that media content into their own lives in ways that address their particular needs. For example, in countries such as Qatar, people tend to use Snapchat far more as a social media platform than Facebook or Twitter (Dennis et al., 2020). One reason for this, interviewees in our sample commented on, was that messages disappear and could not be traced back to them. Another participant suggested that people using Snapchat could express their views with less fear of being singled out. These findings correlate to other studies in the region that indicate important level of subtleness in the way audience engage with and use media according to their collective and individual context (Dennis et al., 2020; Karolak, 2017; Viewed & Hodges, 2016).

In MENA, it is the case that audiences today choose media outlets, channels and platforms to meet their needs to achieve gratification. In relation to science news, people in the region show differences with regard to scientific and environmental issues according to their level of education, their age, gender and socio-economic status, among other factors, something that also happens in the West (Metag & Schäfer, 2018). As is the case in other parts of the world, income is still a defining factor in determining levels of access to communication and information. For years, scholars have well established that income comes to define levels of media literacy and therefore the ability to fulfil the potential of the media to inform and educate (Mansell, 2020; Schramm, 1964).

In her study on migrant workers in Qatar, for example, Professor Susan Dun (2018) noticed how access to, and utilisation of, health information and resources was determined by and limited to not only the level of income and education but also by common perception about what the authorities could do to them if they accessed and input data. Equally, another of her papers on car seatbelts suggests a very different approach to media uses from other segments of the population, namely, young Arabs (Dun & Ali, 2018). All this goes to highlight the importance of analysing media audiences in MENA in a more stratified manner. MENA is far more than the Arab world and in some countries they are not even the majority of the population, while all of these societies—with no exceptions—show levels of diversity in terms of ethnicity and cultural background as well as socio-economic disparities that problematise any analysis of audiences.

Hence, to understand the ways in which science journalism reaches the public and how these same audiences engage and respond to science news, we first need to assess general levels of education and interest in science in these countries. In this sense, there is good news and bad news emanating from the region. On the positive side, we find that most nations in that region have adopted a standard curriculum that incorporates sciences at all levels from primary and secondary schools to a variety of provisions in the higher education sector. We also found that STEM subjects have a greater intake of young women than in many other parts of the world, including the west. For example, girls are more likely than boys to be interested in science in Tunisia and Qatar (Hillman et al., 2017; Rahmouni & Aleid, 2020).

On the negative side, several scholars have pointed out the overall 'poor quality of STEM education' in the region (Wang et al., 2020), where old-fashioned learning methods based on crude memorising, weak teacher training, misinterpretations of Islam in relation to science education and other issues have hindered good practices in teaching and deterred many from pursuing a pathway into science (Karafyllis, 2015). The fact remains that countries in the MENA region have been slow to make science part of a more widespread culture within society, despite a push from the top to do so.

We do know from studies in other parts of the world that science literacy—that is, how well the population is educated in STEM subjects—is a central variable in determining to what degree the public is engaged with science news and the degree to which they can make sense of, and use, that information in their daily lives (Bellová et al., 2021; Chetcuti & Kioko,

2012; Osborne et al., 2003). In countries with higher levels of education in general and where STEM subjects are taught at all levels of the education system, we also find a greater engagement with news (Besley et al., 2013; Land-Zandstra et al., 2016; Osborne & Dillon, 2008). The contrary is also true and in countries where science is not part of the curriculum at all levels or where children do not tend to complete their education cycle, the trend to engage with science is lower (Dawson, 2018; Lo, 2016).

Again, one must highlight that this is not only about a political decision to include STEM or not into the curriculum but also about the result of socio-economic realities in which children are forced to abandon their education because of the pressures to enter work (Heyne et al., 2019; Moore, 2006; Nimeh & Bauchmüller, 2014). In this sense, income is again a central variable in explaining engagement with science by the public, both across the region as well as intra-nationally. In low-income societies in North Africa, we find that this is generally the case but also in countries with very high GDP per capita, where we find, nevertheless, important sections of the population that remain excluded from accessing even very basic scientific knowledge that is relevant and pertinent to their daily lives (Dun, 2018; Dun & Ali, 2018).

Having said all this, equally important to the expansion in public engagement with, and understanding of, science is a greater dissemination of media literacy in the region. It is often assumed that younger generations are more savvy in the use of social media than older generations. However, this is just an assumption and most studies instead suggest that better awareness in relation to media literacy is needed at all levels of the population (Jones-Jang et al., 2021; Mason et al., 2018). In MENA, media literacy is needed not just to make sure that individuals are able to use media effectively to fill their knowledge gaps, but also to be able to recognise and validate truthful content (Alaleeli & Alnajjar, 2020; AlNajjar, 2019).

One of the key problems that the MENA region faces in this respect is that many policy makers continue to approach issues around public understanding of science (PUS) and public engagement with science as a social reproduction of what science communication and science education does in high-income countries, often leaving aside the fact that this means constructing a narrow conceptualisation of what the public is and which reflects the shape, values and practices of dominant groups, all at the expense of marginalised groups in the MENA societies. Henceforth, very large segments of those countries remain excluded from science knowledge and are unable to grasp key information that would greatly improve their lives (Dun, 2018).

However, even when we account for these gaps and the exclusions of these groups, overall interest in science news in Arab societies remains weak at large. This is in terms of being both interested in, and accessing, scientific news. Indeed, one of the most serious problems faced by science journalism in the region is the lack of interest in the subject by the wider public. This lack of a 'news audience' for science also contributes to the lack of investment in the news beat and the weak engagement on the part of the media itself, as we mentioned before. Most of the journalists interviewed for this book believed that the lack of interest in scientific news exists,

> *I don't think that readers care about scientific news, but rather preferred other news beats such as sports. I have written in several areas [news beats] and get a lot of feedback from readers when I write about a variety of issues but I cannot recall a lot of attention or comments when I wrote about science. [INT12]*

Most research shows that lack of 'interest' in serious news on the part of readers derives from their inability to understand and contextualise the meaning of these stories in what the literature refers to as public understanding of science. Here is where science journalists play an important role, both as storytellers and pedagogical agents, who can convey scientific news in simple and contextualised ways to their audiences, making science news not only accessible but also relevant within the community. This is where the scientific community in MENA needs to acknowledge that it is not only the gaps in PUS that determine lack of PES but also, and perhaps more importantly, how relevant does the public find particular scientific knowledge (Nguyen & McIlwaine, 2011).

In other words, to address the disinterest on the part of readers who believe that it is not relevant, science journalists need to find angles and narratives that make these stories appealing while linking them to society itself. The lay public needs a science journalism 'that can adopt fresh mindsets and new techniques to make science news relevant to its daily life' (Nguyen & McIlwaine, 2011, p. 224). In the case of MENA, large audiences who have limited schooling years and exposure to STEM, in principle will find it extremely difficult to connect with topics that seem to them alien, distant and, at times, convoluted.

As we have seen here, this problem of low science literacy is linked to lower scores in natural sciences at the schooling levels and an overall deficient delivery of STEM at early school, primary and secondary education. This in turn has an impact on the degree of awareness with STEM subjects in general among the public and this correlates with the level of engagement with science news across national and regional audiences. Key to addressing this is by underlining the fact that schooling is available to particular segments of the population. Most migrant workers in GCC countries do not have the sufficient knowledge to engage with science news nor do they find it particularly relevant to their own settings. The challenge for governments, organisations and the news media is to develop strategies that can address those segments of the population that remain excluded.

Overall, it is clear that there is simply not a market for dedicated traditional science news provision in the region or enough to allow the legacy media to dedicate resources to provide science content in a regular manner, although this might change in the light of COVID. However, experience in other countries shows that market failures in the media industry can and must be addressed by state and organisational interventions that subsidise alternative provision (Doyle, 2013; Pickard, 2014). That is, if we are serious about delivering science to the public. There is also evidence to suggest that these alternatives can emerge from the civil society itself, where we can see an increasing presence of independent journalists, bloggers and scientists reaching important segments of the population (Allan, 2009; Dunwoody, 2021; Shneiderman, 2008). The issue then becomes not how they reach the public, but what they say to them.

Indeed, beyond the problems associated with people's lack of interest and engagement with STEM, there is also the very important issue of public access to science information in MENA. To be clear, limitations and constraints accessing public information relate to all news beats in this region and are mostly associated with the way political regimes operate and the historical configuration of institutions and political cultures. In other sections of this book, we have discussed the limited access and problems faced by journalists trying to engage with scientific sources in MENA. These problems are even more present in the case of the general public given not only the lack of channels for science dissemination but also a prevalent culture in which authorities and officials—including key research institutions and universities—are simply not used to sharing their work and information about science with the public.

It might be assumed that general issues regarding access to information in Arab countries is that there are no clear policies or procedures that guarantee citizens transparent ways to reach content and information. In most cases, policies that have been put in place are seen as 'window-dressing' (Bebawi, 2016, p. 11) and in practice pay lip-service to the needs of most citizens to access science information. The region presents a particular political setting that intrinsically limits access to information in general and exhibits a political culture in which most people do not feel entitled to request information that otherwise would be considered a basic right in many other countries.

A UNESCO (2013) report pointed out that in comparison to other parts of the world, progress on freedom of information legislation has been slow in Arab states. Even Jordan, which passed an FOI law in 2007, has seen very little progress in this realm, and the law itself has gone through a difficult implementation stage for the past decade or so. In Tunisia, a decree on FOI was enacted in 2011, but today we see a serious retreat in overall civil liberties. Following this, Yemen also passed an FOI law in 2012 but soon after that saw all promises of access to content buried under the rubble of war.

However, the problem of accessing science information is not only about making it accessible but also about creating the interest and capabilities among the audiences to want to access it. This is not only a problem of Arab countries alone but also one that is very present in many places around the globe. Neither is it restricted to a political culture that has been defined by government censorship but that is also linked to an education system that poorly underperforms in STEM subjects. Limited capabilities hinder the ability of many to engage with science news and this in turn is a major obstacle to the creation of a marketplace for science news. To address this, the MENA region needs to implement policies and dedicate resources that make science part of daily life and help elucidate public debate based on scientific knowledge. These efforts, however, cannot only be undertaken nationally or just by nation-states. Instead, they need to be based in collaborative approaches that link the regional with the global. Indeed, while countries such as Qatar, the UAE and Saudi Arabia are discussing the possibility of rail links that interconnect these and other countries, it might be also useful to think about knowledge links that create a true common space for scientific knowledge in the region. If they do so, these countries could set a well-informed debate in the public sphere. One that fosters engagement with science on a much-needed scale and in a more comprehensive form.

## Bibliography

Abdulmajid, A. (2018). A Study on religious diversity and conflict in the middle east. *International Journal of Social Science and Humanities Research*, 6(3), 1–7.

Ahmad, M. I. (2015). The magical realism of body counts: How media credulity and flawed statistics sustain a controversial policy. *Journalism*, 1464884915593237.

Alaleeli, S., & Alnajjar, A. (2020). The Arab digital generation's engagement with technology: The case of high school students in the UAE. *JOTSE: Journal of Technology and Science Education*, 10(1), 159–178.

Allan, S. (2009). The future of science journalism. *Journalism*, 10(3), 280–282.

Almond, G., & Verba, S. (1989). *The Civic Culture Revisited*. Sage.

AlNajjar, A. (2019). Abolish censorship and adopt critical media literacy: A proactive approach to media and youth in the Middle East. *Journal of Media Literacy Education*, 11(3), 73–84.

Al-Sayegh, F. (1999). Diversity in unity: Political institutions and civil society. *Middle East Policy*, 6(4), 14.

Ashwell, D. (2016). The challenges of science journalism: The perspectives of scientists, science communication advisors and journalists from New Zealand. *Public Understanding of Science*, 25(3), 379–393.

Bebawi, S. (2016). *Investigative Journalism in the Arab World: Issues and Challenges*. Springer.

Bellová, R., Balážová, M., & Tomčík, P. (2021). Are attitudes towards science and technology related to critical areas in science education? *Research in Science & Technological Education*, 1–16.

Besley, J. C., Oh, S. H., & Nisbet, M. (2013). Predicting scientists' participation in public life. *Public Understanding of Science*, 22(8), 971–987.

Boczkowski, P. (2021). *Abundance: On the Experience of Living in a World of Information Plenty*. Oxford University Press.

Boczkowski, P. J., & Mitchelstein, E. (2017). The gap between the media and the public. In C. Peters & M. Broersma (Eds.), *Rethinking Journalism Again: Societal role and public relevance in a digital* (pp. 175–186). Routledge.

Chetcuti, D. A., & Kioko, B. (2012). Girls' attitudes towards science in Kenya. *International Journal of Science Education*, 34(10), 1571–1589.

Cook, G., Pieri, E., & Robbins, P. T. (2004). 'The scientists think and the public feels': Expert perceptions of the discourse of GM food. *Discourse & Society*, 15(4), 433–449.

Dawson, E. (2018). Reimagining publics and (non) participation: Exploring exclusion from science communication through the experiences of low-income, minority ethnic groups. *Public Understanding of Science*, 27(7), 772–786.

Dennis, E., Martin, J., & Allagui, I. (2020). *Media Use in the Middle East*.

Deuze, M. (2011). Media life. *Media, Culture & Society*, 33(1), 137–148.

Douai, A. (2019). Global and Arab media in the post-truth era: Globalization, authoritarianism and fake news. *IEMed: Mediterranean Yearbook, 2019*, 124–132.

Doyle, G. (2013). *Understanding media economics.* Sage.

Dun, S. (2018). *Assessing and improving migrant workers access to and utilization of health information and resources. 2018*(4), SSAHPD443.

Dun, S., & Ali, A. Z. (2018). 'Seatbelts don't save lives': Discovering and targeting the attitudes and behaviors of young Arab male drivers. *Accident Analysis & Prevention, 121*, 185–193.

Dunwoody, S. (2014). *Science journalism.* Routledge.

Dunwoody, S. (2021). Science journalism: Prospects in the digital age. In *Routledge handbook of public communication of science and technology* (pp. 14–32). Routledge.

El Oifi, M. (2019). Influence without power: Al Jazeera and the Arab public sphere. In *The Al Jazeera Phenomenon* (pp. 66–79). Routledge.

Essam, B. A., & Abdo, M. S. (2021). How do Arab tweeters perceive the COVID-19 pandemic? *Journal of Psycholinguistic Research, 50*(3), 507–521.

Fandy, M. (2000). Information technology, trust, and social change in the Arab world. *The Middle East Journal*, 378–394.

Friedman, S., Dunwoody, S., & Rogers, C. L. (1986). *Scientists and journalists.* American Association for the Advancement of Science.

Fuchs, C., Boersma, K., Albrechtslund, A., & Sandoval, M. (2013). *Internet and surveillance: The challenges of Web 2.0 and social media, 16*, Routledge.

Gamal, M. Y. (2020). *The Earth turns and the world has changed: Egyptian and Arab Science journalism in the digital age.* Arab Media & Society. https://www.arabmediasociety.com/the-earth-turns-and-the-world-has-changed-egyptian-and-arab-science-journalism-in-the-digital-age/

Gökengin, D., Doroudi, F., Tohme, J., Collins, B., & Madani, N. (2016). HIV/AIDS: Trends in the Middle East and North Africa region. *International Journal of Infectious Diseases, 44*(21), 66–73.

Gray, M. (2010). *Conspiracy theories in the Arab world: Sources and politics.* Routledge.

Heyne, D., Gren-Landell, M., Melvin, G., & Gentle-Genitty, C. (2019). Differentiation between school attendance problems: Why and how? *Cognitive and Behavioral Practice, 26*(1), 8–34.

Hillman, S., Salama, G., Eibenschutz, E. O., Awadh, S. M. A., & El Said, L. (2017). *Being female and an engineering student in Qatar: Successes, challenges, and recommendations.* 2017 ASEE Annual Conference & Exposition.

Humm, C., Schrögel, P., & Leßmöllmann, A. (2020). Feeling left out: Underserved audiences in science communication. *Media and Communication, 8*(1), 164–176.

Jones, D. A. (2004). Why Americans don't trust the media: A preliminary analysis. *Harvard International Journal of Press/Politics, 9*(2), 60–75.

Jones-Jang, S. M., Mortensen, T., & Liu, J. (2021). Does media literacy help identification of fake news? Information literacy helps, but other literacies don't. *American Behavioral Scientist, 65*(2), 371–388.

Kalathil, S., & Boas, T. C. (2010). *Open networks, closed regimes: The impact of the Internet on authoritarian rule.*.

Karafyllis, N. C. (2015). Tertiary education in the GCC countries (UAE, Qatar, Saudi Arabia): How economy, gender and culture affect the field of STEM. In *International Science and Technology Education* (pp. 138–159). Routledge.

Karolak, M. (2017). The use of social media from revolution to democratic consolidation: The Arab Spring and the case of Tunisia. *Journal of Arab & Muslim Media Research, 10*(2), 199–216.

Katz, E., Blumler, J., & Gurevitch, M. (1974). Uses and gratification theory. *Public Opinion Quarterly, 34*(4), 509–523.

Khalil, J. F., & Zayani, M. (2021). De-territorialized digital capitalism and the predicament of the nation-state: Netflix in Arabia. *Media, Culture & Society, 43*(2), 201–218.

Land-Zandstra, A. M., Devilee, J. L., Snik, F., Buurmeijer, F., & van den Broek, J. M. (2016). Citizen science on a smartphone: Participants' motivations and learning. *Public Understanding of Science, 25*(1), 45–60.

Lassoued, M. (2021). Control of corruption, microfinance, and income inequality in MENA countries: Evidence from panel data. *SN Business & Economics, 1*(7), 1–19.

Lee, A. M. (2013). News audiences revisited: Theorizing the link between audience motivations and news consumption. *Journal of Broadcasting & Electronic Media, 57*(3), 300–317.

Livingstone, S. (2019). Audiences in an age of datafication: Critical questions for media research. *Television & New Media, 20*(2), 170–183.

Lo, A. Y. (2016). National income and environmental concern: Observations from 35 countries. *Public Understanding of Science, 25*(7), 873–890.

Loukinas, P. (2017). Surveillance and drones at Greek borderzones: Challenging human rights and democracy. *Surveillance & Society, 15*(3/4), 439–446.

Lugo-Ocando, J. (2013). Reflexivity in the digital world: Rethinking journalism teaching and learning in an interactive world. *Journal of Applied Journalism & Media Studies, 2*(2), 207–214.

Madani, N. (2018). Gender equality is crucial to the fight for better HIV treatment access and outcomes in the MENA region. *Journal of the International AIDS Society, 21*(3), 1–2.

Maillé, M.-È., Saint-Charles, J., & Lucotte, M. (2010). The gap between scientists and journalists: The case of mercury science in Québec's press. *Public Understanding of Science, 19*(1), 70–79.

Mansell, R. (2020). *Making open development inclusive: Lessons from IDRC research*. MIT Press.

Mason, L. E., Krutka, D., & Stoddard, J. (2018). Media literacy, democracy, and the challenge of fake news. *Journal of Media Literacy Education, 10*(2), 1–10.

Masoud, T. (2015). Has the door closed on Arab democracy? *Journal of Democracy, 26*(1), 74–87.

Mellor, N. (2005). *The making of Arab news*. Rowman & Littlefield Publishers.

Metag, J., & Schäfer, M. S. (2018). *Audience segments in environmental and science communication: Recent findings and future perspectives*.

Miladi, N., & Mellor, N. (2020). *Routledge Handbook on Arab Media*. Routledge.

Mirkin, B. (2013). *Arab Spring: Demographics in a region in transition*. United Nations Development Programme, Regional Bureau for Arab States. United Nations Development Program Regional Bureau for Arab States. https://arab-hdr.org/wp-content/uploads/2020/12/AHDR-ENG-Arab-Spring-Mirkinv3.pdf

Moore, R. (2006). Class attendance: How students' attitudes about attendance relate to their academic performance in introductory science classes. *Research and Teaching in Developmental Education*, 19–33.

Neaime, S., & Gaysset, I. (2018). Financial inclusion and stability in MENA: Evidence from poverty and inequality. *Finance Research Letters, 24*, 230–237.

Nee, R. C. (2013). Creative destruction: An exploratory study of how digitally native news nonprofits are innovating online journalism practices. *International Journal on Media Management, 15*(1), 3–22.

Nguyen, A., & McIlwaine, S. (2011). Who wants a voice in Science issues—And why? A survey of European citizens and its implications for science journalism. *Journalism Practice, 5*(2), 210–226.

Nimeh, Z., & Bauchmüller, R. (2014). School enrolment and child labour. In *Agency and participation in childhood and youth: International applications of the capability approach in schools and beyond* (p. 204). Bloomsbury Publishing.

Osborne, J., & Dillon, J. (2008). *Science education in Europe: Critical reflections* (Vol. 13). The Nuffield Foundation.

Osborne, J., Simon, S., & Collins, S. (2003). Attitudes towards science: A review of the literature and its implications. *International Journal of Science Education, 25*(9), 1049–1079.

Pavlik, J. V., Dennis, E. E., Mersey, R. D., & Gengler, J. (2018). *Mobile disruptions in the Middle East: Lessons from Qatar and the Arabian Gulf Region in mobile media content innovation*. Routledge.

Pentina, I., & Tarafdar, M. (2014). From 'information' to 'knowing': Exploring the role of social media in contemporary news consumption. *Computers in Human Behavior, 35*, 211–223.

Peters, C., & Christian Schrøder, K. (2018). Beyond the here and now of news audiences: A process-based framework for investigating news repertoires. *Journal of Communication, 68*(6), 1079–1103.

Picard, R. G. (2003). Cash cows or entrecote: Publishing companies and disruptive technologies. *Trends in Communication, 11*(2), 127–136.

Pickard, V. (2014). The great evasion: Confronting market failure in American media policy. *Critical Studies in Media Communication, 31*(2), 153–159.

Rahmouni, M., & Aleid, M. A. (2020). Teachers' practices and children's motivation towards science learning in MENA countries: Evidence from Tunisia and UAE. *International Journal of Educational Research, 103*, 101605.

Rakedzon, T., Segev, E., Chapnik, N., Yosef, R., & Baram-Tsabari, A. (2017). Automatic jargon identifier for scientists engaging with the public and science communication educators. *PloS One, 12*(8), e0181742.

Ransohoff, D. F., & Ransohoff, R. M. (2001). Sensationalism in the media: When scientists and journalists may be complicit collaborators. *Effective Clinical Practice, 4*(4), 185–188.

Ruddock, A. (2007). *Investigating audiences*. Sage.

Ruggiero, T. E. (2000). Uses and gratifications theory in the 21st century. *Mass Communication & Society, 3*(1), 3–37.

Russell, F. M. (2019). The new gatekeepers: An Institutional-level view of Silicon Valley and the disruption of journalism. *Journalism Studies, 20*(5), 631–648.

Said, E. (2008). *Covering Islam: How the media and the experts determine how we see the rest of the world (Fully revised edition)*. Random House.

Sakr, N. (2022). Purposes and practices of MENA television: Components of an ever-evolving medium. In K. Gholam & T. Guaaybess (Eds.), *The handbook of media and culture in the middle east*. John Wiley and Sons Ltd.

Schramm, W. (1964). *Mass media and national development: The role of information in the developing countries*. Stanford University Press.

Shapin, S. (2020). *Science and the public*. Routledge.

Shneiderman, B. (2008). Science 2.0. *Science, 319*(5868), 1349–1350.

Splendore, S., & Curini, L. (2020). Proximity between citizens and journalists as a determinant of trust in the media. An Application to Italy. *Journalism Studies, 21*(9), 1167–1185.

Stoycheff, E. (2016). Under surveillance: Examining Facebook's spiral of silence effects in the wake of NSA internet monitoring. *Journalism & Mass Communication Quarterly, 93*(2), 296–311.

Treisman, R. (2021). *The UAE is adopting a 4.5-day workweek and a Saturday-Sunday weekend* [News]. National Public Radio. https://www.npr.org/2021/12/08/1062435944/uae-work-week-change-saturday-sunday-weekends-global-markets?t=1640105054377

UNESCO. (2013). *Freedom of Information in Arab States*.

Vieweg, S., & Hodges, A. (2016). *Surveillance & modesty on social media: How Qataris navigate modernity and maintain tradition.* 527–538. https://dl.acm.org/doi/abs/10.1145/2818048.2819966?casa_token=zHxgVUKhtnsAAAA-A%3AJEJbfgi1lh8qE5P0V4NC4cMJ5kWGRHUOffEzFRrnDiFZnVh63kRofpa-RfqvCaTqgrCPujRUhH86vEo

Wang, D. R., Hajjar, D. P., & Cole, C. L. (2020). International partnerships for the development of science, technology, engineering, mathematics, and medical education of middle eastern women. *International Journal of Higher Education, 9*(2), 1–15.

## CHAPTER 10

# Conclusion

From all the formats and pathways used to communicate science to the general public, science journalism continues to be perhaps the most comprehensive at underpinning these efforts (Al-Qafari, 2009; Bauer, 2013). So much so, that while other forms of science communication such as media entertainment—for example, films and television shows—might reach wider audiences while others can be very comprehensive—such as museums and exhibitions—all of them either struggle to deliver accurate information, as in the case of movies, or reach wider audiences such as exhibitions.

Only science journalism seems capable of both, encompassing comprehensive and accurate aspects of science—although it certainly gets it wrong on countless occasions—while, at the same time, being able to disseminate that information across large segments of the public. This is because the news as a commodity, despite audience fragmentation and viewership decline, continues to be widely present in homes and on social media as the primary form used by people to engage with current affairs. News consumption remains the primary factor in setting the agenda in relation to what the public speaks about and, fundamentally responsible for popularising science among the largest audiences (Molek-Kozakowska, 2017; Scheufele & Krause, 2019).

© The Author(s), under exclusive license to Springer Nature Switzerland AG 2023
A. Alhuntushi, J. Lugo-Ocando, *Science Journalism in the Arab World*, Palgrave Studies in Journalism and the Global South, https://doi.org/10.1007/978-3-031-14252-9_10

These important functions of news reporting of science have been widely acknowledged both by experts, scholars and the overall scientific community, despite important reservations about the capacity of journalists to report accurately and comprehensively both the findings and process of producing scientific knowledge (Nguyen & McIlwaine, 2011). Today, many newspapers, television and radio networks and online digital native media outlets in many countries dedicate resources and have space and people dedicated to cover a variety of topics relating to science. In some cases, science news has several specialised beats such as environment, science and health to name some of the most common. Each one with dedicated space, airtime and staff. In this sense, areas such as health, astronomy and even mathematics receive regular news coverage by journalists wholly dedicated to write and produce stories about these topics although with different degrees of presence in the headlines.

However, perhaps the most important function of science journalism is to politicise science and technology. By this, we refer to the Aristotelian notion of politics in which particular topics and issues should be part of the public debates among the members of the 'polis'. Reporters help define and amplify the topics and agendas debated in the public sphere. It is because the way in which science is covered and presented to the public that it becomes a topical and newsworthy issue. One that sparks discussion and debate within the public sphere thanks to the way stories are told.

In this sense, science journalism helps science transcend facts and reach the common people by narrativising—storytelling—and contextualising it in ways that allow the public to make sense of it. In fact, the reporting of science is not just about highlighting discovery, findings and procedures but also about providing contextual meaning within the larger society as to what scientists do and the subjects they research. This entails underlining issues and debates while asking pertinent questions regarding the role of science in the community.

Journalists not only have the right but also the duty to ask the science community hard questions such as why are we trying to put a colony on Mars rather than addressing malaria in sub-Saharan Africa or to question the use of patents developed by state-funded universities with public money by private corporations, the military or the fossil-fuel industry? It is by underlining its political nature that journalists make science and technology relevant and therefore part of our daily news and discussions. It is by making science politically appealing and relevant to their lives that reporters can reach the hearts and minds of audiences with science news stories that open to them the opportunities and possibilities of scientific rationality and method.

In many settings, science news has become central in the questioning of power and public policy such as the use of genetically modified organisms in the food production chain, the emissions of $CO_2$ and the link between smoking and cancer, to mention a few. In many societies, science has become an ally of journalists seeking truth and performing a role of watchdog to power in society. In these countries, science journalists also help popularise science and make accessible complicated notions while asking important questions in relation to the impact of scientific work on the rest of society.

In places such as Australia, Europe, Japan and the United States, science journalists use science to challenge power relations and help improve the wellbeing of society. They are also able to question science itself when its ethics are compromised by greed, power or disdain for others as in the case of the Tuskegee Study where members of the Afro-American community were allowed to die in order to carry out scientific observations of the effects of syphilis (Jones, 1993; Reverby, 2005) or in the case of Chicago Tribune reporter John Crewdson, who uncovered how Dr Robert Gallo, director of research for the National Institutes of Health in the United States had altered records to falsely claim that it was his team and not Dr Luc Montagnier's team at the French Pasteur Institute who first isolated the AIDS virus (Crewdson, 2002).

Central to the dynamics of journalism in relation to bringing science to the public in ways that represent it both accurately and critically is the ability of journalists to access and engage with news sources that include scientists and experts in a diversity of areas. In the case of the Middle East and North Africa (MENA) region, science journalists are normatively expected to fulfil similar functions (El-Awady, 2009; Mellado, 2015; Mellor, 2005). However, they face similar and additional challenges to those of their counterparts in the west so as to fulfil this mission. As we have discussed in this book, these struggles include lack of expertise to engage comprehensively and critically enough with the news sources, opportune and non-mediated access to scientists and expert sources, ability to apply critical interpretation and produce original content around what the sources say, and limitations imposed by the lack of resources (e.g., few newsrooms can access academic journals unless they have open-source agreements) and pressing deadlines.

Therefore, there is a need to assess how journalists in these Arab countries access and engage news sources while covering this newsbeat. All this by trying to explain the nature and characteristics of that relationship. Our book has helped to describe frequent practices in the use of sources and how dependent journalists in the region are on official sources from specific organisations and institutions in order to provide 'expert voices' in the construction of science news. We highlighted that these expert voices are not necessarily scientists or even 'experts' but on many occasions the information and quotations came in the mediated form of press releases and information packages prepared by officials. This dependency on press releases and officials happens in all newsbeats, where reporters have experienced decreasing access to news sources and face a lack of resources and time pressures that limit their own ability to engage directly with, and cross-check, their sources. We should clarify, however, that this is not a particular problem of MENA and that it is very present in many countries, both in the Global South as well as in the west (Lewis et al., 2008, 2008).

Even when journalists develop a diverse pool of sources in their own newsbeat in the Arab region, only the most visible sources are easily reachable. In many cases, the conversation with science becomes mediated by public relations professionals and often limited by constraints imposed by a generalised news culture characterised by deference and opacity. It is important to underline the fact that journalists in MENA are effectively restricted by a set of direct and indirect laws and norms in which their professional autonomy is undermined. The truth is that the current political context in which these reporters operate poses important limitations and barriers on their ability to exercise their professional autonomy when doing their job. These limitations are products of politics, legislation and culture.

Having said that, science journalism does not face the same limitations given that it is not considered as politically sensitive as other newsbeats in the region. All the interviewees were clear on this and unanimously agreed that, contrary to other areas [newsbeats], science and technology rarely see any type of editorial control or state intervention. They pointed to the fact that even within the newsroom, editors, sub-editors and producers rarely intervene except to guarantee that the piece is well written and that it meets the standards of the media outlet.

Hence, we have argued in this book that it is not the constraints and restrictions imposed by politics and culture or religion that really hinder the potential of science journalism in the region but instead the lack of capabilities on the ground and the absence of an audience that creates a viable market for it. Our findings indicate that the lack of educational skills, professional autonomy and low level of interest in science news by the general public are the three most important elements that undermine the ability of science journalism in the Arab world to be able to offer a truly comprehensive, critical and engaging platform for science communication.

To be sure, most of the journalists interviewed for this study are not specialised in scientific news, nor do they have any type of training regarding engagement with, and production of, science news. To make matters worse, limited resources among many mainstream media outlets in the region and the absence of a sufficiently robust market for science news means that there are very few specialised outlets or media spaces in the region in which to practice science news. Instead, science is covered by individuals who must produce these stories alongside the coverage of other very distinctive newsbeats. This leaves no time to prepare beforehand for an interview, cross-check the information they are given or even explore areas that are not normally covered in the daily beat or provided by official sources.

## Accuracy and Rigour

The effect of the limitations in properly engaging with scientists and experts together with the overall inability to understand science is that journalists and even press officials in MENA at times get it wrong. Scientific news in the region may be problematic in terms of accuracy and interpretation as well as credibility and understanding. However, it is the lack of rigour in exploring the themes that these reporters cover that seems to create most of the problems in this regard. To explore this, we used the Delphi Panel methodology, which allows for the surveying of experts in a high-quality and scientific manner (Hohmann et al., 2018). In so doing, we set up a panel of seven top scientists in the region that included areas such as astronomy, biology, chemistry, medicine, engineering and physics. They were provided with a selected sample of 15 science news stories published in the region and asked to assess and evaluate these pieces in terms of accuracy and general quality in relation to their own expectations as experts.

In simple words, experts were asked if the journalists got it right. Contrary to initial expectations, most of the members of the panel indicated that there were examples of good practices and that in some cases news stories were extremely well written and accurate. As a panel member indicated,

> *Journalists in some of these articles have used the information in this article well and in a way that ordinary readers could understand. In one of the cases, his use of data was actually impressive, as he measured relationships, something that can be challenging for non-specialists. For example, the statistics in that particular story were presented clearly and communicated the science effectively. [DPM3]*

However, the panel found important flaws and limitations in some of the selected articles. Particularly in relation to contextualising the story and clarity about the sources that provided the story,

> *Some sources of the information may be unreliable and unknown at the scientific level. I assumed originally that the journalist knew about the classification of the journals that published these types of studies and whether it is classified as a strong and reliable journal. I assumed as well that he would verify this source or at least search for another reliable source that supports this study. I saw none of this and frankly, I was concerned that the story went without really checking if it was a serious study. I was not sure that the reporter understood how peer-review scientific journals operate or how to distinguish one reputable journal from one that has no credibility as he quoted from journals that literally are unknown in my field. [DPM6]*

Another panel member pointed out the fact that,

> *The story in one article does not cite any scientific sources. Who provided the information? I mean, the information may be correct but there is nothing to confirm it. One expects to see an expert in the story but there were none. More problematic was the fact that some of the figures used in the story were not accurate and there was no consistency among the statistics in the same story! [DPM1]*

All these reflect points from the expert panel that show both strengths and weaknesses in the ability of journalists who are not really specialised in dealing with scientific news. This, together with the lack of public interest in science creates an important challenge to the efforts to communicate science effectively. Having said that, the expert panel also highlighted important and significant differences within MENA countries such as

Egypt, Saudi Arabia and Kuwait. Our panel cannot, of course, be extrapolated to universal assumption in the region and further research in this topic is necessary to properly assess the level of quality.

All in all, in this case it seems to be the lack of skills and education regarding the ability of reporters to understand science and understand its procedures that accounts for the gaps and flaws, and which present the main barriers to providing a high-quality level of science news that contributes effectively to the delivery of knowledge, understanding and engagement with sciences among the general public. There are simply not enough reporters who themselves are dedicated to this newsbeat and the few that are out there are limited by constraints of resources and time pressure. The absence of science news reporters who can remain engaged with science is key to explaining the problems around PUS and PES in the region.

This is, however, excellent news. This is because these are variables that we in the Middle East can control and intervene in effectively to address. Neither politics nor religion is the restricting factor that hinders science journalism in MENA, as it is often assumed in the west. If, well, we do need to account for important limitations and issues derived from history, politics and cultures, it is no less true that as a newsbeat science is far less susceptible to the impositions of time and controls that other subject areas might face.

We are well aware that this challenges common assumptions around contextual limitations in the MENA region, which sees politics and religion as unique culprits for journalism in this part of the world somehow not matching the normative professional expectations set in the west. The lack of political freedom and cultural issues associated with the central role of religion in these societies is often cited to be somehow the only factors in creating directly, or indirectly, adverse effects on news practices and professional autonomy. Many of these voices expect a type of journalism that replicates the western political institutions and normative expectations, given that this has been the trend since 1945 in trying to export a model of news reporting to the Global South (Lugo-Ocando, 2020; Paterson et al., 2018).

We are not for one moment trying to argue that these external factors such as the political system in which reporters operate do not affect their ability to perform. On the contrary, whenever professional autonomy is compromised, journalists are unable to fulfil their normative aspirations and that includes the need to bring accountability into science. Most evidence suggests that, in this part of the world, it is almost impossible for news reporters to meet basic standards regarding their normative aspiration of bringing about transparency and accountability to power. We also understand that certain factors play an important role in undermining good practices in reporting in the region. Political settings, culture and economics account for a great deal of the issues and problems around news gathering in the region.

However, even if we accept those premises, the fact remains that the latter is mostly true for other newsbeats such as politics and economics. Our fieldwork underpins the idea that not all newsbeats are the same in MENA. In fact, science and technology are not as heavily regulated and censored as, let us say, politics or economics in the Arab world. Hence, at least in theory, we could expect a greater quality in science news given the fact that reporters working in this beat enjoy more professional autonomy than their peers. Science news reporting is a completely different ball game in the region as it enjoys far more freedoms and autonomy than other areas, even if many in the newsrooms are too embedded in the political culture to see so.

Indeed, rather than taking advantage of these spaces for professional independence, what we see instead are similar gaps, flaws and malpractices as in any of the other more heavily regulated newsbeats. This last point cannot therefore be attributed solely to the contextual limitations. The problems that science news reporting faces are rather different and from a distinctive nature. To start with, there is the general lack of interest from the public in scientific news (Abdulrahman, 2008; Abu Haseera, 2018; Abu Samra, 1995; Bebawi, 2016; El-Awady, 2009; Mellor, 2005, 2011; Rugh, 2004), which makes it difficult to have dedicated spaces for science and technology in the mainstream news outlets. This in turn has undermined the creation of a sufficient number of sustainable spaces to provide a critical mass of independent science news while contributing to the lack of specialised journalists, as it is infeasible for most media outlets to dedicate individuals to this newsbeat. If, well, it is true that the COVID-19 pandemic might have been a turning point, it remains to be seen if editors and producers, as well as media owners—including governments—are willing to 'put their money where their mouth is' in relation to the creation of proper capabilities for science news.

In relation to the real and evident problems that science journalism faces in MENA, our book has pointed to three that we think are decisive and that could be addressed promptly. The key issues signposted in this book are: (1) the lack of education, training and skills within the newsrooms, (2) the lack of professional autonomy and (3) the lack of interest in science news by the wider public. Only the lack of professional autonomy represents the type of challenge that would be difficult to address in this region given the nature of the political systems. However, even if that were the case, there is a lot that can be done in relation to education and skills as well as the interest of audiences. Indeed, education and training of journalists and the public at large seem to be one way forward. It is clear that the lack of skills among local journalists in relation to science affects their ability to provide sound and comprehensive science news. This is aggravated by the absence of an educational framework in the region that can address those gaps and contribute to the general improvement of science journalism in the region. The creation of provision in terms of specialised Master's, training provisions and resources in Arabic and other languages in the region can be a contributing factor in improving this situation.

In MENA, education and skills are far more important for journalists in providing their ability to articulate science news in ways that are comprehensible to, and accessible by, the readers. One important clarification that emerged from the study is the difference between skills and education. It became clear that this dichotomy is central to the formation of journalists and their news cultures in the region and in their ability to engage with science. In this sense, skills need to be understood as the ability to do something, while education is a way to be able to interpret and critically think about the world. Journalists who arrive at a newsroom might be very good at 'doing' news coverage but not necessarily at critically thinking about that coverage. This is, as we explored here, a persistent problem in the Arab world given that it limits their capacity to develop and set their own news agenda independently from official sources.

To be sure, the educational background and training of journalists can play a crucial role in allowing them to examine and validate important claims made by scientists and experts, as well as contextualise these stories within broader societal discussions. Our own study shows that there is a lack of ability in terms of critically understanding science and to manage key concepts. This trait was displayed by more than half of the Arab journalists we interviewed, who confessed to feeling ill-prepared to deal with the different subjects in science. Several factors contribute to this lack of understanding, such as educational background and the scarcity of training courses in these countries. This knowledge gap among reporters can also help to explain the lack of interest in scientific stories as reporters will tend to prioritise producing stories in newsbeats that they actually feel comfortable writing about.

To be sure, journalism education plays a role in improving professional practices of journalism (Deuze, 2005). In this respect, there has been a noticeable development in media colleges in the Arab world in recent years, particularly at universities in the GCC, which has seen an increase in the number of higher education institutions and total number of students undertaking communication, media and journalism studies across the region. However, there is still a lack of provision in the teaching of science in those degrees and few exhibit dedicated courses to science news reporting. However, it is important to say that the lack of teaching provision in relation to science journalism is not only present in the Arab world, but also at the global level with the exception of STEM-related subjects delivered by liberal programmes that are part of the broader media and journalism degrees.

This is also the case in the Arab world, where science is not directly incorporated as a core area for journalism studies and is rather offered tangentially as part of liberal arts programmes that are complementary, as our cross-national comparative analysis of syllabuses and curriculums in the seven countries suggests. This lack of educational provision in most of the media schools in the Arab world has led to important knowledge and skills gaps, not only because media and journalism students have little exposure to science but also because it wrongly gives the idea that it is not part of what journalists do. In this sense, universities, other educational institutions and newspapers in the region need to offer adequate provision and resources to develop skills and education to improve how journalists engage with statistics.

Here, however, there are some important caveats to address in this discussion. To start with, there is a debate between the scientific community and journalists about not only what to teach in such types of courses, but also, and more fundamentally, who they should be directed at and what should be the nature of the courses on offer. For years, the underlining aim from the scientific community to address the problems in PUS and PES is to cut out the middleperson. Hence, the argument runs, if only scientists would acquire the right media skills, then science communication would be better served.

The problem with this position is that it makes some assumptions while ignoring a series of factors that would undermine this view. To start with, several studies in science communication have highlighted the fact that scientists might be able to communicate their own specialism better than others, but if they were to communicate about a different branch of science outside of their expertise, then this would be as good as (no better than?) any journalist without that expert knowledge (Allan, 2009; Secko et al., 2013; Simis et al., 2016). Thus, a biologist who turns reporter might be excellent at covering issues such as genetics, environment and wildlife but they might be just as ill-prepared to report astronomy as anyone else in the newsroom without a science background.

Secondly, the scientific community's position tends to obviate the political economy that underpins most media outlets' operations. In truth, as we have discussed in this book, few media outlets—not only in Arab countries, but also in the rest of the world—have the capacity to have dedicated reporters, editors and producers solely focused on science and technology. In the newsrooms, people exchange newsbeats and despite ample examples of specialisation in which particular reporters cover a newsbeat for years and even decades, the majority of the news media can hardly afford to do so. Our own conversations with the interviewees in MENA showcase that only two out of all the interviewees had done science constantly as part of their regular beat for at least five years. However, even they shared this beat with others and were often assigned and re-assigned to other areas such as economy, politics and sports (this was particularly the case of newspapers).

The other part of the problem is that education and training is also not available at the upper scale, that is, when the individuals are already working in the field. For years, many organisations and institutions have created important training provision online and offline to support science journalists and enhance their capacity to provide comprehensive and accurate coverage. These include important provision in English, Arabic and other languages spoken in MENA. Having said that, with the news organisations in which reporters work they are rarely open to conceding time and space for professional development in this field. There is, overall, little appetite or organisational culture in the region to take a strategic view of where such organisations want to see their journalists in the future. In most cases, this is because the news organisations themselves lack this longer-term view.

In other cases, journalists do not know about available resources or just struggle with the work–life balance. In a region in which there is a high turnover of staff and where many reporters are not local, even as they stay in one place for decades, the tendency is not to plan ahead in terms of professional development of individuals in the newsroom. Hence, there is an urgent need in MENA for a more concerted approach that brings together journalists, media owners and government so as to make sure that there is a long-term strategy in delivering support to those who want to develop in this area.

## OTHER PROBLEMS AND CHALLENGES

However, even if journalists in MENA had been able to jump through all the hoops and somehow managed to achieve a degree of expertise and specialisation, they would still face a lack of access to resources to provide appropriate coverage of science. This relates to the lack of resources available in the news organisations, such as access to databases beyond the ones offered by official sources, so as to improve critical examination and cross-triangulation. In some cases, these limitations are due to financial shortcomings, which prevent media outlets from acquiring, accessing and managing databases independent of governments and external institutions or opening subscriptions to important publications or peer-review journals.

Of equal hindrance are the internal policies, norms and dynamics of the news media outlets themselves, which differ from one country to another. This is something that we have discussed widely across this book, but something which needs to be emphasised. This is because these dynamics determine the level of freedom or editorial procedures that can affect journalists' ability to perform their aspirational role. To be sure, the news organisation, in the case of science news, plays a much greater role in terms of defining levels of professionalism than any external factors. The organisational cultures in many of the news media in MENA are ones that are mostly characterised by self-restraint and self-censorship, which prevail when it comes to covering any beat, as we have already explained.

Having said that, our findings indicate that current assumptions about the limitations and challenges for journalists in the Arab world do not hold in the case of the science newsbeat and that it is instead education, organisational cultures and broader societal dynamics that determine the shortcomings of news reporting in this beat. Again, just to clarify, we are not suggesting that external factors have no bearing on the ability of science journalists to work independently in MENA. On the contrary, professional autonomy in some newsbeats cannot be exercised at all due to these contextual limitations. Illiberal regimes in these countries impose tight control over the media through draconian, and at times, discretional regulation that leads to censorship and self-censorship (Mellor, 2005; Rugh, 2004; Sakr, 2007). In doing so, these governments aim to control freedom of expression in order to ensure that what is published and broadcast to the public is in line with the government's objectives (Mellor, 2011, p. 164; Sakr, 2007, p. 15). To be sure, there is little doubt that Arab governments today continue to hold control over the media to varying degrees. Even in the midst of the Arab Spring, there were clear examples of the traditional cultures of censorship and press control continuing to be exercised in places such as the Egyptian press under the Muslim Brotherhood. In many of these places, journalists continue to be in a precarious position by exercising professional autonomy. If they transgress particular issues, they may find their career is finished, suffer penalties, face prison or even death.

However, even in some countries where we do not expect to see journalism practices that fulfil the slightest aspiration of being a watchdog, we can still expect at least some degree of professional autonomy in newsbeats such as science that has a low level of external regulation and intervention. After all, science news reporting as a newsbeat is not controversial or as politically sensitive as current affairs. Therefore, political constraints on professional autonomy do bear as much weight on the outputs produced by science reporters. There is a much greater degree of freedom and independence, both across countries as well as intra-nationally. However, this is not the case, and even in places such as Kuwait and Tunisia, where the news media enjoys far more freedom than in other places in the region (RWB, 2017), we can still see important deficiencies and flaws in relation to the news coverage of science. Our content analysis and close reading of a selected sample of news stories indicated similar levels of inaccuracy and misrepresentation of statistics in science news as in other countries, as well as a very timid approach towards accountability of official sources. Kuwaiti journalists interviewed complained that the reason for this was that even this type of news is imposed upon them through press releases and editorial pressures because it is paid for by commercial companies or part of the government agenda; therefore, they are unable to perform further scrutiny of the content of these stories.

It is important to note here that it is not only governments who create censorship pressures in science journalism but also pharmaceutical companies, which have a major role to play in influencing professional autonomy in the Arab world thanks to their powerful role as major advertisers. Interestingly, for example, our analysis showed that newspapers in the region present ads in the form of scientific news, whether in health or technology, without even checking and reviewing the statistical information upon which they are based. Further research is needed to establish how much resources are allocated to promoting corporate agendas by means of advertisement and marketing. We know from studies in other countries that this type of marketing investment can be central to co-opting the news agenda of the media and undermining criticality and independence in the news coverage of areas such as health (Briggs & Hallin, 2016; Hallin & Briggs, 2015).

Indeed, some commercial private companies in a diversity of areas such as health and defence may exploit this tendency by passing on information that serves the promotion of a commodity without mentioning the source name, which is originally the commercial company. Hence, our book also identified corporate interests as an additional element hindering a more comprehensive and critical news reporting of science. In this sense, the news media in MENA share with their Western counterparts in their bending to the corporate world and promoting private agendas.

Indeed, we found that the political economy of the newspapers in the Arab world plays a much greater role than the contextual limitations—politics and culture—although it might also be strongly correlated with them. This is because many Arab newspapers still largely depend on government funding to some extent and they and their owners are deeply dependent on subsidies, government advertisement and particular contracts that make up the economy of these organisations.

It is important to fully identify this aspect given its pervasive effects upon professional autonomy. In our view, persistent government and corporate interventions to shape the science news agenda in their favour weaken the ethical framework among journalists who rarely engage with more critical deontological reflections on what they do because they are under external pressures to reproduce what officials and private companies pass on as news and comply with their agendas. All this, is our view, is detrimental to the whole of society.

## It Is Not Faith Alone

As we have seen, science journalism in MENA faces a series of challenges in a variety of forms; many across the region are very different in nature. This is why the persistent orientalist assumption that places religion at the epicentre of the problems and that seems to be obsessed with a category that only highlights the tensions between religion and science as a rational–irrational dichotomy needs to be fully challenged. For these voices, the role that religion plays in these societies is somehow the best explanation for the failures of science in the region. Accordingly, they often argue, countries in which Islam is so central are unable to incorporate objective and factual truth in their analysis of science and, presumably, which in turn limits science itself as it needs to be subordinated to faith (Dawkins, 2006; Hitchens, 2008).

So, let us start by debunking this view by affirming that religion is a false category that has been used historically to simplify what are, by all accounts, far more complex issues in those societies (Asad, 2020 [2003]; Fitzgerald, 2003; Said, 2003 [1978]). Far from these common narratives, Islam is not responsible for gaps in PUS and PES. Islam, on the contrary, not only allows, but calls for, critical thinking around science. The four main schools of thought in Islamic jurisprudence—Hanafi, Shafi'i, Maliki and Hanbali—all promote engagement with scientific knowledge. So why then is critical thinking among Arab journalists in such a state and what can explain the low level of public engagement with science news? Again, as we have discussed at length here, most of these problems reside in prevalent organisational cultures, the political economy of the media and the deep flaws of education systems with poorly designed provision, that rather promote the shallow memorisation of facts than critical examination of processes and issues in science (Al Zahrani & Elyas, 2017).

This is not to say that religious and cultural backgrounds do not influence and even determine, to an extent, Arab journalists' ability to cover science. After all, we are both cultural and political animals. However, religion does not have the degree of hindering influence that many ascribe to it. Journalists in the region might believe that a disease such as HIV/AIDS, for example, carries a moral weight and therefore that it might be a matter of faith. However, as many theologians and other experts have clarified over the years, this is more to do with a misunderstanding of faith than of religion itself (Aldhaleei & Bhagavathula, 2020; Barmania & Reiss, 2018). Misconceptions about religion also affect the news coverage of other areas such as genetic disorders that occur because of intermarriage between tribes. If, instead, journalists highlighted the real numbers of people with problems due to marriage among relatives, this might establish controls and address some of the issues. Again, these debates have nothing to do with faith and, even within different Islamic countries would certainly find different interpretations.

In the past, religious leaders have had a role in influencing the media in a variety of places such as in MENA. Some suggest that Islam has affected governments in the region through religious leaders who have power as legitimising agents for government's political acts (Awad, 2010, p. 12). As a result, the news media have also been prone to be subject to the influence and pressure of religious leaders when publishing their news stories (Al-Kahtani, 1999, p. 215).

However, in recent decades, globalisation and a limited but sustained process of institutional liberalisation have been instrumental in changing the political settings. Progress is observed, to differing degrees, across the region, although with important setbacks.

Most of the MENA countries, but particularly those in the GCC, have come to draw on the so-called Vision 2030, which encompasses a series of policies and initiatives to modernise these societies and diversify their economies. In all cases, these strategic plans engage with the need to make knowledge a central part of society's future and this means in many cases making STEM education central at all levels. The Vision 2030 plans are also an attempt to push for evidence-based policy and for further engagement with both globalisation and modernisation of the existing institutions within society. Some have pointed out how religious leaders have lost power and are not as influential in politics and policy-making as they once were in many of the Gulf countries, while in others that traditionally had more secularised institutions, there is a push for greater technocracy (Dekmejian, 1994; Lacroix, 2019; Ulrichsen & Sheline, 2019).

How these changes will reshape journalism as a political institution in MENA and what opportunities and challenges they will create for science journalism, remains a matter of future research. Again, not all countries in MENA can be painted with the same brush and important caveats remain need to be accounted for. However, one thing seems certain overall, journalism as a whole, and despite important setbacks and very concerning issues, is in a better place than it was. We can embrace these changes and push forward at times, whether by leaping ahead or by taking baby steps. The direction seems for now to be facing forward.

## Future Research

From the start, we have clearly stated that this book never intended to be the definitive guide or even a comprehensive map of what science journalism does in the MENA region. That is a map that is being developed, as we speak, by many researchers from the region who are making extraordinary contributions to our understanding of this beat in the region. We have tried our best to combine our own research with that of our colleagues, past and present, in an attempt to start building an explanatory theoretical framework that provides some insightful discussion and directionality as where to go from here.

Consequently, our book is rather about opening a much-needed discussion about journalism as a whole and an effort towards a better understanding of the gathering, production and dissemination of science news in a region that is often perceived to be at odds with science. We hope to have debunked these myths regarding the assumed incapability between the region and the practice of science journalism, which, frankly speaking, is nothing more than orientalist and poorly substantiated assumptions. We also hope to have made it plainly clear that the complexities around the coverage of science in MENA both overlap with the west and have distinctive features at the same time from it. We are hoping to incentivise future research around science journalism in the Arab world. However, we have tried to do so by showing that scholars in the region have already produced a robust and significant body of work and that scholars in the west need to engage with this literature that at times challenges or confirms some of the most predominant theories in our field.

We have discussed possible solutions and approaches but all of them need to acknowledge the central role that the state plays in these societies. Having said that, governments alone can do very little unless they coordinate with other governments, institutions and organisations in the region. This, as most of the issues that we have explored here demand regional solutions given the nature and scale of the flows and counter-flows of people who live in MENA. We argue that any solution requires concerted and coordinated efforts, including more collaborative journalistic work between different media outlets and a greater number of exchanges between regional news agencies and media outlets. Energising regional professional science journalism associations that can help put in place a comprehensive programme of continuous education and creating permanent networks and spaces for the different media in the region to exchange science news, can be a good step forward. For us, in academia, the challenge is also to take a more regional approach and to work together to develop sound research that generates the necessary knowledge that leads the way to a better future.

This collaboration is urgent as further research is needed in order to explore the impact of cultural, political and religious factors on articulating science news in the region. The lesson from COVID-19 is unequivocal, and we need to better understand the most effective ways to communicate science to the public. There are also important gaps that require this type of collaboration. Our own research, for example, has not considered sufficiently the power and influence of corporate lobby groups in relation to professional autonomy and how this affects science news in MENA. Particularly considering the impact of commercial companies and enterprises in creating additional constraints on the work of reporters and shaping both news agendas and public debates.

Nevertheless, we consider that the greatest challenge and task for researchers wanting to look at science news is not so much on the production and dissemination of science news but instead on our ability to understand its reception and consumption. This is easier said than done as some MENA countries have little appetite—and tolerance—for the type of surveys of the public that would need to be done. Therefore, recognising readers' capabilities to understand science news may require exploring this topic from a different angle and undertaking alternative methodologies and approaches.

From preliminary works we now know that audiences seem not to be interested in science news. This, we know, affects in turn the ability of journalism as a political institution to develop a more comprehensive and critical reporting of science. Hence, it will be interesting to explore further the causes of this disinterest, such as why nations with relatively high income exhibit low levels of engagement. One possible explanation, as we discussed here, is that many Arab societies host large numbers of immigrants including refugees and migrant workers. In some of these places, they constitute the great majority of the population. These create structural barriers that hinder PES and PUS as most have hardly any educational background at all. Ignoring these segments of the population and only counting the Arabs might be the best recipe for failure in science communication and health campaigns in the region (Dun, 2018; Dun & Ali, 2018).

Finally, it is important to pinpoint the multiple challenges that this newsbeat faces today in many Arab countries, including the shortage of capabilities and skills among journalists, which is by all means one of the most important barriers and limitations to their ability to exercise professional autonomy. The book has highlighted some of the weaknesses and strengths in the Arab scientific media in order to suggest a possible solution for improving journalistic practices. We have discussed here the fact that many of these issues can actually be addressed in those societies despite the nature of their political systems. This gives us very good reasons for optimism.

All in all, we want to reiterate that science journalism deserves our attention as researchers, mostly because of its potential to help improve any society, rich or poor. It is good also for journalism itself as there is ample indication that science news reporting played a role in helping professionalise news institutions and news values in many parts of the world (Dennis & McCartney, 1979; Lugo-Ocando, 2020). This is why we need to underline the role it can play in helping the Arab world develop, in broader terms, a type of science communication that can serve its people, even as science news reporting is practised within particular circumstances and rigid contexts in the region.

## Bibliography

Abdulrahman, A. (2008). *Arab women journalists' concerns and challenges: Realistic testimonies.* Al-Arabi.

Abu Haseera, R. (2018). *The reality of scientific journalism in the Palestinian daily newspapers: A comparative analytical and field study.* Islamic University of Gaza.

Abu Samra, N. (1995). *Media performance obstacles of female Egyptian journalists.* Assiut University.

Al Zahrani, B., & Elyas, T. (2017). The implementation of critical thinking in a Saudi EFL context: Challenges and opportunities. *IJELTAL (Indonesian Journal of English Language Teaching and Applied Linguistics), 1*(2), 133–141.

Aldhaleei, W. A., & Bhagavathula, A. S. (2020). HIV/AIDS-knowledge and attitudes in the Arabian Peninsula: A systematic review and meta-analysis. *Journal of Infection and Public Health, 13*(7), 939–948.

Al-Kahtani, A. M. (1999). *The performance of the Saudi Arabian press during the Gulf Conflict, 1990–1991.* University of Leeds.

Allan, S. (2009). The future of science journalism. *Journalism, 10*(3), 280–282.

Al-Qafari, A. (2009). *Science media in Saudi journalism.* King Abdul-Aziz City for Science and Technology (KACST).

Asad, T. (2020). *Formations of the secular.* Stanford University Press.

Awad, T. (2010). *The Saudi press and the Internet: How Saudi journalists and media decision makers at the Ministry of Culture and Information evaluate censorship in the presence of the Internet as a news and information medium.* The University of Sheffield.

Barmania, S., & Reiss, M. J. (2018). *Islam and health policies related to HIV prevention in Malaysia*. Springer.

Bauer, M. W. (2013). The knowledge society favours science communication, but puts science journalism into a clinch. *Science Communication Today, Paris, CNRS*, 145–166.

Bebawi, S. (2016). *Investigative Journalism in the Arab World: Issues and Challenges*. Springer.

Briggs, C., & Hallin, D. (2016). *Making health public: How news coverage is remaking media, medicine, and contemporary life*. Routledge.

Crewdson, J. (2002). *A scientific mystery, a massive coverup, and the dark legacy of Robert Gallo*. Little, Brown & Co.

Dawkins, R. (2006). *The God delusion*. Bantam Books.

Dekmejian, R. H. (1994). The rise of political Islamism in Saudi Arabia. *Middle East Journal, 48*(4), 627–643.

Dennis, E. E., & McCartney, J. (1979). Science journalists on metropolitan dailies: Methods, values and perceptions of their work. *The Journal of Environmental Education, 10*(3), 9–15.

Deuze, M. (2005). What is journalism? Professional identity and ideology of journalists reconsidered. *Journalism, 6*(4), 442–464.

Dun, S. (2018). *Assessing and improving migrant workers access to and utilization of health information and resources. 2018*(4), SSAHPD443.

Dun, S., & Ali, A. Z. (2018). 'Seatbelts don't save lives': Discovering and targeting the attitudes and behaviors of young Arab male drivers. *Accident Analysis & Prevention, 121*, 185–193.

El-Awady, N. (2009). Science journalism: The Arab boom. *Nature, 459*, 1057.

Fitzgerald, T. (2003). *The ideology of religious studies*. Oxford University Press.

Hallin, D. C., & Briggs, C. L. (2015). Transcending the medical/media opposition in research on news coverage of health and medicine. *Media, Culture & Society, 37*(1), 85–100.

Hitchens, C. (2008). *God is not great: How religion poisons everything*. McClelland & Stewart.

Hohmann, E., Brand, J. C., Rossi, M. J., & Lubowitz, J. H. (2018). Expert opinion is necessary: Delphi panel methodology facilitates a scientific approach to consensus. *Arthroscopy: The Journal of Arthroscopic & Related Surgery, 34*(2), 349–351.

Jones, J. H. (1993). *Bad blood*. Simon and Schuster.

Lacroix, S. (2019). Saudi Arabia and the limits of religious reform. *The Review of Faith & International Affairs, 17*(2), 97–101.

Lewis, J., Williams, A., & Franklin, B. (2008). A compromised fourth estate? UK news journalism, public relations and news sources. *Journalism Studies, 9*(1), 1–20.

Lewis, J. M. W., Williams, A., Franklin, R. A., Thomas, J., & Mosdell, N. A. (2008). *The quality and independence of British journalism*. Cardiff School of Journalism, Media and Cultural Studies.

Lugo-Ocando, J. (2020). *Foreign aid and journalism in the global south: A mouthpiece for truth*. Lexington Books.

Mellado, C. (2015). Professional roles in news content: Six dimensions of journalistic role performance. *Journalism Studies, 16*(4), 596–614.

Mellor, N. (2005). *The making of Arab news*. Rowman & Littlefield Publishers.

Mellor, N. (2011). *Arab media: Globalization and emerging media industries* (Vol. 1). Polity.

Molek-Kozakowska, K. (2017). Journalistic practices of science popularization in the context of users' agenda: A case study of New Scientist. *Acta Universitatis Lodziensis. Folia Litteraria Polonica, 43*(5), 93–109.

Nguyen, A., & McIlwaine, S. (2011). Who wants a voice in Science issues—And why? A survey of European citizens and its implications for science journalism. *Journalism Practice, 5*(2), 210–226.

Paterson, C., Gadzekpo, A., & Wasserman, H. (2018). Journalism and Foreign Aid in Africa. *African Journalism Studies, 39*(2), 1–8.

Reverby, S. M. (2005). 'Misrepresentations of the Tuskegee Study'—Distortion of analysis and facts? *Journal of the National Medical Association, 97*(8), 1180.

Rugh, W. (2004). *Arab mass media: Newspapers, radio, and television in Arab politics*. Greenwood Publishing Group.

RWB. (2017). The 2017 World Press Freedom Index. Reporters Without Borders. https://rsf.org/en/2017-pressfreedom-index-ever-darker-world-map-0

Said, E. (2003). *Orientalism: Western conceptions of the Orient*. Penguin Books Limited.

Sakr, N. (2007). *Arab television today*. IB Tauris.

Scheufele, D. A., & Krause, N. M. (2019). Science audiences, misinformation, and fake news. *Proceedings of the National Academy of Sciences, 116*(16), 7662–7669.

Secko, D. M., Amend, E., & Friday, T. (2013). Four models of science journalism: A synthesis and practical assessment. *Journalism Practice, 7*(1), 62–80.

Simis, M. J., Madden, H., Cacciatore, M. A., & Yeo, S. K. (2016). The lure of rationality: Why does the deficit model persist in science communication? *Public Understanding of Science, 25*(4), 400–414.

Ulrichsen, K. C., & Sheline, A. R. (2019). In J. A. Baker III (Ed.), *Mohammed Bin Salman and religious authority and reform in Saudi Arabia* (pp. 1–9). Institute for Public Policy of Rice University. https://scholarship.rice.edu/bitstream/handle/1911/108116/bi-report-092319-cme-mbs-saudi.pdf?sequence=1

# Bibliography

Abd Al-Elah, H. R. H., & Al-Saraj, S. K. (2021). Science Journalism within the framework of Media Richness Theory. *PalArch's Journal of Archaeology of Egypt/Egyptology, 18*(7), 2835–2844.

Abdallah, H. (2021). Qatari women 'outnumber men' at local universities [News]. *Doha News*. Retrieved May 12, 2022, from https://www.dohanews.co/qatari-women-outnumber-men-at-local-universities/

Abdel Rahman Qanchouba, K. R. (2021). COVID-19 crisis: The need for science media. *Journal of Human Sciences, 21*(1), 824–840.

Abdul Hafeez, H. (2016). Journalistic treatment of scientific topics in the Sudanese Press. *Journal of the Humanities, 1*(1), 109–118.

Abdulmajid, A. (2018). A Study on religious diversity and conflict in the middle east. *International Journal of Social Science and Humanities Research, 6*(3), 1–7.

Abdulrahman, A. (2008). *Arab women journalists' concerns and challenges: Realistic testimonies*. Al-Arabi.

Abu Haseera, R. (2018). *The reality of scientific journalism in the Palestinian daily newspapers: A comparative analytical and field study*. Islamic University of Gaza.

Abu Saiba, S. N. (2016). The Lebanese press in the stage of leadership and establishment: A study in the archives of the Lebanese National Archives. *Journal of the College of Education for Girls for Human Sciences, 10*(18), 401–448.

Abu Samra, N. (1995). *Media performance obstacles of female Egyptian journalists*. Assiut University.

Adler-Nissen, R., Andersen, K. E., & Hansen, L. (2020). Images, emotions, and international politics: The death of Alan Kurdi. *Review of International Studies, 46*(1), 75–95.

© The Author(s), under exclusive license to Springer Nature Switzerland AG 2023
A. Alhuntushi, J. Lugo-Ocando, *Science Journalism in the Arab World*, Palgrave Studies in Journalism and the Global South,
https://doi.org/10.1007/978-3-031-14252-9

Afridi, M. (2013). Contribution of Muslim scientists to the world: An overview of some selected fields. *Revelation and Science, 3*(01).

Ahmad, M. I. (2015). The magical realism of body counts: How media credulity and flawed statistics sustain a controversial policy. *Journalism*, 1464884915593237.

Aistrope, T., & Bleiker, R. (2018). Conspiracy and foreign policy. *Security Dialogue, 49*(3), 165–182.

Ajwa, I. A., Liu, Z., & Wang, P. S. (2003). *Gröbner Bases Algorithm* (pp. 1–14). The Institute for Computational Mathematics.

Al Rawi, K. H. (2010). *History of the press and media in Iraq from the Ottoman era until the second Gulf War*. Pages House for Studies and Publishing.

Al Zahrani, B., & Elyas, T. (2017). The implementation of critical thinking in a Saudi EFL context: Challenges and opportunities. *IJELTAL (Indonesian Journal of English Language Teaching and Applied Linguistics), 1*(2), 133–141.

Alaleeli, S., & Alnajjar, A. (2020). The Arab digital generation's engagement with technology: The case of high school students in the UAE. *JOTSE: Journal of Technology and Science Education, 10*(1), 159–178.

Alaqil, F., & Lugo-Ocando, J. (2021). Using statistics in business and financial news in the Arabian Gulf: Between normative journalistic professional aspirations and 'real' practice. *Journalism Practice*, 1–24. https://doi.org/10.1080/17512786.2021.1930572

Alaqil, F. A., & Lugo-Ocando, J. (2019). Challenges and opportunities for teaching data and statistics within journalism education in Saudi Arabia: Fostering new capabilities in the region. *Journalism Education, 8*(2), 55–66.

Aldhaleei, W. A., & Bhagavathula, A. S. (2020). HIV/AIDS-knowledge and attitudes in the Arabian Peninsula: A systematic review and meta-analysis. *Journal of Infection and Public Health, 13*(7), 939–948.

Alexakos, K., & Antoine, W. (2005). The golden age of Islam and science teaching. *The Science Teacher, 72*(3), 36.

Al-Hassan, I. M. (2010). *Specialized press*. Zahran Publishing and Distribution House.

Alheezan, M. (2007). Teaching media in the Saudi and American universities. *Arabic Journal for Media and Communication, 2*, 187–230.

Alhumood, A., Shami, A., & Safia, A. (2016). *Media framing of the national economic projects in the Arab World*. Seventh Annual Forum of the Saudi Association for Media and Communication: The Media and the Economy—Integration Roles in the Service of Development, 11–12 April 2016, Riyadh.

Alhuntushi, A., & Lugo-Ocando, J. (2020). Articulating statistics in science news in Arab newspapers: Cases of Egypt, Kuwait and Saudi Arabia. *Journalism Practice*. https://doi.org/10.1080/17512786.2020.1808857

Aljuaid, K. (2020). *Media in Saudi Arabia: The challenge for female journalists*. PhD Thesis, University of Bedfordshire.

Al-Kahtani, A. M. (1999). *The performance of the Saudi Arabian press during the Gulf Conflict, 1990–1991*. University of Leeds.
Allan, S. (2002). *Media, risk and science*. Open University Press/McGraw-Hill Education.
Allan, S. (2004). *News culture*. Cambridge University of Press.
Allan, S. (2009). The future of science journalism. *Journalism, 10*(3), 280–282.
Allan, S. (2011). Introduction: Science journalism in a digital age. *Journalism, 12*(7), 771–777.
Allard, A. (1997). L'influence des mathématiques arabes dans l'Occident médiéval. *Histoire Des Sciences Arabes, 2*, 199–229.
Allen, L. (2008). Getting by the occupation: How violence became normal during the Second Palestinian Intifada. *Cultural Anthropology, 23*(3), 453–487.
Al-Malki, A., Kaufer, D., Ishizaki, S., & Dreher, K. (2012). *Arab women in Arab news: Old stereotypes and new media*. A&C Black.
Almond, G., & Verba, S. (1989). *The Civic Culture Revisited*. Sage.
Al-Mutairi, R. (2009). *Job satisfaction among Saudi female journalists and influencing factors*. Imam University.
AlNajjar, A. (2019). Abolish censorship and adopt critical media literacy: A proactive approach to media and youth in the Middle East. *Journal of Media Literacy Education, 11*(3), 73–84.
Al-Najjar, A. (2011). Contesting patriotism and global journalism ethics in Arab journalism. *Journalism Studies, 12*(6), 747–756.
Al-Qafari, A. (2009). *Science media in Saudi journalism*. King Abdul-Aziz City for Science and Technology (KACST).
Alqudsi-Ghabra, T. (1995). Information control in Kuwait: Dialectic to democracy. *Journal of South Asian and Middle Eastern Studies, 18*(4).
Al-Rawi, A. K. (2010). Iraqi women journalists' challenges and predicaments. *Journal of Arab & Muslim Media Research, 3*(3), 223–236.
AL-Salem, K., & Abu-Saab, A. (2007). Science Magazine. *AAL—Bahith AL—A'alami, 1*(3), 31–48.
Al-Sayegh, F. (1999). Diversity in unity: Political institutions and civil society. *Middle East Policy, 6*(4), 14.
Al-Suaid, I. M. (2016). Emirati media: Its origin and development. *The Scientific Journal of Public Relations and Advertising Research, 2016*(8), 437–467.
Altınbaş, N. (2014). Marriage and divorce in the late Ottoman Empire: Social upheaval, women's rights, and the need for new family law. *Journal of Family History, 39*(2), 114–125.
Alyan, H. (2012). History of science journalism in Kuwait. *Al Taqaddum Al-Ilmi Journal, 76*.
Alzougool, B., AlMansour, J., & AlAjmi, M. (2021). Women leadership styles in the public sector in Kuwait: The perspective of their subordinates. *Management Science Letters, 11*(2), 465–472.

Amr, S. S., & Tbakhi, A. (2007). Abu Bakr Muhammad Ibn Zakariya Al Razi (Rhazes): Philosopher, Physician and Alchemist. *Annals of Saudi Medicine, 27*(4), 305–307.

Amrane-Minne, D. D., & Abu-Haidar, F. (1999). Women and politics in Algeria from the War of Independence to our day. *Research in African Literatures, 30*(3), 62–77.

Anderson, A., Peterson, A., David, M., & Allan, S. (2005). Communication or spin? Source-media relations in science journalism. *Journalism: Critical Issues*, 188–198.

Anderson, C. (2018). *Apostles of certainty: Data journalism and the politics of doubt*. Oxford University Press.

Anema, A., Freifeld, C. C., Druyts, E., Montaner, J. S. G., Hogg, R. S., & Brownstein, J. S. (2010). An assessment of global Internet-based HIV/AIDS media coverage: Implications for United Nations Programme on HIV/AIDS'Global Media HIV/AIDS Initiative. *International Journal of STD & AIDs, 21*(1), 26–29.

Angler, M. W. (2017). *Science Journalism. An Introduction*. Routledge.

AP. (2020). China cuts Uighur births with IUDs, abortion, sterilization. *The Associated Press*. Retrieved June 1, 2022, from https://apnews.com/article/ap-top-news-international-news-weekend-reads-china-health-269b3de1af34e17c1941a514f78d764c

Asad, T. (2003). *Formations of the secular: Christianity, Islam, modernity*. Stanford University Press.

Asad, T. (2020). *Formations of the secular*. Stanford University Press.

Ashwell, D. (2016). The challenges of science journalism: The perspectives of scientists, science communication advisors and journalists from New Zealand. *Public Understanding of Science, 25*(3), 379–393.

Ateş, H., Es, M., & Bayraktar, Y. (2005). Dependency Theory: Still an appropriate tool for understanding the political economy of the middle-east? *Atatürk Üniversitesi İktisadi ve İdari Bilimler Dergisi, 19*(2), 247–262.

Atkins, P. (1995). Science as truth. *History of the Human Sciences, 8*(2), 97–102.

Atwater, T. (1988). Reader interest in environmental news. *Newspaper Research Journal, 10*(1), 31–38.

Autzen, C., & Weitkamp, M. (2018, June 7). *Science communication, public relations, journalism: Exploring blurry boundaries*. Current Challenges to Mediatised Science Communication Conference, Rostock.

AW. (2021). GCC sees women's rights progress in wake of reforms. *The Arab Weekly*. https://thearabweekly.com/gcc-sees-womens-rights-progress-wake-reforms

Awad, T. (2010). *The Saudi press and the Internet: How Saudi journalists and media decision makers at the Ministry of Culture and Information evaluate cen-*

sorship in the presence of the Internet as a news and information medium. The University of Sheffield.
Azzouz, H. (2016). The Algerian press specialized in the era of the French occupation. *Al-Turath Magazine, 22*(1), 190–181.
Badran, A. (2014). *The reality of scientific journalism in Kuwait from the perspective of journalists working in Kuwait.* Middle East University.
Baker, N., & Scott, H. (2018). Media capacity building in Sudan: A measure of success? *African Journalism Studies, 39*(2), 130–137.
Ballon, P., & Duclos, J. (2016). A comparative analysis of multidimensional poverty in Sudan and South Sudan. *African Development Review, 28*(S2), 132–161.
Barel-Ben David, Y., Garty, E. S., & Baram-Tsabari, A. (2020). Can scientists fill the science journalism void? Online public engagement with science stories authored by scientists. *PloS One, 15*(1), e0222250.
Barmania, S., & Reiss, M. J. (2018). *Islam and health policies related to HIV prevention in Malaysia.* Springer.
Bauer, M., & Bucchi, M. (2008). *Journalism, science and society: Science communication between news and public relations.* Routledge.
Bauer, M., Howard, S., Ramos, R., Jessica, Y., Massarani, L., & Amorim, L. (2013). *Global science journalism report: Working conditions & practices, professional ethos and future expectations.* Science and Development Network.
Bauer, M. W. (2013). The knowledge society favours science communication, but puts science journalism into a clinch. *Science Communication Today, Paris, CNRS*, 145–166.
Bauer, M. W., & Howard, S. (2009). *The Sense of Crisis among Science Journalists. A survey conducted on the occasion of WCSJ_09 in London. StePS. London School of Economics and Political Science.* Institute of Social Psychology.
Bebawi, S. (2016). *Investigative Journalism in the Arab World: Issues and Challenges.* Springer.
Beer, D. G. (2016). How should we do the history of big data? *Big Data & Society, 3*(1), 1–10.
Bellová, R., Balážová, M., & Tomčík, P. (2021). Are attitudes towards science and technology related to critical areas in science education? *Research in Science & Technological Education*, 1–16.
Bennato, D. (2017). The shift from public science communication to public relations. The Vaxxed case. *Journal of Science Communication, 16*(2), C02.
Benson, R., & Neveu, E. (2005). *Bourdieu and the journalistic field.* Polity Press.
Berkowitz, D., & Beach, D. W. (1993). News sources and news context: The effect of routine news, conflict and proximity. *Journalism & Mass Communication Quarterly, 70*(1), 4–12.
Bernadas, J. M. A. C., & Ilagan, K. (2020). Journalism, public health, and COVID-19: Some preliminary insights from the Philippines. *Media International Australia, 177*(1), 132–138.

Besley, J. C., Oh, S. H., & Nisbet, M. (2013). Predicting scientists' participation in public life. *Public Understanding of Science, 22*(8), 971–987.

Bibbo, B. (2008). *Call for creation of journalists' association in Qatar*. World Gulf. https://gulfnews.com/world/gulf/qatar/call-for-creation-of-journalists-association-in-qatar-1.84882

Boczkowski, P. (2021). *Abundance: On the Experience of Living in a World of Information Plenty*. Oxford University Press.

Boczkowski, P. J., & Mitchelstein, E. (2017). The gap between the media and the public. In C. Peters & M. Broersma (Eds.), *Rethinking Journalism Again: Societal role and public relevance in a digital* (pp. 175–186). Routledge.

Borges, R. E. (2017). Towards an epistemology of data journalism in the devolved nations of the UK: Changes and continuities in materiality, performativity and reflexivity. *Journalism*. https://doi.org/10.1177/1464884917693864

Borges-Rey, E. (2016). Unravelling Data Journalism: A study of data journalism practice in British newsrooms. *Journalism Practice, 10*(7), 833–843.

Borges-Rey, E., Heravi, B., & Uskali, T. (2018). Periodismo de datos iberoamericano: Desarrollo, contestación y cambio social. Presentación. *La Revista ICONO 14: Revista de Comuncacion y Tecnologias Emergentes, 16*(2), 1–13.

Bou Tebakalt, T. (2013). The role of the press in the modern Arab renaissance or when cultures cross. *Turjuman Magazine, 22*(2), 11–48.

Bouhaila, R. (2017). History of the specialized written press in general and sports in particular in Europe and the Arab world: Egypt and Algeria as a model., Issue 15. *Al-Maaref Journal for Research and Historical Studies, 15*(1), 289–309.

Brand, R. (2008). The numbers game: A case study of mathematical literacy at a South African newspaper. *Communication: South African Journal for Communication Theory and Research, 34*(2), 210–221.

Brandao, R. (2016). *Study shows: How statistics are used to articulate and shape discourses of science in the newsroom*. University of Sheffield.

Briggs, C., & Hallin, D. (2016). *Making health public: How news coverage is remaking media, medicine, and contemporary life*. Routledge.

Bro, P., & Wallberg, F. (2014). Digital gatekeeping: News media versus social media. *Digital Journalism, 2*(3), 446–454.

Brossard, D., & Scheufele, D. A. (2013). Science, new media, and the public. *Science, 339*(6115), 40–41.

Bubela, T., Nisbet, M. C., Borchelt, R., Brunger, F., Critchley, C., Einsiedel, E., Geller, G., Gupta, A., Hampel, J., & Hyde-Lay, R. (2009). Science communication reconsidered. *Nature Biotechnology, 27*(6), 514–518.

Bucchi, M. (1998). *Science and the media: Alternative routes in scientific communication*. Routledge.

Bucchi, M., & Mazzolini, R. (2003). Big science, little news: Science coverage in the Italian daily press, 1946–1997. *Public Understanding of Science, 12*(1), 7–24.

Burns, T., O'Connor, D., & Stocklmayer, S. (2003). Science communication: A contemporary definition. *Public Understanding of Science, 12*(2), 183–202.
Byerly, C. (2016). Jordan: Towards Gender Balance in the Newsroom. In C. Byerly (Ed.), *The Palgrave International Handbook of Women and Journalism*. Palgrave Macmillan.
Çakır, S. (2007). Feminism and feminist history-writing in Turkey: The discovery of Ottoman feminism. *Aspasia, 1*(1), 61–83.
Calvo Hernando, M. (2002). El periodismo del tercer milenio. Problemas de la divulgación científica en Iberoamérica. *Interciencia, 27*(2), 57–61.
Carlson, M. (2015). Introduction: The many boundaries of journalism. In M. Carlson & S. Lewis (Eds.), *Boundaries of Journalism: Professionalism, Practices and Participation* (pp. 1–18). Routledge.
Carrion-Alvarez, D., & Tijerina-Salina, P. X. (2020). Fake news in COVID-19: A perspective. *Health Promotion Perspectives, 10*(4), 290.
Carver, R. B. (2014). Public communication from research institutes: Is it science communication or public relations? *Journal of Science Communication, 13*(3), C01.
Chaney, E. (2016). *Religion and the rise and fall of Islamic science*. Harvard University.
Charrad, M. (2001). *States and women's rights: The making of postcolonial Tunisia, Algeria, and Morocco*. University of California Press.
Chetcuti, D. A., & Kioko, B. (2012). Girls' attitudes towards science in Kenya. *International Journal of Science Education, 34*(10), 1571–1589.
Citino, N. J. (2008). The Ottoman Legacy in cold war modernization. *International Journal of Middle East Studies, 40*(4), 579–597.
Claussen, J., Cooney, P., Defilippi, J., Fox, S., Glaser, S., Hawkes, E., Hutt, C., Jones, M., Kemp, I., & Lerner, A. (2013). Science communication in a digital age: Social media and the American Fisheries Society. *Fisheries, 38*(8), 359–362.
Cohn, V. (1989). *News & numbers: A guide to reporting statistical claims and controversies in health and other fields*. Iowa State University Press.
Cole, J. R. (1981). Feminism, class, and Islam in turn-of-the-century Egypt. *International Journal of Middle East Studies, 13*(4), 387–407.
Cook, G., Pieri, E., & Robbins, P. T. (2004). 'The scientists think and the public feels': Expert perceptions of the discourse of GM food. *Discourse & Society, 15*(4), 433–449.
Crewdson, J. (2002). *A scientific mystery, a massive coverup, and the dark legacy of Robert Gallo*. Little, Brown & Co.
Curtin, P. A., & Maier, S. R. (2001). Numbers in the newsroom: A qualitative examination of a quantitative challenge. *Journalism & Mass Communication Quarterly, 78*(4), 720–738.
Cushion, S., & Lewis, J. (2017). Impartiality, statistical tit-for-tats and the construction of balance: UK television news reporting of the 2016 EU referendum

campaign. *European Journal of Communication, 32*(3), 208–223. https://doi.org/10.1177/0267323117695736

Dajani, R., Dhawan, S., & Awad, S. M. (2020). The increasing prevalence of girls in stem education in the Arab World: What can we learn? *Sociology of Islam, 8*(2), 159–174.

Dallal, A. (2010). *Islam, science, and the challenge of history*. Yale University Press.

Davey-Quantick, J. (2020, March 24). *Censorship in the Islamic world, through the eyes of journalist Jessica Davey-Quantick*. [Recording]. Spotify. https://open.spotify.com/episode/2FA1XVGFixhntNAlua5PJl

Davey-Quantick, J. (2020, March 24). Censorship in the Islamic World, Through the Eyes of Journalist Jessica Davey-Quantick [Recording]. Spotify. https://open.spotify.com/episode/2FA1XVGFixhntNAlua5PJl

Davis, P., & Hersh, R. (2005). *Descartes' dream: The world according to mathematics*. Courier Corporation.

Davis, U. (2003). *Apartheid Israel: Possibilities for the struggle within*. Zed Books.

Dawkins, R. (2006). *The God delusion*. Bantam Books.

Dawson, E. (2018). Reimagining publics and (non) participation: Exploring exclusion from science communication through the experiences of low-income, minority ethnic groups. *Public Understanding of Science, 27*(7), 772–786.

De Angelis, E. (2015). Introduction: The hybrid system of Egypt and 'cultural chaos'. *Égypte/Monde Arabe, 12*, 21–33.

De Baets, A. (2016). Censorship by European states of views on their past as colonizers. In *La censure des États européens sur leur passé colonial* (pp. 229–245). Presses Universitaires de Rennes.

Dekmejian, R. H. (1994). The rise of political Islamism in Saudi Arabia. *Middle East Journal, 48*(4), 627–643.

Dennis, E., Martin, J., & Allagui, I. (2020). *Media Use in the Middle East*.

Dennis, E., Martin, J., & Allagui, I. (2020). Media Use in the Middle East. Northwestern University in Qatar. https://www.mideastmedia.org/survey/2019/ [Accessed on January 18, 2022]

Dennis, E. E., & McCartney, J. (1979). Science journalists on metropolitan dailies: Methods, values and perceptions of their work. *The Journal of Environmental Education, 10*(3), 9–15.

Determann, J. M. (2015). *Researching biology and evolution in the Gulf states: Networks of science in the Middle East*. Bloomsbury Publishing.

Determann, J. M. (2018). *Space Science and the Arab World: Astronauts, observatories and nationalism in the middle east*. Bloomsbury Publishing.

Deuze, M. (2005). What is journalism? Professional identity and ideology of journalists reconsidered. *Journalism, 6*(4), 442–464.

Deuze, M. (2011). Media life. *Media, Culture & Society, 33*(1), 137–148.

Díaz del Campo Lozano, J. (2012). Professionalization process of the journalist in Spain or the History with no end. *Anagramas-Rumbos y Sentidos de La Comunicación, 11*(21), 69–80.

Di-Capua, Y. (2015). Nahda: The Arab project of enlightenment. In *The Cambridge Companion to Modern Arab Culture* (pp. 54–74). Cambridge University Press.

Dickson, D. (2005). The case for a 'deficit model' of science communication. *SciDev.Net, 27*.

Dimitrova, D. V., & Strömbäck, J. (2009). Look who's talking: Use of sources in newspaper coverage in Sweden and the United States. *Journalism Practice, 3*(1), 75–91.

Dorling, D., & Simpson, S. (1999). *Statistics in society: The arithmetic of politics.* .

Douai, A. (2019). Global and Arab media in the post-truth era: Globalization, authoritarianism and fake news. *IEMed: Mediterranean Yearbook, 2019*, 124–132.

Douai, A., & Moussa, M. B. (2016). *Mediated identities and new journalism in the Arab world*. Palgrave Macmillan.

Dowling, D. O. (2020). When news became literature: The tumultuous ascent of narrative journalism in the twentieth century. *American Periodicals: A Journal of History & Criticism, 30*(2), 168–172.

Doyle, G. (2013). *Understanding media economics*. Sage.

Dun, S. (2018). Assessing and improving migrant workers access to and utilization of health information and resources. *2018*(4), SSAHPD443.

Dun, S., & Ali, A. Z. (2018). 'Seatbelts don't save lives': Discovering and targeting the attitudes and behaviors of young Arab male drivers. *Accident Analysis & Prevention, 121*, 185–193.

Dunwoody, S. (2014). *Science journalism*. Routledge.

Dunwoody, S. (2020). Science journalism and pandemic uncertainty. *Media and Communication, 8*(2), 471–474.

Dunwoody, S. (2021). Science journalism: Prospects in the digital age. In *Routledge handbook of public communication of science and technology* (pp. 14–32). Routledge.

Dunwoody, S., & Ryan, M. (1983). Public information persons as mediators between scientists and journalists. *Journalism Quarterly, 60*(4), 647–656.

Ekmeleddin İhsanoğlu, H. A. (2020). The birth of the tradition of printed books in the Ottoman Empire Transition from manuscript to print (1729–1848). In *Studies on Ottoman Science and Culture*. Routledge.

El Hajj, M. C. (2019). Digital media and freedom of expression: Experiences, challenges, resolutions. *Global Media Journal, 17*(32), 185.

El Oifi, M. (2019). Influence without power: Al Jazeera and the Arab public sphere. In *The Al Jazeera Phenomenon* (pp. 66–79). Routledge.

El Saadawi, N., & Saʿdāwī, N. (2007). *The hidden face of Eve: Women in the Arab world*. Zed Books.

El-Awady, N. (2009). Science journalism: The Arab boom. *Nature, 459*, 1057.

El-Feki, S. (2008). *Strong medicine*.

El-Nawawy, M. (2007). Between the newsroom and the classroom: Education standards and practices for print journalism in Egypt and Jordan. *International Communication Gazette, 69*(1), 69–90.

Essam, B. A., & Abdo, M. S. (2021). How do Arab tweeters perceive the COVID-19 pandemic? *Journal of Psycholinguistic Research, 50*(3), 507–521.

Esser, F., & Umbricht, A. (2014). The evolution of objective and interpretative journalism in the Western press: Comparing six news systems since the 1960s. *Journalism & Mass Communication Quarterly, 91*(2), 229–249.

Fahy, D., & Nisbet, M. C. (2011). The science journalist online: Shifting roles and emerging practices. *Journalism, 12*(7), 778–793.

Falagas, M., Zarkadoulia, E., Samonis, G., & The FASEB Journal. (2006). Arab science in the golden age (750–1258 CE) and today. *The FASEB Journal, 20*(10), 1581–1586.

Fandy, M. (2000). Information technology, trust, and social change in the Arab world. *The Middle East Journal*, 378–394.

Fargues, P. (2005). Women in Arab countries: Challenging the patriarchal system? *Reproductive Health Matters, 13*(25), 43–48.

Fatih, Z. (2012). Peering into the Mosque: Enlightenment views of Islam. *The French Review*, 1070–1082.

Figenschou, T. U. (2013). *Al Jazeera and the global media landscape: The South is talking back.* Routledge.

Fioramonti, L. (2013). *Gross domestic problem: The politics behind the world's most powerful number.* Zed Books Ltd.

Fioramonti, L. (2014). *How numbers rule the world: The use and abuse of statistics in global politics.* Zed Books Ltd.

Fischhoff, B., & Scheufele, D. (2013). The science of science communication. *Proceedings of the National Academy of Sciences, 110*, 14031–14032.

Fitzgerald, T. (2003). *The ideology of religious studies.* Oxford University Press.

Fitzgerald, T. (2007). *Discourse on civility and barbarity.* Oxford University Press.

Fjæstad, B. (2007). 12 Why journalists report science as they do. In *Journalism, Science and Society* (p. 123). Routledge.

Franklin, B., & Carlson, M. (2010). *Journalists, sources, and credibility: New perspectives.* Routledge.

Friedman, S., Dunwoody, S., & Rogers, C. L. (1986). *Scientists and journalists.* American Association for the Advancement of Science.

Frost, C. (2015). *Journalism ethics and regulation.* Routledge.

Fuchs, C., Boersma, K., Albrechtslund, A., & Sandoval, M. (2013). *Internet and surveillance: The challenges of Web 2.0 and social media, 16*, Routledge.

Galison, P. (2015). The journalist, the scientist, and objectivity. In F. Padovani, A. Richardson, & J. Tsou (Eds.), *Objectivity in Science. New perspectives from Science and Technology Studies* (pp. 57–75). Springer.

Galtung, J., & Ruge, M. H. (1965). The structure of foreign news: The presentation of the Congo, Cuba and Cyprus crises in four Norwegian newspapers. *Journal of Peace Research, 2*(1), 64–90.

Gamal, M. Y. (2020). *The Earth turns and the world has changed: Egyptian and Arab Science journalism in the digital age*. Arab Media & Society. https://www.arabmediasociety.com/the-earth-turns-and-the-world-has-changed-egyptian-and-arab-science-journalism-in-the-digital-age/

Garcés Prettel, M. E., & Arroyave Cabrera, J. (2017). Autonomía profesional y riesgos de seguridad de los periodistas en Colombia. *Perfiles Latinoamericanos*, 25(49), 35–53.

García-Marín, J. (2017). Media and media freedom. In *Political change in the Middle East and North Africa: After the Arab Spring* (pp. 231–251). Edinburgh University Press.

Genis, A. (2001). *Numbers count: The importance of numeracy for journalists*. Stellenbosch University.

Ghalioun, B. (2004). Debate: The persistence of Arab authoritarianism. *Journal of Democracy*, 15(4), 126–132.

Ghosh, S. M., & Qadeer, I. (2020). Public good perspective of public health evaluating health systems response to COVID-19. *Economic and Political Weekly*, 40–48.

Gibney, E. (2020). UAE announces first Arab Moon Mission. *Nature*, 587(7833), 186–187.

Gigerenzer, G., Gaissmaier, W., Kurz-Milcke, E., Schwartz, L., & Woloshin, S. (2007). Helping doctors and patients make sense of health statistics. *Psychological Science in the Public Interest*, 8(2), 53–96.

Giles, J. (2006). Islam and Science: Oil rich, science poor. *Nature*, 444(7115), 28–29.

Glasser, T. L. (1980). The aesthetics of news. *ETC: A Review of General Semantics*, 37, 238–247.

Gohlman, W. (1986). *The Life of Ibn Sina*. Suny Press.

Gökengin, D., Doroudi, F., Tohme, J., Collins, B., & Madani, N. (2016). HIV/AIDS: Trends in the Middle East and North Africa region. *International Journal of Infectious Diseases*, 44(21), 66–73.

Goldacre, B. (2009). *Bad Science*. Harper Perennial.

Golley, N. A. (2004). Is feminism relevant to Arab women? *Third World Quarterly*, 25(3), 521–536.

Gray, J. (2007). *Black Mass: Apocalyptic religion and the death of Utopia*. Macmillan.

Gray, J. (2015). *Al Qaeda and what it means to be modern* (Vol. 2). Faber & Faber.

Gray, M. (2010). *Conspiracy theories in the Arab world: Sources and politics*. Routledge.

Gregory, J., & Miller, S. (1998). *Science in public: Communication, culture, and credibility*. Plenum Press.

Guessoum, N. (2008). The Qur'an, science, and the (related) contemporary Muslim discourse. *Zygon*, 43(2), 411–431.

Halabi, N. (2015). Media privatization and the fate of social democracy in Egypt. *Arab Media & Society, 21*, 1–10.

Hallin, D. C., & Briggs, C. L. (2015). Transcending the medical/media opposition in research on news coverage of health and medicine. *Media, Culture & Society, 37*(1), 85–100.

Hamdan, J. M. (2011). Newspaper stories on HIV/AIDS in Jordan: A look into the Lexicon. *International Journal of Arabic-English Studies (IJAES), 12*.

Hamdy, N. (2013). Arab investigative journalism practice. *Journal of Arab & Muslim Media Research, 6*(1), 67–93.

Hamilton, J. F. (2020). Drone journalism as visual aggregation: Toward a critical history. *Media and Communication, 8*(3), 64–74.

Hamwi, A. (2009). Translation and the problem of the scientific term in media. Science Media. *Journal of Scientific Progress*, 67–71.

Hanitzsch, T. (2007). Deconstructing journalism culture. Toward a Universal Theory. *Communication Theory, 17*, 367–385.

Hanitzsch, T., Hanusch, F., Ramaprasad, J., & de Beer, A. (2019). *Worlds of journalism: Journalistic cultures around the globe*. Columbia University Press.

Hansen, A. (2016). The changing uses of accuracy in science communication. *Public Understanding of Science, 25*(7), 760–774.

Hanssen, J., & Weiss, M. (2018). *Arabic Thought Against the Authoritarian Age: Towards an Intellectual History of the Present*. Cambridge University Press.

Harb, Z. (2019). Challenges facing Arab journalism, freedom, safety and economic security. *Journalism, 20*(1), 110–113.

Harcup, T., & O'neill, D. (2001). What is news? Galtung and Ruge revisited. *Journalism Studies, 2*(2), 261–280.

Harrison, S. (2014). History of numeracy education and training for print journalists in England. *Numeracy: Advancing Education in Quantitative Literacy, 7*(2), 2.

Hassan, I. M. (2013). *Specialized Press*. Zahran House for Publishing and Distribution.

Hasso, F. (2000). Modernity and gender in Arab accounts of the 1948 and 1967 defeats. *International Journal of Middle East Studies, 32*(4), 491–510.

Herman, E. S., & Chomsky, N. (2010). *Manufacturing consent: The political economy of the mass media*. Random House.

Hermida, A. (2010). Revitalizing science journalism for a digital age. In D. Kennedy & G. Overholser (Eds.), *Science and the Media* (pp. 80–87). American Academy for Arts and Sciences.

Heyne, D., Gren-Landell, M., Melvin, G., & Gentle-Genitty, C. (2019). Differentiation between school attendance problems: Why and how? *Cognitive and Behavioral Practice, 26*(1), 8–34.

Hillman, S., Salama, G., Eibenschutz, E. O., Awadh, S. M. A., & El Said, L. (2017). *Being female and an engineering student in Qatar: Successes, challenges, and recommendations.* 2017 ASEE Annual Conference & Exposition.

Hitchens, C. (2008). *God is not great: How religion poisons everything.* McClelland & Stewart.

Hohmann, E., Brand, J. C., Rossi, M. J., & Lubowitz, J. H. (2018). Expert opinion is necessary: Delphi panel methodology facilitates a scientific approach to consensus. *Arthroscopy: The Journal of Arthroscopic & Related Surgery, 34*(2), 349–351.

Hough, G. (1995). *News writing* (Vol. 5, 5th ed.). Houghton Mifflin.

Hovden, J. F., & Kristensen, N. N. (2021). The cultural journalist around the globe: A comparative study of characteristics, role perceptions, and perceived influences. *Journalism, 22*(3), 689–708.

Howell, M., & Prevenier, W. (2001). *From reliable sources: An introduction to historical methods.* Cornell University Press.

Hoyland, R. (2002). *Arabia and the Arabs: From the Bronze Age to the coming of Islam.* Routledge.

Huff, T. (2017). *The rise of early modern science: Islam, China, and the West.* Cambridge University Press.

Humm, C., Schrögel, P., & Leßmöllmann, A. (2020). Feeling left out: Underserved audiences in science communication. *Media and Communication, 8*(1), 164–176.

Hunter, P. (2016). The communications gap between scientists and public: More scientists and their institutions feel a need to communicate the results and nature of research with the public. *EMBO Reports, 17*(11), 1513–1515.

Huntington, S. P. (1981). *The soldier and the state: The theory and politics of civil–military relations.* Harvard University Press.

Ibnrubbian, A. (2016). *Economic media in the Kingdom of Saudi Arabia: The reality and development opportunities.* Seventh Annual Forum of the Saudi Association for Media and Communication: The Media and the Economy—Integration Roles in the Service of Development, 11–12 April 2016, Riyadh.

Inalcik, H. (2019). *The Ottoman Empire and Europe.* Kronik.

Ings, S. (2016). *Stalin and the scientists: A history of triumph and tragedy 1905–1953.* Faber & Faber.

Iqbal, F., Khaliq, A., & Al-Ain, M. N. (2021). An evaluation of political modernization of Asian Islamic states in postmodern era. *Journal of Religious Studies, 3*(2), 163–172.

Iqbal, M. (2007). *Science and Islam.* Greenwood Publishing Group.

Islam, S. I. (2017). Arab women in Science, Technology, Engineering and Mathematics fields: The way forward. *World Journal of Education, 7*(6), 12–20.

Jebril, N., & Loveless, M. (2017). Media audiences and media consumption during political transitions: The case of Egypt. *Interactions: Studies in Communication & Culture, 8*(2–3), 151–167.

Jenks, C. (2002). *Visual culture*. Routledge.
Jjuuko, M. (2020). Environmental journalism in East Africa: Opportunities and challenges in the 21st century. In *Routledge Handbook of Environmental Journalism* (pp. 354–365).
Jones, D. A. (2004). Why Americans don't trust the media: A preliminary analysis. *Harvard International Journal of Press/Politics, 9*(2), 60–75.
Jones, J. H. (1993). *Bad blood*. Simon and Schuster.
Jones-Jang, S. M., Mortensen, T., & Liu, J. (2021). Does media literacy help identification of fake news? Information literacy helps, but other literacies don't. *American Behavioral Scientist, 65*(2), 371–388.
Joss, S. (1999). Public participation in science and technology policy- and decision-making—Ephemeral phenomenon or lasting change? *Science and Public Policy, 26*(5), 290–293.
Kalathil, S., & Boas, T. C. (2010). *Open networks, closed regimes: The impact of the Internet on authoritarian rule.* .
Kandiyoti, D. (1991). *Women, Islam and the state* (Vol. 105). Temple University Press.
Karafyllis, N. C. (2015). Tertiary education in the GCC countries (UAE, Qatar, Saudi Arabia): How economy, gender and culture affect the field of STEM. In *International Science and Technology Education* (pp. 138–159). Routledge.
Karolak, M. (2017). The use of social media from revolution to democratic consolidation: The Arab Spring and the case of Tunisia. *Journal of Arab & Muslim Media Research, 10*(2), 199–216.
Kasrils, R., Ben-Dor, D. O., Cook, J., Farsakh, L., Löwstedt, A., Badran, A., Friedman, S., Tilley, V. Q., & Greenstein, R. (2015). *Israel and South Africa: The many faces of Apartheid*. Bloomsbury Publishing.
Katsakioris, C. (2010). Soviet lessons for Arab modernization: Soviet educational aid towards Arab countries after 1956. *Journal of Modern European History, 8*(1), 85–106.
Katz, E., Blumler, J., & Gurevitch, M. (1974). Uses and gratification theory. *Public Opinion Quarterly, 34*(4), 509–523.
Kennedy, E. (1970). *The Arabic heritage in the exact sciences*. American University of Beirut.
Khairy, L. (2020). Applying the four models of science journalism to the publics' interaction with coronavirus news. *Arab Media & Society, 28*(6), 71–88.
Khalil, J. F., & Zayani, M. (2021). De-territorialized digital capitalism and the predicament of the nation-state: Netflix in Arabia. *Media, Culture & Society, 43*(2), 201–218.
Khamis, S. (2013). Gendering the Arab Spring: Arab women journalists/activists, 'cyberfeminism,' and the sociopolitical revolution. In C. Cynthia, S. Linda, & M. Lisa (Eds.), *The Routledge companion to media & gender* (pp. 583–594). Routledge.

Khan, M. A. I. A. A. (2019). Dynamics encouraging women towards embracing entrepreneurship: Case study of Mena countries. *International Journal of Gender and Entrepreneurship*, *11*(4), 379–389. https://pustaka-sarawak.com/eknowbase/attachments/1584599252.pdf

Khazen, J. (1999). Censorship and state control of the press in the Arab world. *Harvard International Journal of Press/Politics*, *4*(3), 87–92.

Khun, T. (2012). *The structure of scientific revolutions*. University of Chicago Press.

Kiernan, V. (2003). Embargoes and science news. *Journalism & Mass Communication Quarterly*, *80*(4), 903–920.

Kilpatrick, J. (1999). *Números e escritores não somam*. Barganca: Fundação Calouste Gulbenkian.

Kirat, M. (2018). The world of women public relations practitioners in Qatar. *International Journal of Business and Social Science*, *9*(9), 81–94.

Koblitz, A. H. (2016). Life in the fast lane: Arab women in science and technology. *Bulletin of Science, Technology & Society*, *36*(2), 107–117.

Koetsenruijter, A. W. M. (2011). Using numbers in news increases story credibility. *Newspaper Research Journal*, *32*(2), 74–82.

KoKaz, S. (2008). The specialized press in Iraq after the events of April 9. *AL—Bahith AL—A'alami*, *1*(4), 126–145.

Komorowski, M. (2017). A novel typology of media clusters. *European Planning Studies*, *25*(8), 1334–1356.

Kuehn, T. (2011). *Empire, Islam, and politics of difference: Ottoman rule in Yemen, 1849–1919*. Brill.

Lacroix, S. (2019). Saudi Arabia and the limits of religious reform. *The Review of Faith & International Affairs*, *17*(2), 97–101.

Land-Zandstra, A. M., Devilee, J. L., Snik, F., Buurmeijer, F., & van den Broek, J. M. (2016). Citizen science on a smartphone: Participants' motivations and learning. *Public Understanding of Science*, *25*(1), 45–60.

Lassoued, M. (2021). Control of corruption, microfinance, and income inequality in MENA countries: Evidence from panel data. *SN Business & Economics*, *1*(7), 1–19.

Lawson, B. (2021). Hiding behind databases, institutions and actors: How journalists use statistics in reporting humanitarian crises. *Journalism Practice*, 1–21.

Lee, A. M. (2013). News audiences revisited: Theorizing the link between audience motivations and news consumption. *Journal of Broadcasting & Electronic Media*, *57*(3), 300–317.

Levy-Aksu, N., Lévy-Aksu, N., & Georgeon, F. (2017). *The Young Turk Revolution and the Ottoman Empire: The Aftermath of 1908*. Bloomsbury Publishing.

Lévy-Leblond, J. (1992). About misunderstandings about misunderstandings. *Public Understanding of Science*, *1*(1), 17–21.

Lewenstein, B. (2003). Models of public communication of science and technology. *Public Understanding of Science*.

Lewis, B. (1980). The Ottoman Empire and its aftermath. *Journal of Contemporary History, 15*(1), 27–36.

Lewis, B. (1982). The question of Orientalism. *New York Review of Books, 24*(6) https://www.nybooks.com/articles/1982/06/24/the-question-of-orientalism/

Lewis, B. (2009). Free at last-the Arab world in the twenty-first century. *Foreign Affairs, 88*, 77.

Lewis, B. (2018). *The political language of Islam.* University of Chicago Press.

Lewis, J., Williams, A., & Franklin, B. (2008). A compromised fourth estate? UK news journalism, public relations and news sources. *Journalism Studies, 9*(1), 1–20.

Lewis, J. M. W., Williams, A., Franklin, R. A., Thomas, J., & Mosdell, N. A. (2008). *The quality and independence of British journalism.* Cardiff School of Journalism, Media and Cultural Studies.

Lewis, N. P., & Nashmi, E. A. (2019). Data journalism in the Arab region: Role conflict exposed. *Digital Journalism, 7*(9), 1200–1214.

Lewis, S. C., & Westlund, O. (2015). Big data and journalism: Epistemology, expertise, economics, and ethics. *Digital Journalism, 3*(3), 447–466.

Lind, R., & Danowski, J. (1998). The representation of Arabs in US electronic media. In R. Yahya & C. Theresa (Eds.), *Cultural diversity and the US media* (pp. 157–168). State University of New York Press.

Lippmann, W. (1992). *Public opinion.* Routledge.

Lippmann, W. (2018). *Liberty and the news.* Routledge.

Littlejohn, S., & Foss, K. (2010). *Theories of human communication.* Waveland Press.

Livingston, C., & Voakes, P. (2011). *Working with numbers and statistics: A handbook for journalists.* Routledge.

Livingstone, S. (2019). Audiences in an age of datafication: Critical questions for media research. *Television & New Media, 20*(2), 170–183.

Lo, A. Y. (2016). National income and environmental concern: Observations from 35 countries. *Public Understanding of Science, 25*(7), 873–890.

Long, M. (1995). Scientific explanation in US newspaper science stories. *Public Understanding of Science, 4*(2), 119–130.

Losurdo, D. (2014). *Liberalism: A counter-history.* Verso.

Loukinas, P. (2017). Surveillance and drones at Greek borderzones: Challenging human rights and democracy. *Surveillance & Society, 15*(3/4), 439–446.

Lublinski, J., Reichert, I., Denis, A., Fleury, J., Labassi, O., & Spurk, C. (2014). Advances in African and Arab science journalism: Capacity building and new newsroom structures through digital peer-to-peer support. *Ecquid Novi: African Journalism Studies, 35*(2), 4–22.

Lugo-Ocando, J. (2008). *The Media in Latin America.* McGraw-Hill Education (UK).

Lugo-Ocando, J. (2013). Reflexivity in the digital world: Rethinking journalism teaching and learning in an interactive world. *Journal of Applied Journalism & Media Studies, 2*(2), 207–214.

Lugo-Ocando, J. (2015). Journalists do live in a parallel universe: A response to practitioner critiques of journalism academics. *Journal of Applied Journalism & Media Studies, 4*(3), 369–379.

Lugo-Ocando, J. (2017). *Crime statistics in the news: Journalism, numbers and social deviation.* Palgrave Macmillan.

Lugo-Ocando, J. (2020). *Foreign aid and journalism in the global south: A mouthpiece for truth.* Lexington Books.

Lugo-Ocando, J., & Brandão, R. (2016). STABBING NEWS: Articulating crime statistics in the newsroom. *Journalism Practice, 10*(6), 715–729.

Lugo-Ocando, J., & Faria Brandão, R. (2016). STABBING NEWS: Articulating crime statistics in the newsroom. *Journalism Practice, 10*(6), 715–729.

Lugo-Ocando, J., & Lawson, B. (2017). Poor numbers, poor news: The ideology of poverty statistics in the media. In A. Nguyen (Ed.), *News, Numbers and Public Opinion in a Data-Driven World.* Bloomsbury Publishing Inc.

Lugo-Ocando, J., Mohsin, A., Nguyen, A., & Hamadeh, S. (2019). *Assessing the Qatari news media's capacities for fostering public understanding of and engagement with science: Issues, challenges, opportunities and their socio-political implications.* QNRF, Doha. NPRP12S-0317-190381.

Lugo-Ocando, J., Cañizales, A., & Lohmeier, C. (2010). When PSB is delivered by the hand of God: The case of Roman Catholic broadcast networks in Venezuela. *International Journal of Media & Cultural Politics, 6*(2), 149–167.

Lynch, M. (2015). How the media trashed the transitions. *Journal of Democracy, 26*(4), 90–99.

Madani, N. (2018). Gender equality is crucial to the fight for better HIV treatment access and outcomes in the MENA region. *Journal of the International AIDS Society, 21*(3), 1–2.

Mahmood, S. (2008). *Scientific media.* Alfagar Publishing.

Mahmoud, N. (2018). *The credibility of scientific and technological news in electronic and paper newspapers among scientific elites and the general public.* .

Maier, S. (2002). Numbers in the news: A mathematics audit of a daily newspaper. *Journalism Studies, 3*(4), 507–519.

Maier, S. (2003). Numeracy in the newsroom: A case study of mathematical competence and confidence. *Journalism & Mass Communication Quarterly, 80*(4), 921–936.

Maillé, M.-È., Saint-Charles, J., & Lucotte, M. (2010). The gap between scientists and journalists: The case of mercury science in Québec's press. *Public Understanding of Science, 19*(1), 70–79.

Majetic, C., & Pellegrino, C. (2014). When science and information literacy meet: An approach to exploring the sources of science news with non-science majors. *College Teaching, 62*(3), 107–112.

Malik, S. I. (2012). Writing from inside out: Accounts of Sudanese women working in the media. *Journal of Arts and Humanities, 1*(2), 68–83.

Manning, P. (2000). *News and news sources: A critical introduction*. Sage.

Manning, P. (2001). *News and news sources: A critical introduction*. Sage.

Mansell, R. (2020). *Making open development inclusive: Lessons from IDRC research*. MIT Press.

Marcinkowski, F., & Steiner, A. (2014). Mediatization and political autonomy: A systems approach. In H. Kriesi (Ed.), *Mediatization of politics: Understanding the transformation of western democracies* (pp. 74–89). Palgrave Macmillan.

Margit, M. (2021). Women changing the face of Science in the middle east and north Africa. *The Media Line*. https://themedialine.org/top-stories/women-changing-the-face-of-science-in-the-middle-east-and-north-africa/

Marshall, J., & Wickenden, M. (2018). Services for people with Communication Disabilities in Uganda: Supporting a new Speech and Language Therapy profession. *Disability and the Global South, 5*(1), 1215–1233.

Martin, J. (2016). A census of statistics requirements at US journalism programs and a model for a 'statistics for journalism' course. *Journalism & Mass Communication Educator, 72*(4), 461–479.

Martínez, A. A. (2018). *Burned Alive: Bruno, Galileo and the Inquisition*. Reaktion Books.

Martinisi, A., & Lugo-Ocando, J. A. (2020). *Statistics and the quest for quality journalism: A study in quantitative reporting*. Anthem Press.

Martisini, A. (2018). *Journalism, statistics and quality in the news*. University of Leeds.

Mason, L. E., Krutka, D., & Stoddard, J. (2018). Media literacy, democracy, and the challenge of fake news. *Journal of Media Literacy Education, 10*(2), 1–10.

Masood, E. (2017). *Science and Islam (Icon Science): A History*. Icon Books.

Masoud, T. (2015). Has the door closed on Arab democracy? *Journal of Democracy, 26*(1), 74–87.

Massarani, L., & Boys, B. (2007). La ciencia en la prensa de América Latina: Un estudio en 9 países. *Reunión de La Red de Popularización de La Ciencia y La Tecnología En América Latina y El Caribe, 10*, 1–12. Retrieved March 11, 2022, from https://www.cientec.or.cr/pop/2007/BR-LuisaMassarani.pdf

Massarani, L., & Peters, H. P. (2016). Scientists in the public sphere: Interactions of scientists and journalists in Brazil. *Anais Da Academia Brasileira de Ciências, 88*, 1165–1175.

Masuzawa, T. (2005). *The invention of world religions: Or, how European universalism was preserved in the language of pluralism*. University of Chicago Press.

Matter. (2017). Science and sports news most trusted by British public. https://www.techmezine.com/top-10-news/science-sports-news-trusted-british-public/ [Accessed on March 12, 2022]

Matthews, O. (2020). *Britain Drops Its Go-It-Alone Approach to Coronavirus. Foreign Policy.*
Mawlawi, R. (1988). Arab scientific journalism: Achievements and aspirations. *Impact of Science on Society, 38*(4), 397–409.
Maziad, M. (2021). Qatar in Egypt: The politics of Al Jazeera. *Journalism, 22*(4), 1067–1087.
Mbarga, G., Lublinski, J., & Fleury, J.-M. (2012). New perspectives on strengthening science journalism in developing countries: Approach and first results of the 'SjCOOP' mentoring project. *Journal of African Media Studies, 4*(2), 157–172.
McCallie, E., Bell, L., Lohwater, T., Falk, J. H., Lehr, J. L., Lewenstein, B. V., Needham, C., & Wiehe, B. (2009). *Many experts, many audiences: Public engagement with science and informal science education.* A CAISE Inquiry Group Report. https://digitalcommons.calpoly.edu/cgi/viewcontent.cgi?article=1011&context=eth_fac
McChesney, R. W. (2015). *Rich media, poor democracy: Communication politics in dubious times.* New Press.
McCluskey, J., & Swinnen, J. (2011). The media and food-risk perceptions: Science & society series on food and Science. *EMBO Reports, 12*(7), 624–629.
McDevitt, M. (2003). In defense of autonomy: A critique of the public journalism critique. *Journal of Communication, 53*(1), 155–164.
McNair, B. (1998). *The sociology of journalism.* Oxford University Press.
MEE. (2021). Egypt detains former al-Ahram editor after he called on Sisi to step down [News]. *Middle East Eye.* https://www.middleeasteye.net/news/egypt-ahram-nasser-salama-sisi-criticism-ethiopia-dam-detained
Mehran, Z. (2018). *How to introduce science to the Arab child.* Academic Library.
Melki, J., & Hitti, E. (2021). The domestic tethering of Lebanese and Arab women journalists and news managers. *Journalism Practice, 15*(3), 288–307.
Melki, J., & Mallat, S. E. (2018). When Arab women (and men) speak: Struggles of women journalists in a gendered news industry. In Steiner L, Carter C, & S. Allan (Eds.), *Journalism, Gender and Power* (pp. 33–48). Routledge.
Melki, J. P., & Mallat, S. E. (2016). Block her entry, keep her down and push her out: Gender discrimination and women journalists in the Arab world. *Journalism Studies, 17*(1), 57–79.
Mellado, C. (2015). Professional roles in news content: Six dimensions of journalistic role performance. *Journalism Studies, 16*(4), 596–614.
Mellado, C., & Humanes, M. L. (2012). Modeling perceived professional autonomy in Chilean journalism. *Journalism, 13*(8), 985–1003.
Mellado, C., Salinas, P., Del Valle, C., & González, G. (2010). Estudio comparativo de cuatro regiones: Mercado laboral y perfil del periodista. *Cuadernos. Info, 26,* 45–64.
Mellor, N. (2005). *The making of Arab news.* Rowman & Littlefield Publishers.

Mellor, N. (2007). *Modern Arab journalism: Problems and prospects: Problems and prospects.* Edinburgh University Press.

Mellor, N. (2008). Arab journalists as cultural intermediaries. *The International Journal of Press/Politics, 13*(4), 465–483.

Mellor, N. (2010). More than a parrot The case of Saudi women journalists. *Journal of Arab & Muslim Media Research, 3*(3), 207–222.

Mellor, N. (2011). *Arab media: Globalization and emerging media industries* (Vol. 1). Polity.

Mellor, N. (2019). The (in) visibility of Arab women in political journalism. In L. Steiner, C. Carter, & S. Allan (Eds.), *Journalism, Gender and Power*. Routledge.

Merskin, D. (2004). The construction of Arabs as enemies: Post-September 11 discourse of George W. Bush. *Mass Communication & Society, 7*(2), 157–175.

Metab, H. S. (2019). *Haider Shallalientific press in Iraq.* Karbala Channel. https://www.youtube.com/watch?v=kxSsK7itcPk

Metag, J., & Schäfer, M. S. (2018). *Audience segments in environmental and science communication: Recent findings and future perspectives.*

Meyer, G. (2018). *The Science communication challenge: Truth and disagreement in democratic knowledge societies.* Anthem Press.

Meyer, K., Rizzo, H., & Ali, Y. (2007). Changed political attitudes in the Middle East: The case of Kuwait. *International Sociology, 22*(3), 289–324.

Meyer, P. (1989). Precision journalism and the 1988 US elections. *International Journal of Public Opinion Research, 1*(3), 195–205.

Meyer, P. (2002). *Precision journalism: A reporter's introduction to social science methods.* Rowman & Littlefield.

Mikhail, A., & Philliou, C. M. (2012). The Ottoman empire and the imperial turn. *Comparative Studies in Society and History, 54*(4), 721–745.

Miladi, N., & Mellor, N. (2020). *Routledge Handbook on Arab Media.* Routledge.

Miles, H. (2010). *Al Jazeera: How Arab TV news challenged the world.* Hachette UK.

Miller, K., Kyriazi, T., & Paris, C. M. (2017). Arab women employment in the UAE: Exploring opportunities, motivations and challenges. *International Journal of Sustainable Society, 9*(1), 20–40.

Miller, R. (2010). *Britain.* Ashgate Surrey.

Minces, J. (1982). *The house of obedience: Women in Arab society.* Palgrave Macmillan.

Mir-Hosseini, Z. (2006). Muslim women's quest for equality: Between Islamic law and feminism. *Critical Inquiry, 32*(4), 629–645.

Mirkin, B. (2013). *Arab Spring: Demographics in a region in transition. United Nations Development Programme, Regional Bureau for Arab States.* United Nations Development Program Regional Bureau for Arab States. https://arab-hdr.org/wp-content/uploads/2020/12/AHDR-ENG-Arab-Spring-Mirkinv3.pdf

Moaddel, M. (1998). Religion and women: Islamic modernism versus fundamentalism. *Journal for the Scientific Study of Religion*, 108–130.

Močnik, N. (2019). Occupying the Land, Grabbing the Body: The Female Body as a Disposable Place of Colonialization in Post-Ottoman Bosnia-Herzegovina. *Southeastern Europe*, 43(2), 93–110.

Moghadam, V. M. (2015). Women, work and family in the Arab region: Toward economic citizenship. *DIFI Fam Res Proc*, 7, 1–20.

Molek-Kozakowska, K. (2017). Journalistic practices of science popularization in the context of users' agenda: A case study of New Scientist. *Acta Universitatis Lodziensis. Folia Litteraria Polonica*, 43(5), 93–109.

Mooney, C. (2007). *The Republican war on science*. Basic Books.

Moore, R. (2006). Class attendance: How students' attitudes about attendance relate to their academic performance in introductory science classes. *Research and Teaching in Developmental Education*, 19–33.

Moore-Gilbert, K., & Abdul-Nabi, Z. (2021). Authoritarian downgrading,(self) censorship and new media activism after the Arab Spring. *New Media & Society*, 23(5), 875–893.

Mortensen, M., & Trenz, H.-J. (2016). Media morality and visual icons in the age of social media: Alan Kurdi and the emergence of an impromptu public of moral spectatorship. *Javnost-The Public*, 23(4), 343–362.

Mostyn, T. (2002). *Censorship in Islamic Societies*. Saqi Books.

Muchtar, N., Hamada, B., Hanitzsch, T., Galal, A., & Masduki, & Ullah, M. (2017). Journalism and the Islamic worldview: Journalistic roles in Muslim-majority countries. *Journalism Studies*, 18(5), 555–575.

Murcott, T. (2009). Science journalism: Toppling the priesthood. *Nature*, 459(7250), 1054–1055.

Mutsvairo, B. (2019). Challenges facing development of data journalism in non-western societies. *Digital Journalism*, 7(9), 1289–1294.

Muwahed, J. (2020). Coronavirus pandemic goes viral in the age of social media, sparking anxiety. *ABC News*. https://abcnews.go.com/Politics/coronavirus-pandemic-viral-age-social-media-sparking-anxiety/story?id=69580796

Na'ik, Z. (2001). *Qur'an and modern science: Compatible or incompatible*. Dar-US-Salaam.

Nafadi, A. (1996). *Press Emirates upbringing and artistic and historical evolution*. Publications of the Cultural Foundation.

Najjar, F. (2004). Lbn Rushd (Averroes) and the Egyptian Enlightenment Movement. *British Journal of Middle Eastern Studies*, 31(2), 195–213.

Nasr, S., & De Santillana, G. (1968). *Science and civilization in Islam* (Vol. 16). Harvard University Press.

Neaime, S., & Gaysset, I. (2018). Financial inclusion and stability in MENA: Evidence from poverty and inequality. *Finance Research Letters*, 24, 230–237.

Nee, R. C. (2013). Creative destruction: An exploratory study of how digitally native news nonprofits are innovating online journalism practices. *International Journal on Media Management, 15*(1), 3–22.

Nelkin, D. (1995). *Selling science: How the press covers science and technology*. Rev. Ed. Freeman.

Ng, A. (2021). Saudi Arabia sees a spike in women joining the workforce, Brookings study shows. *CNBC News*. https://www.cnbc.com/2021/04/29/saudi-arabia-sees-a-spike-in-women-joining-the-workforce-study-says.html

Nguyen, A. (2017). *News, numbers and public opinion in a data-driven world*. Bloomsbury Publishing.

Nguyen, A., & Lugo-Ocando, J. (2015). Introduction: The state of statistics in journalism and journalism education–issues and debates. *Journalism, 1*(14), 1464884915593234.

Nguyen, A., & Lugo-Ocando, J. (2016). The state of data and statistics in journalism and journalism education: Issues and debates. *Journalism, 17*(1), 3–17.

Nguyen, A., & McIlwaine, S. (2011). Who wants a voice in Science issues—And why? A survey of European citizens and its implications for science journalism. *Journalism Practice, 5*(2), 210–226.

Nguyen, A., & Tran, M. (2019). Science journalism for development in the Global South: A systematic literature review of issues and challenges. *Public Understanding of Science, 28*(8), 973–990.

Nimeh, Z., & Bauchmüller, R. (2014). School enrolment and child labour. In *Agency and participation in childhood and youth: International applications of the capability approach in schools and beyond* (p. 204). Bloomsbury Publishing.

Nisbet, M., & Scheufele, D. (2009). What's next for science communication? Promising directions and lingering distractions. *American Journal of Botany, 96*(10), 1767–1778.

Nölleke, D., Grimmer, C. G., & Horky, T. (2017). News sources and follow-up communication: Facets of complementarity between sports journalism and social media. *Journalism Practice, 11*(4), 509–526.

Nygren, G. (2012). Autonomy—A crucial element of professionalization. In G. Nygren & B. Dobek-Ostrowska (Eds.), *Journalism in Russia, Poland and Sweden—Traditions, cultures and research* (pp. 73–95). Peter Lang.

Nygren, G. (2015). Media development and professional autonomy. *Journalism in Change. Journalistic Culture in Poland, Russia and Sweden*, 119–152.

Nygren, G., Dobek-Ostrowska, B., & Anikina, M. (2015). Professional autonomy. *Nordicom Review, 36*(2), 79–95.

O'Neil, C. (2016). *Weapons of math destruction: How big data increases inequality and threatens democracy*. Broadway Books.

O'Reilly, A. (2020). *Trump calls for restarting economy by Easter: 'We have to get back to work.'*

Odine, M. (2011). Middle East media: Press freedom in Kuwait. *Journal of Advanced Social Research, 1*(2), 177–190.
Oliver, J. E., & Wood, T. J. (2014). Conspiracy theories and the paranoid style (s) of mass opinion. *American Journal of Political Science, 58*(4), 952–966.
Olsen, R. K., Pickard, V., & Westlund, O. (2020). Communal news work: COVID-19 calls for collective funding of journalism. *Digital Journalism, 8*(5), 673–680.
Ong, A. (1999). Muslim Feminism: Citizenship in the shelter of corporatist Islam. *Citizenship Studies, 3*(3), 355–371.
Onyebadi, U., & Alajmi, F. (2016). Gift solicitation and acceptance in journalism practice: An assessment of Kuwaiti journalists' perspective. *Journalism, 17*(3), 348–365.
Oreskes, N., & Conway, E. M. (2010). Defeating the merchants of doubt. *Nature, 465*(7299), 686–687.
Oreskes, N., & Conway, E. M. (2011). *Merchants of doubt: How a handful of scientists obscured the truth on issues from tobacco smoke to global warming*. Bloomsbury Publishing.
Ortaylı, İ. (2019). *Ottoman studies, 10*, Kronik.
Osborne, J., & Dillon, J. (2008). *Science education in Europe: Critical reflections* (Vol. 13). The Nuffield Foundation.
Osborne, J., Simon, S., & Collins, S. (2003). Attitudes towards science: A review of the literature and its implications. *International Journal of Science Education, 25*(9), 1049–1079.
Otto, S. L. (2016). *The war on Science: Who's waging it, why it matters, what we can do about it*. .
Paris, T. J. (2004). *Britain, the Hashemites and Arab rule: The sherifian solution*. Routledge.
Paterson, C., Gadzekpo, A., & Wasserman, H. (2018). Journalism and Foreign Aid in Africa. *African Journalism Studies, 39*(2), 1–8.
Pavlik, J. V., Dennis, E. E., Mersey, R. D., & Gengler, J. (2018). *Mobile disruptions in the Middle East: Lessons from Qatar and the Arabian Gulf Region in mobile media content innovation*. Routledge.
Pentina, I., & Tarafdar, M. (2014). From 'information' to 'knowing': Exploring the role of social media in contemporary news consumption. *Computers in Human Behavior, 35*, 211–223.
Peters, C., & Christian Schrøder, K. (2018). Beyond the here and now of news audiences: A process-based framework for investigating news repertoires. *Journal of Communication, 68*(6), 1079–1103.
Peters, H. P. (2013). Gap between science and media revisited: Scientists as public communicators. *Proceedings of the National Academy of Sciences, 110*(Supplement 3), 14102–14109.

Picard, R. G. (2003). Cash cows or entrecote: Publishing companies and disruptive technologies. *Trends in Communication, 11*(2), 127–136.

Picard, R. G., & Barkho, L. (2011). Dubai media city: Creating benefits from foreign media developments. In *Media Clusters*. Edward Elgar Publishing.

Pickard, V. (2014). The great evasion: Confronting market failure in American media policy. *Critical Studies in Media Communication, 31*(2), 153–159.

Pierce, J., Lee-Sammons, L., & Lovrich, N., Jr. (1988). US and Japanese source reliance for environmental information. *Journalism Quarterly, 65*(4), 902–908.

Pintak, L. (2014). Islam, identity and professional values: A study of journalists in three Muslim-majority regions. *Journalism, 15*(4), 482–503.

Pintak, L. (2019). Middle Eastern and North African Journalism. In *The International Encyclopedia of Journalism Studies* (pp. 1–12). John Wiley & Sons.

PISA. (2015). *PISA 2015 Results (Volume III)*.

Plackett, B. (2020). [News]. Al-Fanar Media. https://www.al-fanarmedia.org/2020/03/talk-to-me-urges-a-science-journalist-working-in-the-arab-world/

Popper, K. (2005). *The logic of scientific discovery*. Routledge.

Porlezza, C., Maier, S., & Russ-Mohl, S. (2012). News accuracy in Switzerland and Italy: A transatlantic comparison with the US press. *Journalism Practice, 6*(4), 530–546.

Potter, D. (2010). *News with numbers*.

Pratt, N. C. (2007). *Democracy and authoritarianism in the Arab world*. Lynne Rienner Publishers.

Provence, M. (2011). Ottoman modernity, colonialism, and insurgency in the interwar Arab East. *International Journal of Middle East Studies, 43*(2), 205–225.

Qabbanji, J. A. (2011). Research in Lebanon: Scientific groups, researchers and creativity: The current situation in the social sciences. *The Arab Journal of Sociology—Additions, 15*(1), 173–176.

Quataert, D. (2005). *The Ottoman Empire, 1700–1922*. Cambridge University Press.

Quigley, J. (1991). Apartheid outside Africa: The case of Israel. *Indiana International & Comparative Law Review, 2*, 221.

Radford, T. (2007). Scheherazade: Telling stories, not educating people. In M. W. Bauer & M. Bucchi (Eds.), *Journalism, Science and Society* (pp. 95–100). Routledge.

Rahmouni, M., & Aleid, M. A. (2020). Teachers' practices and children's motivation towards science learning in MENA countries: Evidence from Tunisia and UAE. *International Journal of Educational Research, 103*, 101605.

Rakedzon, T., Segev, E., Chapnik, N., Yosef, R., & Baram-Tsabari, A. (2017). Automatic jargon identifier for scientists engaging with the public and science communication educators. *PloS One, 12*(8), e0181742.

Randall, D. (2000). *The universal journalist*. Pluto Press.

Ransohoff, D. F., & Ransohoff, R. M. (2001). Sensationalism in the media: When scientists and journalists may be complicit collaborators. *Effective Clinical Practice, 4*(4), 185–188.

Rāshid, R., & Jolivet, J. (1997). *Oeuvres philosophiques et scientifiques d'Al-Kindi: L'optique et la catoptrique* (Vol. 29). Brill.

Reid, M., Walsh, C., Raubenheimer, J., Bradshaw, T., Pienaar, M., Hassan, C., Nyoni, C., & Le Roux, M. (2018). Development of a health dialogue model for patients with diabetes: A complex intervention in a low-/middle income country. *International Journal of Africa Nursing Sciences, 8*, 122–131.

Reinisch, L. (2010). Environmental journalism in UAE. *Arab Media & Society, 11*, 1–19.

Renima, A., Tiliouine, H., & Estes, R. (2016). The Islamic golden age: A story of the triumph of the Islamic civilization. In H. Tiliouine & R. Estes (Eds.), *The State of Social Progress of Islamic Societies* (pp. 25–52). Springer.

Requejo-Alemán, J. L., & Lugo-Ocando, J. (2014). Assessing the sustainability of Latin American Investigative Non-profit Journalism. *Journalism Studies, 15*(5), 522–532.

Reverby, S. M. (2005). 'Misrepresentations of the Tuskegee Study'—Distortion of analysis and facts? *Journal of the National Medical Association, 97*(8), 1180.

Riccio, B. D. (1994). *Walter Lippmann: Odyssey of a liberal*. Transaction Publishers.

Rizvi, A. (2018). UAE bucks global trend as women lead the way in science studies [News]. *The Nation*. https://www.thenationalnews.com/uae/uae-bucks-global-trend-as-women-lead-the-way-in-science-studies-1.745043

Rodrigues, U. M., & Xu, J. (2020). Regulation of COVID-19 fake news infodemic in China and India. *Media International Australia, 177*(1), 125–131.

Rogacheva, M. (2017). *The private world of Soviet scientists from Stalin to Gorbachev*. Cambridge University Press.

Ross, K., & Carter, C. (2011). Women and news: A long and winding road. *Media, Culture & Society, 33*(8), 1148–1165.

Rowe, A. (2008). Meet the Arab Agency for Science News [Magazine]. *Wired*. https://www.wired.com/2008/11/meet-the-arab-a/

Ruddock, A. (2007). *Investigating audiences*. Sage.

Rudin, R., & Ibbotson, T. (2002). *An introduction to journalism: Essential techniques and background knowledge*. Focal Press.

Ruggiero, T. E. (2000). Uses and gratifications theory in the 21st century. *Mass Communication & Society, 3*(1), 3–37.

Rugh, W. (2004). *Arab mass media: Newspapers, radio, and television in Arab politics*. Greenwood Publishing Group.

Russell, F. M. (2019). The new gatekeepers: An Institutional-level view of Silicon Valley and the disruption of journalism. *Journalism Studies, 20*(5), 631–648.

Saber, N. (2013). The scientific media crisis: A study of the scientific press discourse in Al-Ahram newspaper from October–December 2012. *Arab Journal for Media and Communication Research, 2*, 192–215.

Said, E. (2003). *Orientalism: Western conceptions of the Orient*. Penguin Books Limited.

Said, E. (2008). *Covering Islam: How the media and the experts determine how we see the rest of the world (Fully revised edition)*. Random House.

Sakr, N. (2007). *Arab television today*. IB Tauris.

Sakr, N. (2022). Purposes and practices of MENA television: Components of an ever-evolving medium. In K. Gholam & T. Guaaybess (Eds.), *The handbook of media and culture in the middle east*. John Wiley and Sons Ltd.

Sakr, N., & De Burgh, H. (2005). The changing dynamics of Arab journalism. In *Making journalists: Diverse models, global issues* (pp. 142–157). Routledge.

Saleh, I. (2010). Journalism education in MENA: Walking on eggshells. *Brazilian Journalism Research, 6*(1), 78–88.

Salem, R., & Yount, K. M. (2019). Structural accommodations of patriarchy: Women and workplace gender segregation in Qatar. *Gender, Work & Organization, 26*(4), 501–519.

Saviano, M., Nenci, L., & Caputo, F. (2017). The financial gap for women in the MENA region: A systemic perspective. *Gender in Management: An International Journal, 32*(3), 203–217.

Sayyid, S. (2014). *Recalling the Caliphate: Decolonisation and world order*. Oxford University Press.

Scheufele, D. A., & Krause, N. M. (2019). Science audiences, misinformation, and fake news. *Proceedings of the National Academy of Sciences, 116*(16), 7662–7669.

Schlesinger, P. (1978). *Putting 'Reality' together: BBC News. Series: Communication and society*. Constable.

Schlesinger, P. (1999). Putting 'reality' together: BBC News. In H. Tumber (Ed.), *News. A Reader* (pp. 121–133). Sage.

Schramm, W. (1964). *Mass media and national development: The role of information in the developing countries*. Stanford University Press.

Schudson, M. (2003). *The sociology of news*. Norton.

Scott, J. M., & Carter, R. G. (2015). From cold war to Arab Spring: Mapping the effects of paradigm shifts on the nature and dynamics of US democracy assistance to the Middle East and North Africa. *Democratization, 22*(4), 738–763.

Seale, C. (2010). How the mass media report social statistics: A case study concerning research on end-of-life decisions. *Social Science & Medicine, 71*(5), 861–868.

Secko, D. M., Amend, E., & Friday, T. (2013). Four models of science journalism: A synthesis and practical assessment. *Journalism Practice, 7*(1), 62–80.

Sedki, H. (2018). *Scientific journalism between theory and practice*. Academic Library.

Şentürk, R., & Bilal, M. S. (2020). *Human rights in the Ottoman reform: Foundations, motivations and formations.* İbn Haldun Üniversitesi Yayınları.

Seyb, R. (2015). Trouble with the statistical curve: Walter Lippmann's Blending of History and Social Science during Franklin Roosevelt's First Term. *American Journalism, 32*(2), 138–160.

Seyb, R. P. (2015). What Walter Saw: Walter Lippmann, The New York world, and scientific advocacy as an alternative to the news-opinion dichotomy. *Journalism History, 41*(2), 58.

Shaaban, A. M. (2009). The trends of the Iraqi press in the first decade of the royal era: A descriptive study of the newspapers of Baghdad. *Al-Adab Journal, University of Baghdad, 88*(1), 492–511.

Shahsavari, S., Holur, P., Wang, T., Tangherlini, T. R., & Roychowdhury, V. (2020). Conspiracy in the time of corona: Automatic detection of emerging COVID-19 conspiracy theories in social media and the news. *Journal of Computational Social Science, 3*(2), 279–317.

Shapin, S. (2020). *Science and the public.* Routledge.

Sharkey, H. J. (1999). A century in print: Arabic journalism and nationalism in Sudan, 1899–1999. *International Journal of Middle East Studies, 31*(4), 531–549.

Sherwood Taylor, F. (1956). An alchemical work of Sir Isaac Newton. *Ambix, 5*(3–4), 59–84.

Shipman, M. (2014). Public relations as science communication. *Journal of Science Communication, 13*(3), C05.

Shirky, C. (2014). Last call: The end of the printed newspaper. *Medium. Com,* August, 21.

Shneiderman, B. (2008). Science 2.0. *Science, 319*(5868), 1349–1350.

Sidqi, H. (2009). *Scientific journalism between theory and practice.* Academic Library.

Silva, M. F., & Eldridge, S. A. (2020). *The ethics of photojournalism in the digital age.* Routledge.

Simis, M. J., Madden, H., Cacciatore, M. A., & Yeo, S. K. (2016). The lure of rationality: Why does the deficit model persist in science communication? *Public Understanding of Science, 25*(4), 400–414.

Sjøvaag, H. (2013). Journalistic autonomy. *Nordicom Review, 34,* 155–166.

Skalli, L. (2006). Communicating gender in the public sphere: Women and information technologies in the MENA. *Journal of Middle East Women's Studies, 2*(2), 35–59.

Slater, J. (1990). The Superpowers and an Arab-Israeli political settlement: The cold war years. *Political Science Quarterly, 105*(4), 557–577.

Soloski, J. (1989). Sources and channels of local news. *Journalism Quarterly, 66*(4), 864–870.

Spirer, H., & Spirer, L. (1998). *Misused statistics.* CRC Press.

Splendore, S., & Brambilla, M. (2021). The hybrid journalism that we do not recognize (anymore). *Journalism and Media*, *2*(1), 51–61.

Splendore, S., & Curini, L. (2020). Proximity between citizens and journalists as a determinant of trust in the media. An Application to Italy. *Journalism Studies*, *21*(9), 1167–1185.

Spurr, D. (1993). *The rhetoric of empire: Colonial discourse in journalism, travel writing, and imperial administration.* Duke University Press.

Sreberny, A. (2000). Television, gender, and democratization in the Middle East. *De-Westernizing Media Studies*, 63–78.

Stearns, P. (2015). *Gender in world history*. Routledge.

Stecula, D. A., & Pickup, M. (2021). How populism and conservative media fuel conspiracy beliefs about COVID-19 and what it means for COVID-19 behaviors. *Research & Politics*, *8*(1), 2053168021993979.

Stein, R. A., Ometa, O., Shetty, S. P., Katz, A., Popitiu, M. I., & Brotherton, R. (2021). Conspiracy theories in the era of COVID-19: A tale of two pandemics. *International Journal of Clinical Practice*, *75*(2) https://www.ncbi.nlm.nih.gov/pmc/articles/PMC7995222/

Stephens, M. (2020). A geospatial infodemic: Mapping Twitter conspiracy theories of COVID-19. *Dialogues in Human Geography*, *10*(2), 276–281.

Sternadori, M., & Thorson, E. (2009). Anonymous sources harm credibility of all stories. *Newspaper Research Journal*, *30*(4), 54–66.

Stilgoe, J., Lock, S., & Wilsdon, J. (2014). Why should we promote public engagement with science? *Public Understanding of Science*, *23*(1), 4–15.

Stoycheff, E. (2016). Under surveillance: Examining Facebook's spiral of silence effects in the wake of NSA internet monitoring. *Journalism & Mass Communication Quarterly*, *93*(2), 296–311.

Sturgis, P., & Allum, N. (2004). Science in society: Re-evaluating the deficit model of public attitudes. *Public Understanding of Science*, *13*(1), 55–74.

Suleski, J., & Ibaraki, M. (2010). Scientists are talking, but mostly to each other: A quantitative analysis of research represented in mass media. *Public Understanding of Science*, *19*(1), 115–125.

Summ, A., & Volpers, A. (2016). What's science? Where's science? Science journalism in German print media. *Public Understanding of Science*, *25*(7), 775–790.

Suran, M. (2010). The separation of church and science: Science and religion offer different worldviews, but are they opposite or complementary? *EMBO Reports*, *11*(8), 586–589.

Tasseron, M., & Lawson, B. T. (2020). Legitimizing military action through statistics and discourse in the 2014 IDF assault on Gaza. *Media, War & Conflict*, 1750635220917692.

Tharoor, S. (2018). *Inglorious Empire: What the British did to India*. Penguin.

Thompson, T. (2016). Conducting the Conversation: Insights from the Historical and Theological Contextualization of Edward Said's Orientalism. *The Muslim World*, *106*(2), 255–270.

Thomson, E. A., White, P. R., & Kitley, P. (2008). 'Objectivity' and 'hard news' reporting across cultures: Comparing the news report in English, French, Japanese and Indonesian journalism. *Journalism Studies, 9*(2), 212–228.

Tibi, B. (1997). *Arab nationalism: Between Islam and the nation-state*. Palgrave Macmillan.

Tibi, S. (2006). Al-Razi and Islamic medicine in the 9th century. *Journal of the Royal Society of Medicine, 99*(4), 206–207.

Tignor, R. L. (1980). Dependency Theory and Egyptian Capitalism, 1920 to 1950. *African Economic History, 9*, 101–118.

Tillier, B., & Nicholson-Smith, D. (2012). The impact of censorship on painting and sculpture, 1851–1914. *Yale French Studies, 122*, 79–103.

Treise, D., & Weigold, M. F. (2002). Advancing science communication: A survey of science communicators. *Science Communication, 23*(3), 310–322.

Treisman, R. (2021). *The UAE is adopting a 4.5-day workweek and a Saturday-Sunday weekend* [News]. National Public Radio. https://www.npr.org/2021/12/08/1062435944/uae-work-week-change-saturday-sunday-weekends-global-markets?t=1640105054377

Trench, B. (2008). Towards an analytical framework of science communication models. In *Communicating science in social contexts* (pp. 119–135). Springer.

Trench, B., & Junker, K. (2001). *How scientists view their public communication*, 1–3.

Tuchman, G. (1972). Objectivity as strategic ritual: An examination of newsmen's notions of objectivity. *American Journal of Sociology, 77*(4), 660–679.

Ulrichsen, K. C., & Sheline, A. R. (2019). In J. A. Baker III (Ed.), *Mohammed Bin Salman and religious authority and reform in Saudi Arabia* (pp. 1–9). Institute for Public Policy of Rice University. https://scholarship.rice.edu/bitstream/handle/1911/108116/bi-report-092319-cme-mbs-saudi.pdf?sequence=1

Umbricht, A. (2014). *Patterns of news making in Western journalism*.

UNESCO. (2013). *Freedom of Information in Arab States*.

UNP. (2020). *Women Empowerment in the KSA*. https://www.my.gov.sa/wps/portal/snp/careaboutyou/womenempowering

Usher, N. (2021). *News for the Rich, White, and Blue: How Place and Power Distort American Journalism*. Columbia University Press.

Utts, J. (2010). *Unintentional lies in the media: Don't blame journalists for what we don't teach*. Proceedings of the Eighth International Conference on Teaching Statistics.

Van Engen, J. (1986). The Christian Middle Ages as an historiographical problem. *The American Historical Review, 91*(3), 519–552.

Van Sertima, I. (1992). *The golden age of the Moor* (Vol. 11). Transaction Publishers.

Vaughan, J. R. (2005). *The Failure of American and British Propaganda in the Arab Middle East, 1945–57*. Palgrave Macmillan.

Verdery, R. N. (1971). The Publications of the Būlāq Press under Muḥammad 'Alī of Egypt. *Journal of the American Oriental Society*, 129–132.

Vieweg, S., & Hodges, A. (2016). Surveillance & modesty on social media: How Qataris navigate modernity and maintain tradition. 527–538. https://dl.acm.org/doi/abs/10.1145/2818048.2819966?casa_token=zHxgVUKhtnsAAAA-A%3AJEJbfgi1lh8qE5P0V4NC4cMJ5kWGRHUOffEzFRrnDiFZnVh63kRofpa-RfqvCaTqgrCPujRUhH86vEo

Vorderstrasse, T. (2014). The archaeology of the Ottoman Empire and its aftermath in the Middle East. *Near Eastern Archaeology*, 77(4), 292–298.

Waisbord, S. (2013). *Reinventing professionalism: Journalism and news in global perspective.* John Wiley & Sons.

Walker, R., & Clokie, T. (2013). *Mentoring for the modern newsroom.* The Age of Mobile News/Jeanz 2013 Conference. http://researcharchive.wintec.ac.nz/3007/

Wang, D. R., Hajjar, D. P., & Cole, C. L. (2020). International partnerships for the development of science, technology, engineering, mathematics, and medical education of middle eastern women. *International Journal of Higher Education*, 9(2), 1–15.

Wasserman, H., & de Beer, A. S. (2010). *Journalism in the global South: South Africa and Brazil.*, 36(2), 143–147.

Watenpaugh, K. D. (2014). *Being Modern in the Middle East.* Princeton University Press.

Weaver, D., & Willnat, L. (2012). *The global journalist in the 21st century.* Routledge New York.

Westfall, R. S. (1994). *The Life of Isaac Newton.* Cambridge University Press.

WFSJ. (2015). *Impact of African and Arab science journalists.*

Wilby, P. (2007). Damn journalists and statistics. *The Guardian.*

Wiseman, A. W., Abdelfattah, F. A., & Almassaad, A. (2016). The intersection of citizenship status, STEM education, and expected labor market participation in Gulf Cooperation Council Countries. *Digest of Middle East Studies*, 25(2), 362–392.

Wolfsfeld, G. (1997). *Media and political conflict: News from the Middle East.* Cambridge University Press.

World Bank. (2020). *Women, Business and the Law.* World Bank. https://wbl.worldbank.org/en/wbl

Worth, A. (2014). *Imperial media: Colonial networks and information technologies in the British literary imagination, 1857–1918.* The Ohio State University Press.

Wright, Z. V. (2020). *Realizing Islam: The Tijaniyya in North Africa and the Eighteenth-century Muslim World.* The University of North Carolina Press.

Yagoob, A., & Zuo, T. (2016). Patterns of economic growth and poverty in Sudan. *Journal of Economics and Sustainable Development*, 7(2).

Yahia, M. (2008). *Arab world debuts its first science news website*. SciDev.Net. https://www.scidev.net/global/news/arab-world-debuts-its-first-science-news-website/

Yari, Y. (2016). A study on the thought and political action of Salama Moussa in the realm of Socialism. *A Quarterly Journal of Historical Studies of Islam*, *8*(29), 151–169.

Yetiv, S. (2002). Kuwait's democratic experiment in its broader international context. *The Middle East Journal*, 257–271.

Yildiz, M. (2018). *Historiography development in Arabic-Islamic history writing*.

Yosmaoğlu, İ. K. (2003). Chasing the printed word: Press censorship in the Ottoman Empire, 1876–1913. *The Turkish Studies Association Journal*, *27*(1/2), 15–49.

Yusoff, M., Yakub, M., & Danehsgar, M. (2011). *Islam and the relation of science and the Qur'an*. International Conference on Humanities, Society and Culture, Singapore.

Zahlan, A. (2012). *Science, development, and sovereignty in the Arab World*. Palgrave Macmillan.

Zelizer, B. (1993). Journalists as interpretive communities. *Critical Studies in Mass Communication*, *10*(3), 219–237. https://doi.org/10.1080/15295039309366865

Ziadat, A., & Jallow, B. (1986). *Western science in the Arab world: The impact of Darwinism 1860–1930*. Palgrave Macmillan.

Zilfi, M. C. (1997). *Women in the Ottoman Empire: Middle Eastern women in the early modern era* (Vol. 10). Brill.

Zillmann, D., & Brosius, H.-B. (2012). *Exemplification in communication: The influence of case reports on the perception of issues*. Routledge.

# Index[1]

**A**
Accreditation Council on Education in Journalism and Mass Communication, 174
Afghanistan, 113
Africa, 4, 5, 8, 13, 50, 60, 111, 168, 193, 198, 210, 211
*Al-Ahram*, 54, 87, 94, 157–159
Alan Kurdi, 166
*Al-Falah*, 57
*Algerian Medical Journal*, 50
*Al-Jawa'ib*, 59
*Al-Jazeera*, 64, 101, 106
al-Khadyu, 80
*Al-Masry Al-Yuom*, 158, 159
*Al-Qabas*, 58, 87, 94, 158
*Al-Qabascame*, 157
*Al-Rai*, 158
*Al Riyadh*, 82
Al-Riyadh, 87, 94, 157, 158
*Al-Waqa al Masriya*, 80
Al-Zawraa, 56
Arab Spring, 105, 221
Arab Union, 61
Australia, 101, 149, 211

**B**
Baath party, 106
Baghdad, 15, 19, 20
Bahrain, 49, 149, 194
Beirut, 60–62
Berges Paris, 59
Broadcast Journalism Training Council, 174

**C**
Censorship, 8, 50, 55, 69, 72, 88, 101, 102, 105–108, 116, 117, 123, 125, 129, 138, 150, 195, 201, 220, 221

---

[1] Note: Page numbers followed by 'n' refer to notes.

Chechen Republic, 114
Cold War, 21, 55, 81, 85
COVID-19, 1, 3, 4, 51, 58, 64, 69, 89, 90, 95, 157, 187, 192, 200, 216, 226
Critical Religion Studies, 81

**D**
Darfur, 66
Defamation laws, 150
Deficit Model, 11, 12
Deontology, 81, 82, 92, 109, 117, 118
Disinformation, 2, 3, 7
*Dunia Al-Alam*, 60

**E**
*Echourouk*, 51
Egypt, 5–7, 14, 18, 50, 54–56, 66, 70, 106, 108, 108n3, 138, 144, 149, 152, 157, 159, 215
Emirates Scientists Council, 71
*Ennahar*, 51
Ethiopia, 107
Europe, 16–18, 20, 54, 66, 81, 85, 101, 109, 112, 114, 115, 117, 149, 166, 168, 170, 191, 211

**F**
Fe y Alegría, 101
Finland, 101
Fox News, 3

**G**
GCC countries, 70, 150, 190, 200
Global South, 4, 22, 63, 82, 85, 118, 168, 170, 212, 215
Gulf War, 57, 58

**H**
HIV/AIDS, 111, 112, 160, 192, 223

**I**
Indonesia, 13, 110, 148
Iran, 13
Iranian Revolution, 114
Islamic Golden Age, 15
Israel, 61, 109, 113

**J**
Japan, 101, 211
Jordan, 110, 149, 175, 176, 201

**K**
Kuwait, 5, 50, 58–59, 87, 90, 103, 110, 124, 144, 149, 152, 215, 221

**L**
Lebanon, 59–61, 149, 175, 176
LGTB, 111
LIFE, 165

**M**
Malaysia, 148
Middle Ages, 14, 115, 117
Modernization, 113
Morocco, 149
mRNA, 2
Muslim Brotherhood, 221

**N**
Nakba, 61
National Council for the Training of Journalists, 174

News culture, 78–81, 84, 85, 87, 89–93, 95, 129, 138, 212

**O**
Oman, 5, 50, 149
*Oqaz*, 83, 87, 94, 157, 158
Orientalist
  Orientalism, 15

**P**
Pakistan, 148
Palestine, 61–63, 149
*Palestinian Medical Journal*, 62
*Petroleum and Industry News*, 70
Post-colonial, 21, 81, 108, 147
Public Engagement with Science (PES), 49, 199, 215, 218, 223, 226
Public Understanding of Science (PUS), 3, 61, 198, 199, 215, 218, 223, 226

**Q**
Qatar, 22, 50, 63–64, 71, 89, 95, 101, 103, 106, 106n2, 114, 127, 149, 175, 176, 191, 194, 196, 197, 201
Qatar National Research Fund, 22

**R**
*Reporters Sans Frontières*, 103

**S**
Saudi Arabia, 22, 50, 64–65, 87, 94, 109, 110, 124, 144, 148, 152, 154, 155, 158, 174, 175, 201, 215

Science, Technology, Engineering, and Mathematics (STEM), 49, 58, 72, 114, 124, 131, 133, 134, 144, 150, 151, 155, 156, 176, 197–201, 218, 224
Shura Council, 106
Supreme Council for Women, 149
Supreme Press Council, 106, 107
Syria, 68–70, 114

**T**
*Tawila*, 57
Tunisia, 103, 108, 149, 175, 176, 197, 201, 221

**U**
UAE, 50, 70–72, 106, 149, 158, 191, 194
*Umm al-Qura*, 64
United Arab Emirates, 50, 70, 149, 175, 176, 194
United Kingdom, 3, 80, 125, 146, 174
United States, 4, 80, 109, 114, 191, 211
Uses and Gratifications Theory, 196

**W**
Watchdog, 4, 77, 188, 211, 221
World Federation of Science Journalists, 111
World War II, 55

**Y**
YLE, 101